*A Poetics of Impasse in Modern
and Contemporary American Poetry*

A Poetics of Impasse
in Modern and Contemporary
American Poetry

SUSAN M. SCHULTZ

THE UNIVERSITY OF ALABAMA PRESS

Tuscaloosa

to my mother and to Radhika

Typeface: Minion

∞

The paper on which this book is printed meets the minimum requirements of American
National Standard for Information Sciences—Permanence of Paper for Printed Library
Materials, ANSI Z39.48–1984.

Library of Congress Cataloging-in-Publication Data

Schultz, Susan M., 1958–
A poetics of impasse in modern and contemporary American poetry / Susan M. Schultz.
p. cm. — (Modern and contemporary poetics)
Includes bibliographical references and index.
ISBN 0-8173-1470-9 (alk. paper) — ISBN 0-8173-5198-1 (pbk. : alk. paper)
1. American poetry—20th century—History and criticism. 2. American poetry—
21st century—History and criticism. 3. Experimental poetry, American—History and
criticism. 4. Poetics. I. Title. II. Series.
PS325.S38 2005
811'.50911—dc22

2005002056

Contents

Acknowledgments

As BEFITS A BOOK with the title *A Poetics of Impasse,* this one has been a long time in finishing. The Introduction explains, I hope, the most fruitful of the intellectual impasses I have dealt with over the past dozen years, my work at the University of Hawaiʻi. As an autobiographical piece of criticism, it takes its place alongside essays by my colleague and former colleagues Cynthia Franklin, Juliana Spahr, and Rob Wilson, whose models have proved bracing and inspiring. Living and teaching and editing in Hawaiʻi have forced me to reconsider my readings of American poetry generally, not just the poetry written in this state. For helping to break the impasses that made this book difficult to bring together, I owe a tremendous debt to Hank Lazer, who encouraged and nagged me over the final hurdles, and made crucial suggestions for revision. He is the most generous of poet-critic-editors. Marjorie Perloff has offered much encouragement and some tough readings across the years, as have Charles Bernstein, Alan Gilbert, Juliana Spahr, John Ernest, Ann Vickery, Craig Watson, Deborah Meadows, Jonathan Morse, Miriam Fuchs, Kristin MacAndrews, and many others. Rob Wilson's work on Bamboo Ridge poets and American poetry has proved invaluable. An anonymous reader for the press offered up recipes for reading on subjects that had gathered some fuzz over time, but quickly regained their fizz. Thanks also to the editors of publications in which earlier versions of these essays appeared, among them Ann Vickery, Eric Selinger and Joel Bettridge, and John Tranter and John Kinsella. Journals and books in which the essays have appeared, in other form, are *Raritan, Arizona Quarterly, Contemporary Literature, How(2), Salt and Jacket; Close Listening* (Oxford University

Press) and the National Poetry Foundation's forthcoming volume on the work of Ronald Johnson (Orono, Maine). Permissions to reprint have been granted. Many colleagues and students in the English department at the University of Hawai'i have been supportive during my time in Hawai'i, as have—among others—writers Lisa Linn Kanae and Lee Tonouchi, whom I've had the pleasure to publish through Tinfish Press, as well as Marie Hara and Eric Chock. I thank the staff of the University of Alabama Press, and I owe a debt of gratitude to the copyeditor, Debbie Posner, as well. Thanks to my mother, Martha J. Schultz and to the rest of my family, for their support. For being the greatest, and most loving, of my impasses, I thank my husband, Bryant Webster Schultz, our son, Sangha, and our daughter, Radhika.

PERMISSIONS

John Ashbery, for permission to quote from *Flow Chart,* Georges Borchardt; to quote from other poems, W. W. Norton & Co., Carcanet Press, Ltd.

Charles Bernstein kindly gave permission to quote from his work, published and unpublished.

Ronald Johnson, for permission to quote from *ARK* (1996), *RADI OS* (1977), *Up to Now* (unpublished, 2004), and *Valley of the Many-Colored Grasses,* from Peter O'Leary, executor of Johnson's estate.

Gertrude Stein, for permission to quote, from the law firm of Levin & Gann, P.A.

For permission to quote from e-mails, I would like to thank Anselm Berrigan, Allison Cobb, Rod Smith, K. Silem Mohammad, and Juliana Spahr.

Introduction

Introducing Impasse[1]

Call this point *impasse,*
The place where nothing is natural,
Artificial rest from which to locate artifice
In the outer suburbs. Yet artifice is not what
Fascinates me, nor the process by which
Its difficulties lead us to participate in the work
Of art we see constructed before us, as if
It were a perpetual site of cement mixers
And Bob the Builder types imitating
That poet in the wilderness, if it's re-
Figured as any urban setting, almost an
Inverse reality where the jar gives chaos
Back to its rightful owners. Rather, what
I want to think about is the fact of
What is called *writer's block,*
Generally described in clinical
Terms as "condition" or as "obstacle" or
A state of (non)being from which one wants quick
Exit. To be stuck as a writer is to fail that course
Of study you'd banked on to navigate an institution's
Requirements, and then (if you're lucky) to make
A career of them within or without the academy.

Before turning my full attention to *writer's block,* I want
To propose that avant-garde writing, with its focus
On the reader as coproducer of meaning, uses a method
One might call "reader's block," whereby the reader's desire
To be "absorbed" into a text is deflected (artificially,
According to Charles Bernstein in his "Artifice of Absorption")
By means of writing that is "anti-absorptive."[2] It's as if the expected
Sponge were really a ball bearing, except it's a ball bearing
That lends itself to analysis, to critique, to addition rather than
The subtractions that "reading" often presumes in the classroom,
Where "deep meaning" is shorthand for "and the answer is!"
Poetry reduced to the status of game show, with teacher
As host, students at their buttons, and everyone pretending
To have good fun. Thus is "meaning" assumed to involve
"Winning," either good grades or vacations in tropical places
(Read "tropic" not in its "trop(e)-ical" sense but literally), where
The avant-garde poet asks the reader to eschew this economic
Model of reading for what Juliana Spahr terms an "anarchic"
Process[3] or which Ron Silliman describes as "torque,"[4] where
Meaning becomes an activity, free but controlled play if you will,
Inscribed into the political realm, where communities of readers
Are assumed to share leftist politics (when Charles Bernstein
Came to Hawai'i in 1993, the flyer emphasized his status
As a left, Marxist thinker, and Silliman's
Work in Socialist journalism is well known). If being
"Absorbed" into a text is the reader's version of free-writing,
Where the reader in some sense *becomes* the text as it appears
On the page (as the writer extends herself into text while
Being absorbed in the process of writing), then "reader's block"
Prevents that identification between reader and language from
Occurring. That this block is necessary to the process of
Recovering, uncovering, creating meaning, is something argued
By most recent defenders of the avant-garde,
But its relationship to a prior block, experienced by the writer
Him- or herself, is a subject not as well considered. If reading
And writing are to be aligned as part of the same process
(Adrienne Rich's lesbian continuum comes to mind here
As a model for ranges within identity formations), then consider the

Writer as reader, the writer as a blocked reader, the reader
As someone whose texts become opaque to her even as she
Produces them. The fruit of this block is silence, just as
The aftermath of any reading of Stein's *Tender Buttons* in the college
Classroom is so often an interlude of quiet. The way this
Silence operates—its process, like the course of Cage's 4′33″—
Is not unlike the way a poet like Susan Howe approaches
The historical archive, where her interests lie more in absences
Than presences, more in the shards ("syllable from sound")[5]
Than in the well-wrought urns of traditional narrative histories.
Tender Buttons is archive, albeit of another content than that of
Hope Atherton's wanderings, but wordplay unites them
In linguistic histories where history is backdated prophecy
And fossil poetry is not figured, but presumes an actual
Ground (Emerson's house, not his ideas, in other words).
The student detective learns to organize her clues
Not toward closure but a refusal of it
(See Hejinian's essay against[6]), but in that very
Move to foreclose it, meaning's mortgage gets paid.
Silence generally presumes privacy; we read in silence,
Are not supposed to move our lips, mutter under our breaths,
Have any manner of bad reading hygienes. But if we assume
That silence is a public property, that its ownership matters,
And that any talk of silence is itself an opening out of impasse,
Then, I think, we are getting somewhere.
Writer's block is an impasse in the act a writer generally
Assumes to be natural, spontaneous, or artificial and constructed
(Little matter here, as I believe the artifice vs. nature opposition often
Gets overstated for effect or affect). But let's assume that the block is itself
The natural or artificial result of the writer's coming into knowledge,
And that one comes into knowledge through silence rather than speech,
That what the block offers is an education (if not a BA) in
A new awareness, whether political or cultural or personal.
Or, if not an education in and of itself, then a sabbatical
In which to learn, by way of its powerful anxieties,
Where and what next to write.

The agent of this block is often an enemy: the Visiting Distinguished
Writer at UH who told Lois-Ann Yamanaka that her English was
    "bad,"
That she should never write in Pidgin because it was "bad English"
And her work wouldn't sell in New York, is only example among
    many.[7]
The point of my rumination is not to refigure the enemy as a hero,
But to suggest that the enemy, while remaining one, forces us
To find value in the language we use: the writer is a survivalist,
Banished to the woods or words of her own making, who emerges,
    like
Susan Howe's scout (in *Singularities*), with earned knowledge.

In his small book *Living Pidgin,* local Hawaiʻi writer Lee Tonouchi
(Gen-X writer, teacher, and editor of the magazine, *Hybolics,*
Which comes from the Pidgin word meaning
"Exaggerated language"), begins with a block, a literal
Block. The concrete poem that inaugurates his collection of
Lectures and poems about speaking and writing in Pidgin
Is called "Test Your Pidgin P.O.V." The only text
Is

N O

CAN

Which translates into standard English as "I/you can't."
The "no can" that fascinates Lee involves the silencing
Of local students, some of whom he encounters when he teaches
At Kapiolani Community College in Honolulu. Tonouchi
Has his students write a group poem about the things they can't do:
Among them are "BE SMART / BE IMPORTANT /
BE SUCCESSFUL / BE PROFESSIONAL / BE TAKEN
SERIOUSLY / BE ONE TEACHER/ BE ONE DOCTOR."
Tonouchi's book is polemical: he argues for a counterhistorical
Mainstreaming of Pidgin, including a Department of Pidgin
At the university level, thus (implicitly) dismantling the
Heretofore inextricable link between "Pidgin-speaker"
And "local," a link that is racial and class-based (Asian,
Hawaiian, and working class). Tonouchi adopts and adapts
The language of hip-hop and academic discourse to make

His arguments; what the reader of the book cannot hear
Is his performance, less polemical than comical, in the
Tradition of local ethnic humor as much as that
Of language politics as it's usually played in this state.
Whereas the first poem in the book poses a block,
"NO CAN," the last poem, "DA KINE,"[8]
(Phrase meaning everything from "you know" to "that kind
Of thing") is blank, white space. This space is silent,
But there is not nothing there; rather, Tonouchi, it seems
To me, has revalued silence over the course of his book,
Moving from the POV of a student who has been silenced
To that of a writer who uses silence to spring open
A place for "People BORN Pidgin," who "gotta be free
For LIVE Pidgin," as Lee, AKA "Da Pidgin Guerrilla"
Puts it on the penultimate page of the book.

Lisa Linn Kanae's *Sista Tongue* is both more
Traditional and revolutionary a presentation of the issues
Tonouchi raises in his book. On the one hand, Kanae's method
Is historical; she writes about the history of Pidgin in Hawai'i,
Pidgin's origins in the plantation system of the nineteenth and early
    twentieth
Centuries, the way in which the educational system attempted to sup-
    press,
Or at least segregate, Pidgin speakers. On the other hand, her method
Is metaphorical: she uses her brother's experience as a "late talker,"
Sent to remedial classes in a bus with severely handicapped children,
As an analogue to "the Pidgin speaker" in Hawai'i. Her argument,
Then, is both grounded in history and extremely suggestive.[9]
The book's designer, Kristin Kaleinani Gonzales, took her text,
Formed of collages of personal narrative (in Pidgin), academic dis-
    course
(Standard English) and pep talk, and intervened in it. She altered
What appeared to be a linear argument to bring forward its nonlinear
Movement; the book appears in pieces, chunks, scattered across
Pages, sutured with gaps. She enacts the "reader's block," that is,
In discussions of Pidgin better termed "speaker's block";
Readers gather no momentum in their experience of this book,

Forced as they are to stop on each page, to turn the book to one
Side or to gaze on images of mouths, tongues, teeth, the very
   mechanics
Of talk. The book "embodies" its subject, as well
As our process of experiencing that subject.
There is a link to Language writing here,
Though it's a dangerous one to make: while
Charles Bernstein's use of ideolect and nonstandard English
Is *not* a Pidgin or the expression of a communal working-class
Identity, it attempts a similar kind of nonstandard deviation
From the norms by which our linguistic lives are run. Spatially,
Parts of Kanae's and Gonzales's book resemble pages 56 and 57
Of Susan Howe's *Singularities,* where words
Are pictures and the reader creates the torque by turning,
Not pages, but the entire book.

As editor and publisher of a journal of "experimental" writing
In a state where "experiment" usually denotes "New York" or
"San Francisco" rather than Honolulu, I'm sometimes asked
Why I put together poetry by poets as different from one another
As Caroline Sinavaiana-Gabbard from Bill Luoma, or Kathy
Banggo from Geraldine MacKenzie (the list of apparent
Mismatches goes on). "Is writing in Pidgin inevitably experimental?"
Goes one version of this question. "Experiments differ," I say.
Having come to Hawai'i in 1990, freshly excited about Language
writing, Hawai'i's literary and cultural politics/poetics seemed
   anathema
To the goals of Language writing; here, words like "identity"
And "authenticity" and "blood" *mean.* Pomo
Presumptions that identity is an essentialist gag
Find no welcome here, and language (in literary terms)
Is presumed to be clear, to transmit values cultural and
Historical; to get things "wrong" is the sin
One does not want to commit. Tinfish Press has been my
Attempt to synthesize these apparent oppositions; what
It taught me is that words like "experimental" are not fixed,
But wobble into being depending on the needs of place.
What might be an experimental poem in Sydney is not one
In San Francisco; what is avant-garde in Los Angeles

May be retro in Honolulu and vice versa. Alan
Sondheim's recent web experiments with writing
In Hawaiian (see "Colonialism and Theology" on
The poetics list, June, 2003),which he considers
Liberatory (the language is, after all written by
Hawaiians) would be considered colonial here
(The language was, after all, stolen by a white guy
From the North American continent).[10] With
Experiment, then, comes responsibility. We
Cannot liberate each other, though
We can write from the same neighborhood, as
Juliana Spahr does in "Dole Street," where she walks
A street that is not hers, acutely aware of herself
As a settler, thereby honoring both this place
And the possibilities for poetry by "outsiders."

And I'm asked again what *is* experimental
About Hawai'i writing, a question that perhaps leads me
To bleed the category of "experiment" to a point where
It no longer functions in the way many critics would like
It to, namely as a boundary between the avant-garde,
Which experiments, and the so-called mainstream,
Which likes to present the results of its experiments,
Postpaid. Within the literary history of Hawai'i
There are moments when using the actual languages
Of place—Pidgin, Hawaiian—can be termed "experiments,"
I think, where foregrounding language, as well as place-
Based content, is experimental, even if the end result
Is an attempt at "authenticity" rather than describing
Fluid identities, which come to think of it
Are also often based on "authenticities" that
Are simply not named. Pierre Joris's "nomadism,"
Or Bernstein's Reznikoff, are instances of language
Rooted not to place so much as to exile, the poet's
Removal from one to another place, sometimes from
One to another language.

Which is not to say there is not an "avant" poetry
In Hawai'i, by whatever definition you use. Barry

Masuda's "Holoholo Style," in *Tinfish* 1, riffs off
Eric Chock's "The Meaning of Fishing," even as
It argues for another kind of local writing than that
Canonized in Eric Chock's journal, *Bamboo Ridge*[11]
(Named after the coast on the windward side of Oahu
Where fisherman worked with their bamboo poles).
Chock's poem uses "fishing" as a metaphor
For "feeling" and, finally, for the art of writing
Poetry: "You know when you go fishing and you
Whitewash, / nothing. / You know the feeling, right?"
The poem ends: "Even if you woulda let em go anyway
After you caught em,
And if you never catch em
And hold em in your hands,
You think you know da meaning of fishing?" (*Last Days Here,* 30)
Masuda's take on meaning is even *more* local
Than is Chock's, his poetry less lyrical, more "encumbered"
By a starker Pidgin than Chock ever uses, by more Hawaiian words,
More academic discourse ("I stay feeling da dialectic" is surely
A play on "You know the feeling, right?") than in the "traditional"
Local poem.

> *Bamboo Ridge not da only place fo' catch* ulua, *brah—get oddah*
>   *places*
> *too. Get Lone Kiawe, get Lone Pine, get Makena*
> *Lighthouse, get OP10, get plenny odda places, bu'. Da*
> *meaning of fishing not only* papio *or* ulua *too—it's using*
> ha'ukeuke *fo' go catch* panunu uhu, *den grinding da*
> ha'ukeuke *cuz da* uhu *no bite cuz get couple Japanee touris'*
> *wi' dakine hot pink snorkle splashing around. It's going*
> *Makena side fo' go hook mu and no can find "public access"*
> *cuz get some moa hotels wen grow ovahnight.* (29)

Masuda perceives
an impasse in the local version of what Charles Altieri calls "the scenic
    mode,"
That Chock's brand of lyricism, in this poem at any rate, cannot cri-
    tique

The "growing hotels" (artifice masquerading as natural process)
Or the tourist economy, disrupting the economy of fishing, its exis-
    tence
Prior to literary figuration. I would say that in work like "Poem for
George Helm: Aloha Week 1980" (in *Last Days Here*), Chock combines
    his lyric impulse
With his own political critique, showing how his love
For the word "aloha" has been destroyed by the "servants of the USA"
Who bombed Kahoolawe for so many years. (Helm was a singer
And martyr to the cause of Hawaiian sovereignty who drowned off
Kahoolawe during protests against the bombing, well over a decade
Before the first President Bush called it off in a transparent and unsuc-
    cessful
Attempt to get a Republican elected to the Senate from this heavily
Democratic state.)[12] These investigations of politics through language
Are not dissimilar from those efforts by Language writers to
Alter political consciousness through disruptions of Language;
For the Hawai'i poet, however, language has already been disrupted
To such an extent that transparencies operate in much the way
That translucencies do in Language writing; poets like Masuda
And, more recently, Ida Yoshinaga, combine modes,
Intervening in local politics by way of writing practices
Taken from Bamboo Ridge *and* the "traditional" avant-garde,
The synthesis of avant-garde practice (associated with an international
Art movement) with local and Hawaiian politics is exciting, though
It behooves us to remain aware of its dangers (watering
Down politics with "craft" is one; blunting the
Language critique with too great a transparency being
Another.)

I mean to get away from categories like "local" and "avant-
Garde," however, in my own critical practice, because they close
Off the very junction that I want to explore, an intersection of
The two and their spin-offs, which are too idiosyncratic to have
Names of their own. Some critics' efforts to patrol the boundaries
Of the avant-garde, while rigorous in their own right, don't interest
Me nearly as much as does the comingling of traditions they consider
Incompatible.[13] By this I don't so much mean the fruitful confusion

Now apparent between experimental writing and the fruits of main-
Stream (mainland[14]) MFA programs; Iowa comes to mind as a place
Where Lyn Hejinian and Jorie Graham have converged on students
Open to various modes of thinking; a writer like Claudia Keelan[15]
Embodies this confusion in work that is at once well-crafted,
Politically aware, and difficult. But the mix that fascinates me
Is the even less apparent bringing-together of work by Steve
Evans-certified writers (Jennifer Moxley and Lisa Jarnot spring
To mind) and the writers I've come to know in Hawai'i
Whose work tests the limits of "official verse culture"
In very different ways, by using Pidgin as its primary
Language, say, or by challenging "white" (aka "haole")
Canons that include the very poets considered avant-garde
On the coasts of the North American continent, and more
Recently, by bringing the Hawaiian language into play
As an alternative (historical and most present) to the other
Official language of this place, namely English.

The gathering of tribes, coalitions, communities, draws
Much critical attention (see books by Michael Davidson on
San Francisco poets, by Ann Vickery on women Language poets,
By Libbie Rifkin on poets surrounding Charles Olson, for
Example). Such communities organize themselves around common
Concerns: these are communities of avant-garde writers, mainly men,
Who discover themselves as audiences for each other, then aim
To create larger (if not large) audiences for their work through
The formation of journals or small presses and in academic
Circles coalescing until recently around figures
Like Charles Bernstein and Susan Howe at Buffalo.
Community, following this definition, is at once coherent
And oppositional; poets form allegiances almost as if
They were gated communities (not necessarily plush ones)
To maintain distinct borders between their own practices
As poets and those of writers they perceive as unlike
Themselves. What I propose is a different definition of
Community, less defined, and probably more fictive
Than those described in the books I've mentioned.
Rather than a community of same, I want to describe

A community of difference. In Hawai'i,
For example, there are communities of Hawaiian writers,
Local Asian writers, and white writers; these communities are fluid,
Can be redefined as occasion permits, morphing into communities
Of Gen-X writers (both Hawaiian and local, as in the group
Around Lee Tonouchi and Carrie Takahata), or communities of
Established local and white writers (as one sees in the fitful
Kaimana, occasional publication of the Hawai'i Literary Arts Council).
What is still missing is a sense of community not as poets
Who thrive on their desire to create the same kinds of work,
But as poets who learn from the practices of poets very
Different from themselves: experimental poets from
Narrative poets, Pidgin poets from avant-garde poets,
White poets from Hawaiian poets, and so on. These
Are the communities formed, however tangentially,
By journals such as *Hybolics* and *Tinfish,* which
Call into question old frameworks
Of writing in Hawai'i, necessary to extending
Literary practices between the gates of privileged
Communities, whether they are nearly lily white suburbs
Of the avant-garde or exclusionary neighborhoods of
Local writers who see those suburbs as part
And parcel of the old colonial project. Ironically
Perhaps, Steve Evans's inclusion of Bill Luoma in
His list of favored poets,[16] although his Luoma is
The Bill of Brooklyn, makes this link for me,
For Luoma has written in compelling terms about
Hawai'i, its fruit markets, baseball games, and its Chinese
Cemetery, thus not so far from the world of
Lee Tonouchi (whose writing about his dad touches
On Luoma's in intriguing ways) after all.[17]

Digression (is it?) on difficulty:
John Vincent, in a recent book, *Queer Lyrics:*
Difficulty and Closure in American Poetry,
Refines George Steiner's typology of "difficulty," extending
It into extrapoetic difficulties, having more to do
With being a homosexual writer than with merely

Happening to be a writer of obscure lyrics, so that difficulty
Becomes a term that applies to reading from an identity— a
Position not shared by most critics. As he writes about
Ashbery's queer lyrics, "*Difficult* describes a way lived
Life feels (full of pain, littered with climbable and un-
Climbable obstacles), which corresponds to a kind of
Poetry (full of disjunctions and ellipses, littered with
Climbable and unclimbable obstacles)" (57). If one looks
At this from the perspective of what I'm calling "reader's
Block," difficulty doesn't reside solely in a text that is
By its very "nature" difficult, one like Ashbery's that starts
One place and wanders to another, attired in a new pronoun
That requires new verb agreements. From my station
In Hawai'i, then, the "difficult text" confronts me
From a culture not my own; when I first moved here,
Eric Chock's "Tutu on the Curb"[18] was a difficult poem,
Both for its use of the word "tutu," to mean old woman,
Grandmother figure, but for its being written in Pidgin.
Years later, this seems the most transparent of poems,
The tutu a vehicle of local nostalgia for what has passed,
Is passing, has come. Two days ago, as I bought Gala apples;
The new cashier called them "Gahlah," but the veteran cashier
Corrected her to "Gayla." "Gahlah" is "snot," in Pidgin.
The apple's name introduced a kind of difficulty that is both
Block and opening, the refusal of closure Hejinian advocates
Written into the most ordinary of supermarket exchanges.
The difficulties that interest me, then, are at once those
That are textual (the "this poem is difficult" cited by Steiner
As evidence the poem is) and those that are cultural and social
(whether the reasons stem from the poet's queerness or her
Belonging to a nondominant ethnic culture). These last difficulties
Do not mimic the difficulty lived by the Hawai'i Pidgin writer,
Say, but might access that difficulty for the "haole"
Or outside reader of the Pidgin text. Texts in Hawaiian take
This process a step further, obliging the outside(r) reader to study
That language in order to read them with any understanding.
Difficulty, I suggest, is a kind of silence; the hostile reader
Perceives it as null, sullen, refusing connection
With the reader eager to take the text in, or "penetrate it,"

A phrase John Vincent makes much hay of; the friendly
Reader finds a way in which to enter the silence. Here
I approximate the reader-response emphasis I
Wish otherwise to set aside. What I want to make clear
Is that the writer first participates in silence
When she enters his or her impasse. One could perhaps
Write a narrative of these impasses, silences, order them
Like shrubs on a military base, but I'd rather let them
Remain as moments, instances, alarms set to wake
The writer to her inability to write that way any more,[19]
Not out of some longing for the new
But because social and cultural circumstances
Demand that these silences be voices, much as
Yamanaka's characters overwhelm their listeners
With what explodes out of their mouths,
Knowing what cannot be written is crucial
To any process of composition, silences essential
To whatever poetry comes after. These are
The stories I tell here, not so much as stories
But as explorations of how a writer comes to
Write, or to continue writing, under the stresses
Of the many forces that demand she not do so.

Trouble with the Editor

It is important to separate the creator and the editor or internal
censor when you practice writing, so that the creator has free space
to breathe, explore, and express. If the editor is absolutely annoying
and you have trouble differentiating it from your creative voice, sit
down whenever you need to and write what the editor is saying;
give it full voice—"You are a jerk, who ever said you could write, I
hate your work, you suck, I'm embarrassed, you have nothing valuable to say, and besides you can't spell. . . . " Sound familiar?
—Natalie Goldberg, *Writing Down*
the Bones: Freeing the Writer Within

I sometimes use Goldberg's book to teach creative writing, urging students
Out of the white spaces that envelope them ("You suck" seems

An especially apt phrase for them to use, in this regard), but

The "editor" in me wants to return to passages like this one,

More closely examine the vocabulary of "breath" "exploration" "expression"

And the ways it's juxtaposed against the implied "suffocation" "imprisonment"

And "oppression" of the unwritten "texts" Goldberg is so eager to erase

(And erase them she does in "marathons" of writing, communal writing sessions,

What sound like thousands of pages of journal entries scrivened in cafés

And on kitchen tables). Goldberg's argument is that silence oppresses us,

While writing liberates us; to "write down the bones" is to free the writer's

Very marrow and thus defeat the forces of "editing," or as my students

Translate for me, "the critic." What if we begin our discussion not

From the point of "how do we start writing, given that it's difficult?"

But that of "why is it that we are having such difficulty writing,

And how is it that we can meaningfully begin to write about subjects

That are not easy to tackle?" At the level of the beginning writer,

Perhaps it's best simply to set pen or pixel to paper and scribble,

But for any serious writer, the question of block is not simply

A technical, or even a psychological, problem, but one that

Leads us to consider the larger forces that inform our writing,

Or our lack of it. The notion that any writing, however private,

Is "free," while it may result in words on paper, does not ask

The hard questions about "freedom" (or any such abstract noun/

Concept) that need to be addressed before or during our hoped-for

Move from writer's block to writing practice. What Goldberg ignores

Is the *content* of the block, even as she offers remedies

For the block's *effects*. Get at that content, my argument goes,

And the reason behind the block becomes the content

Of the writing that follows; at the least, writing resumes

At the moment one recognizes why it has stopped in the first

Place, and the content of that writing inscribes both reason

And release, is not perhaps liberation but a means to elucidate

Ways in which we are implicated in the larger structures
That silence us.

Ronald Johnson is, at times, more "editor" than "creator,"
Reversing Goldberg's process by becoming a writer *of*
The block, in large measure Milton's block, manifested
In his erasures of *Paradise Lost* into his own epic,
RADI OS. To compose by erasing a previous text
Does more than introduce writer's and reader's blocks
Into the very process of composition, however. Johnson's
Title, *RADI OS,* condensation of *Paradise Lost,* but also
The name for the boxes that talk to us, suggests that the
Erasure of writing leads back to oral expression, that
By highlighting what is left out—creating silences, in
Other words—what remains is vocable, performative,
A score to hear as much as read (see Cage, see Retallack).
Johnson's work does not rest on a historical crux,
The way Susan Howe's does, but her uses of silences
Inside the text resemble his; while he
Is the poet with the eraser, she is the editor/reviser
Recovering texts that always already were erased,
Or never existed, the words of women and native
Americans lost in wo(o)(r)dland. A conscious silence,
In these instances, cannot anymore suppress speech,
And the performances that grow from these silences,
If they do not precisely fill them in, give us words
To hang on the lines of our syntax.[20]

This is to get ahead of myself, because the problem is
To create actual communities, not fictive ones; the class-
Room is often the best place in which to model a community
Out of the differences I've been engaging in my essay thus
Far. This past semester, my graduate students told me they'd
Come to UH to write, to be "apprenticed" to a "master"
In the art; one said he'd dreamed of the writer's
Version of "fat camp" where everything you did was geared
To a single goal, whether of losing or (in this case) gaining . . .
Midway through the second semester of their lives here,

They stopped writing: "I cannot write about Hawai'i because I am
a) a settler, b) a local but also a settler, c) Polynesian but not Hawaiian,
d) knowledgeable about Hawai'i, but unable to speak the languages of
The place." "If I were to write, I'd get it wrong." Outbreaks of block
Punctuated each week's responses. I came here to write but I stopped.
I cannot be responsible and write about this place. So that, as
Provocateur self-assigned to make their lives just uncomfortable
   enough
To consider their responsibilities as writers in a "state" (word much
Maligned, as it is not in, say, Virginia) where ownership
Of the land and "ownership" of the literature are equally vexed,
Where Haunani-Kay Trask, the Hawaiian activist, several years ago
Told local writers (most of them Asian Americans, born and raised
Here) that they, like the haoles (your fair writer is one of them)
Are settlers, have no claim on the land, nor right to the "subject"
That inhabits most of their work (see Bamboo Ridge Press's
List, or read issues of its journal). While the venue for her speech
Was an international MELUS conference,[21] populated mostly by
Visitors from other places, her words echoed in other attacks on
Bamboo Ridge Press for not publishing enough work by Hawaiian
   writers,
And on writers like Yamanaka, who not only are seen by some
Local Asians to perpetuate stereotypes of Filipinos, but also
To ignore the myths and histories that wander like ghosts
Around the edges of her narratives (or "poetic novellas,"
As she calls her poems). In a place where literature is crucial,
However, silence is not an option; what had been a lack of
Writing, decade after decade, exploded into book after book in
The 1970s, 1980s, and 1990s, and around each book the heat
Of reception was stronger than I have ever witnessed at any
Book launch or writers' group meeting. Still, I thought my
Students, while their passions were apt, overreacted by laying
Claim to the otherwise privileged position of *not* writing about
Hawai'i, another way to reach the safety of base
Via the theft of one's own words, their investment elsewhere.
The real crux is that we write out of this place to which we are
Attached, either by blood or self-"adoption" into
Place (adoption a contentious issue, especially
Where indigenous and foreigner meet and sometimes become

Family). Anne Brewster writes about the "anxiety of whiteness"[22]
(For which substitute any "outsider," to some degree or other)
But, at the same time, writes out of a profound sense
Of "witness," both as an intelligence ("wit") and as one
Who attempts to write (sic) and anthologize
Those writers whose voices have remained a mumble under
The monologues of mainstream culture. Whiteness, as she
Writes about it, is potentially a mechanism of self-silencing,
Though white writers are notorious more for their inability
To stop chattering. But the impasse that she reaches is one
She navigates by writing what is called in Australia "fictocriticism,"
Word that acknowledges both the fictitiousness of criticism and
The critical apparatus that can be brought to bear on one's own
Experiences. In my class we called it "positioning," and I asked
The students to write a statement in which they presented
The reader with evidence of their authority for writing
About place. Later, they turned these position papers into
Collages, melding (almost) memoir and myth, history and fiction
In ways that worked toward "truths," if not Platonic certitude.

While I empathized with their frustrations, having experienced them
During my early years here, and almost every week since, I believe
That such a block is necessary to becoming a writer
Aware of the political ramifications of possessing a certain identity
(Whether or not you know it, acknowledge it, or honor it) in this
   place.
Arguments against critiques of writing here almost always invoke si-
   lence
As a bad thing, as if silence were always an act of censorship.

Career Trouble

> Verse writing in the postmodern era, it is plausible to claim, is less
> a visionary or sacramental art than a highly competitive industry.
> —Walter Kalaidjian (1989) as quoted by
> Hank Lazer, *Opposing Poetries,* vol. 1, 83

Not all poets can be silenced: Charles Bernstein is the most garrulous
   of writers,

Yet, I would argue, his work feeds off of the possible impasses
In his own practice. His hatred of ready-mades could "inspire" him
To stop writing, since the language itself is ready-made
(Buy your words and receive the free gift of syntax),
Taxed almost beyond recognition by Bushes I and II.
His response is to go overboard
The other way, to take all the ways in which the language has been mis-
Used, misplaced, misspelled, and to combine them in a kind of rococo
Salad that reinvigorates the discourse. That his practice is rife with self-
Contradiction goes without saying. *Why do you keep talking about his
Career?* writes a correspondent, who wonders what a poetry career
Might be. Ask Hank Lazer, who has one, about Charles Bernstein's
Career, and he'll ventriloquize the following questions: "Isn't poetry a small
Business with plenty of indirect economic benefits (prizes, reading
Fees, academic positions, grants, residencies, publication) that usually
Go unacknowledged?" (*Opposing Poetries* 2: 131) The career that Bern-
stein
At once wants and finds most dangerous, the installation of the poet
In the very institution that propagates "official verse culture," inspires
The question of how to make of that career something other
Than expected, becomes a discipline, a pit into which one sometimes
Falls, skins one's literary knees and then rises up, the comic laughing
At his own tendency to tell jokes, or the MLA panelist who so abhors
MLA panels that his appearance on one is farce. Career, then, is itself
A kind of block, blockage, blocage (an arterial bypass is called for, is performed
As a balloon-therapy, the language becoming full and fuller until,
Like Rover on the 1960s show, *The Prisoner,* the ball comes
To take over the prison camp that is also a vacation colony for old
Chess players and opera singers). And so one's strategy for pursuing
The career is a response to the silence that career enforces,
Whether through committee meetings or the process of dealing
With colleagues, or the inevitable critique of your participation in
The very career you used to deride. There are ways away from this:
Ron Silliman, for example, works in computers, and poets in other
Countries aren't folded into the academy the way they are here,
But I am interested in the way that poets can perform upon this
Apparent paradox (this becomes something of a tongue twister,

Peck of Peter style) by participating in it, not avoiding it, insofar
As it can be avoided (and of course any poet depends upon the
University for his or her "reception," as if the university were
A kind of clear-channel mechanism for spreading the word,
Hegemonically, across reading zones). Again, I want to add
That my emphasis is not on the act of reading, per se,
However crucial that is to any consideration of poetry,
But on the *process* by which a poet reaches an *impasse,*
Whether of language or career or history and then either
Falls into that impasse (Riding is a primary example here)
Or courts it (as do Bernstein and Howe and other writers
Considered here or elsewhere).

Laura (Riding) Jackson showed us that "career" (aka "mammon")
Ropes the poet into writing in particular "styles," those deemed ac-
    ceptable
By poetry's "public." Career can be seen as an attempt to enter into
A poetry public, albeit one now defined by institutional life, but is also
A privatization of that "visionary" impulse that Kalaidjian refers to
In his diagnosis of contemporary poetry. In *Career Moves,* Libbie
Rifkin reads the poems of Zukofsky, Berrigan, et al.
Quite eloquently, but seems to suggest that every line these poets
Wrote or spoke was geared toward that anomaly of their times,
The "poetry career." For them, career was community, the kind
Of nest we envisage, as graduate students, in the academy, only
To realize when we're hired, that we're essentially "one of a kinds"
In our departments, bereft of community in that sense of the term.
Career is not the foundation of community, we come to think,
But enforces individualism by separating us from our peers,
Both geographically and (we fear) intellectually.
Or we find that "community" exists in opposition to other communi-
    ties
In ways that perpetuate colonialism, or sexism, or other modes
Of oppression institutionalized by the university system.
In my department, the hiring of a "local writer" (read non-white,
Born and raised in Hawai'i) in the mid-1990s brought into
The open voices one had always known existed,
But had silenced themselves to consolidate power.
When Eric Chock was appointed Distinguished Visiting Writer

At the UH, in the mid-1990s, the creative writing committee,
Composed at the time of all creative writing teachers in the
Department, argued over whether or not to drop the word
"Distinguished" from Chock's temporary title. Rarely
Are discussions so open; usually, the language
Of *craft* was used to exclude writers whose work's content
And language were utterly *local* (in a place where approximately
90 percent of our students are from the local community).
Presumptions of quality ("aesthetics," as they were called throughout
the debates by the forces of "conservation") were trotted out
In opposition to writers whose qualities were simply other, or,
Ironically, much the same (given that many of the local writers
Studied with the professors who now hoped to keep them off
The faculty). When arguments of "craft" failed, the focus
Turned to departmental "need"; when those failed, one
Committee member threatened to walk out of a meeting
If the Director (then myself) insisted on calling for a vote
To admit new faculty to the program, allow them to teach
Creative writing courses. These tactics were fascinating
For their various strategies of silencing; that they took
Place behind closed doors brought the issue of "block"
Into relief. This is a highly selective and partial rendering
Of a time in departmental history when issues like writing
And race exploded out of the rooms in which they'd been
Talked about or, more frequently, elided, illustrating
For me the power of institutions to silence even those
Writers who write and publish. If to become an academic
Is, to quote my father-in-law, to "court insignificance,"
Then in cases like these, what may seem insignificant on
The outside proves crucial to the relationships between
The university and the community it serves, between
Writers who perceive themselves as working under
Different philosophies of craft, and between members
Of these communities, who stay or go according to
Needs both public and private.

Thus, I find it reductive to consider the block as a problem of craft,
Technique, angle of approach to the page, color of the pen or the pad,

And, while the spirit world is of immense importance to me, this
  group
Of essays does not work off of a spiritual diagnosis of the block, one
Addressed by such books as *Writing Down the Bones,* where the freeing
Of the spirit is tantamount to the freeing of the pen.
Rather, I see the block, here, where I write in a professional space that I
Sometimes call my "career," as a necessary stopping point for the
  writer.
I do not want to suggest that *silence,* a focal point in this conversation
With myself (a silent one, except for the tapping of the keys) is a
  univocal
(as it were) term, for silence needs to be stripped away from *silencing,*
And withheld silences from those that reach out (the difference here
Between guilt, which internalizes and aggrandizes and attempts to em-
  brace
What we so awkwardly call "the other," and action, publication,
Community organization that is not aimed at positioning
The self at the head but at the sides of the table).
So there is the silence of the survivor, a silence that masks remem-
  bering,
Perhaps even prevents it from occurring, a silence that comes out of
Having been silenced. This is the ur-silence, at least in the framework
I'm laying, a destructive silence, whether it comes from the outside
(As it so often does in politics) or the inside (as it did in the cases
Discussed here of Hart Crane and Laura Riding)—of course, it's
A matter of degree here, where inside and outside part ways,
Like the boundaries between holy lands that President Bush
Referred to recently as "that old stuff." These silences, like so much
He does not know, are historical in depth and in feeling.

This is our impasse, this not knowing how to proceed, the lack
Of language as symptom of an oppressive disorder, but I want
To revalue this impasse as a crucial moment of opportunity,
Of exception, a point of launching from the old languages,
Which strangle, into new organizations of words.
Where I wish to change the emphasis
Is by focusing attention back upon the writer, not as a solitary
Walker in the woods or fields, but as one comprised of a kind

Of "cultural negative capability," as Hank Lazer puts it.[23] In order
To achieve that state of not-knowing, one must assume both the
Writer and the reader positions; yes, meaning is produced
Communally, and difficult writing (to be severely reductive)
Can challenge communities into being or, as is the case in my
Classrooms, can force communities to begin their discussions
In anticipation of final projects and other coercive aspects of their
Experiences as students. But to place "difficulty" at the point of
Reception is too easy, or at least not the complete picture, if there
Can be said to be one, since "difficulty" is what generates these
Texts in the first place. And that difficulty is composed (only
In the sense of the word as a verb) of these moments of stasis,
Followed by movement, a kind of evolution by preemption,
Though my language is growing more political in a way
I abhor right now, as "preemption" is now the polite word
For "invading countries lest they attack you later."
I find my poet friends these days wonder all the time
How to write about the political situation
We find ourselves in. Donald Rumsfeld is the muse of the day,
And this is not to say that what he left on the table was worth
Eating. If Donald Rumsfeld silences me, I need a new
Method, which is one of writing and not of reading, at
Least at its origins (which I know are problematic in them-
Selves, but I use the term pointedly to suggest that we need
Pay more attention to the writer, to the mode of production,
To the content of the piece, and less to the formal effects
That engender meaning). If I say I'm less interested in form
Than in content, I separate my poetics from that of many
Of the poets about whom I write, those for whom the trade
Of content-based poetics for formal fascinations were
Necessary to get us away from a shallow scene-based
Poetry, which had come to be generated out of a form
So powerful that it dictated content.

Impasse as Possibility

The impasse, meanwhile, that is both language's creative condition
and its problem can be described as the disjuncture between words

and meaning, but at a particularly material level, one at which the
writer is faced with the necessity of making formal decisions.
—Hejinian, "The Rejection of Closure," 42

One approach to the "problem" of impasse, then, is to
Attack it by formal means. E.g: The fire hose of form
Takes on the wildfire of "nature poetry"[24] and puts it out.
Language *itself* is form, in this instance, as the reader of
Stein and Bernstein will recognize in the manic patterns
Of words covering pages not with their meaning but with
Their syncopation, a kind of spiritual hammer sent to
Wrench (sic) language out of its political morass (at least
In later readings of Stein found in *The L=A=N=G=U=A=G=E Book*
And elsewhere). My book is an homage to these modes
Of reading and writing, but also suggests a way past the
Impasse I find in the form-based poetics of the very poets
Whose work I admire enough to stake my "career" on it.
Where form works best, it seems to me, it offers up an
Enactment of the process of impasse and revision that
I'm suggesting we might, as it were, entertain. The form,
From Shakespeare on, is a farm fence, a barrier against
Which the poet struggles (Annie Finch has much
To say about this in her critical writings); when a sonnet
Comes to be written by a feminist poet, that impasse
Relates directly back to writing a poem in a form
That is historically labeled "male." The silence before
The choice of sonnet is what intrigues me, as much
As the writing of it, because in that silence
"choice," insofar as there are choices,
Becomes available to the poet. And, while
Repeated use of the form in this revolutionary
Way can remain effective over the long-term
(just see how long traditional sonnets packed
Their punch), and repetition, as Stein so brilliantly
Asserted, is less rote than it is insistence, changing
Utterly in context, I still want to cast my torch
Away from the question of form and to a content-based
Poetics, based as it is on responses to current impasses,

Especially those presented in the political sphere.
This is not to say that changes in genre are not
Alterations in thinking; in my experience, the move from
A poetry whose force depended on the drama of the line
Break to another that abandoned the break for the prose
Poem, was likely a move from what Stephen Ellis called
(In private e-mail) a "vertical" to a "horizontal" poetics.
Yet prose is form as the absence of form and, as such, fits
My new poetics as a vehicle for meaning, development,
Expansiveness, that does not call attention to itself
As form but as the form of the content, rather than
What so often seems more to be the content of the form.
Lest I turn the introduction to my volume of essays
Into an argument against it, tempting prospect indeed
As these projects inevitably turn into long rumbles
With one's own ideas, shifting variously as they do,
I propose that, whatever the strategy for overcoming
Impasse, whether it is formal or one that puts
Form on the back burner, that these strategies, which
Become the poems we read, emerge out of a stall
(the balsa glider lifts into the near sky and then
Threatens to halt, falling, then catches its
Breath again before crashing into the field)
That is the place given us, as poets, to reconsider
The next word we put upon the page, the next
Poem, the next book, the next.
That it was possible to write after Auschwitz is now
Evident, but that the question was real, vital, horrible,
Was, as well. Holocaust, or symbolic/actual attack, such as
Those on the Twin Towers (now an empty block)[25] and
The Pentagon, are efforts to destroy content by way of form:
The building is crucial insofar as it represents an idea,
The idea crucial insofar as it sustains the larger form, of government,
Of ethos, of economy, of a daily life spent moving from New
Jersey to Manhattan and back again. Metaphor is,
In this instance, a dangerous method, as actual death
Cannot be mitigated by it, nor can poetry aptly be
Described in the terms it sets; poetry makes more
Than nothing happen, perhaps, but it does not

Operate in the same way as a building, coherent
Or emptied in the chaos of a vacant lot. But
What we are given, then, is a moment of
Choice, the option to build or to leave
Behind, to strike back or to pull in.
These are the choices a poet has, as well,
Given impasse, whether he or she chooses
To begin from the building or from what the building
Enclosed, is less important than the fact of singing
Out of the space and back into being. Not all
Impasses or choices are so like the sublime, as I
See it rise like the Alps on my computer screen;
Some involve more trivial choices, but that of
Writing out of the recognition of impasse
Is the one that most interests me as a poet
And here, as an essayist about poets
Who required me to ask this last,
Most starkly pointed, question.

The poet I describe (and want to be) will always live one block away
From the neighborhood figured as someone else's "community,"
Will partake of qualities admired by transcendentalists (that craggy
Individualism) and by partisans of community (however con-
Figured); the poet I describe will be more outside than inside,
More Whitman than Walt, or Stein than Gertrude,
The poet I describe will be the public editor of texts
That include work from all the streets of all the neighborhoods
In a diverse city of styles and conundrums; the poet I describe
Will privately write a poetry that is both in and out of the game,
A poetics of the outside that acknowledges this as a form
Of community, not its lack. The poet I describe will think
Of community as collage, of postmodernism as a literal
Map of the paintmix of place and unfinished lexicons
Of howzit and aloha and words still unmangled by commerce,
If not the corporate strictures of the university, or
The public's desires for consolation after terror,
An old-fashioned elegy a better buy on this market
Than the self-ravishing artifact of an avowedly "difficult" poet.

Hart Crane and the Impasse of Formalism

MISSING FROM Cleanth Brooks's famous study, *The Well-Wrought Urn: Studies in the Structure of Poetry* (1947), is any mention of Hart Crane's urn poem, "Praise for an Urn," first published in 1922. Brooks's urn, borrowed from Donne and Keats, represents the perfections of poetic form, as of eternal time; what it says to the poet is "that 'formed experience,' or imaginative insight, embodies the basic and fundamental perception of man and nature" (150), a vision that is at once beautiful and true. The urn poem, furthermore, is ultimately unreadable; it teases, rather than tells, its secrets to the beholder, arms him or her with a healthy "distrust" (152). The urn's literary value, then, exists in symbolizing both the artifact of the poem and its reception by the reader. John Donne knew this when he used the urn as part of his mechanism of seduction: "We'll build in sonnets pretty roomes; / As well a well wrought urne becomes / The greatest ashes" (240). The speaker of this poem teases his reader/lover with the specter of death, but only in order to fulfill the more instrumental and seductive intent of his rhetoric. Death is simply one more metaphor for the dangers (and the delights) of evading (or giving in to) love.

Why did Brooks not include a discussion of Crane's "Praise for an Urn" in his book? By the midforties, Crane's star had fallen; Brooks and Warren, in their textbook *Understanding Poetry,* first published in 1938, hardly mentioned Crane, and attacked the Romantics—whom they associated with him—for sentimentality and "immaturity." Crane's poem does not fit Brooks's scheme for quite another reason, however; his urn, unlike that of Donne or Keats, does not represent the perfections of form so much as its ultimate inconsequence in the face of death. Even though Crane writes his praise in the disciplined quatrains that mark much of his best work, these quatrains are the precise vehicle by which Crane undermines the forms in which, and of which, he writes. If Keats's urn offers the consolations of an elegy that promises eternal life to those painted on the urn or written into the poem, then Crane's elegy makes no such claims. Instead, after touching on the "inheritances" that the poet receives from his friend (the poem is dedicated to Ernest Nelson, someone Crane knew in Cleveland), the poem concludes by equating the poet's words with the urn's ashes. The first word of the penultimate stanza is "Still": referring to death's stillness and to an earlier punning line "Of what the dead keep, living still," certainly, but also to the poet's doubts about the efficacy of the urn or poem to keep his friend's memory alive:

> Still, having in mind gold hair,
> I cannot see that broken brow
> And miss the dry sound of bees
> Stretching across a lucid space. (Simon 8)

The power of Keats's urn depended upon just the sight that Crane professes to have lost here; while Keats's urn provides the medium for art, the presentation of a "sylvan scene" to which the eyes of generations can return, Crane's urn can only represent what cannot be seen. Ashes yield no image, and so the poet "cannot see" a brow that is now "broken." Stillness, then, does not figure eternity so much as loss. The final stanza equates the poet's words with the ashes in the urn; he means for his words to be scattered, but the poet hints at no recovery of their meaning:

> Scatter these well-meant idioms
> Into the smoky spring that fills
> The suburbs, where they will be lost.
> They are no trophies of the sun. (8)

"Well-meant" or no, these idioms, like the friend's ashes—and like the memory of his "gold hair"—will be lost. Language does not replenish itself through death, as many elegies argue; rather it too dies. Crane's fears, and his hopes, were tied closely to the central images in the poem, which begins with a mythical description of the friend's face:

> It was a kind and northern face
> That mingled in such exile guise
> The everlasting eyes of Pierrot
> And, of Gargantua, the laughter. (8)

This epitaph, as Crane made clear to Gorham Munson in a letter, was as much for himself as for Nelson: "Here is my sum poetic output for the last three months—two lines—'The everlasting eyes of Pierrot / And of Gargantua,—the laughter.' Maybe it is my epitaph, it is contradictory and wide enough to be. But I hope soon to make it into a poem and thereby, like Lazarus, return. (Hammer and Weber, *O My Land, My Friends: The Selected Letters of Hart Crane* [*Land*] 58–59) Seven years later, having refigured himself as Lazarus at the end of "The Tunnel" section of *The Bridge*, Crane had already entered a period of his own life when resurrection seemed less possible.

What I will do in this chapter is explore reasons for Crane's loss of power as a poet, and point toward a possible renovation (if not resurrection) of poetry in Crane's late, largely unrecognized, work. For what Crane was doing in "Praise for an Urn," in my view, was to write a proleptic elegy to New Critical formalism, given shape by Brooks and others throughout the middle decades of the century. The renovation of his poetry was to come about not by way of the same forms that the New Critics advocated and institutionalized, but through new forms (often disguised as formlessness) later created by Beat poets and by Language poets. This "new formalism," which is not to be confused with the school of Dana Gioa, Brad Leithauser, and others, replaces closed forms represented so artfully by the urn with those better symbolized by the scattered idioms to which Crane alludes in his urn poem. These idioms are not "trophies of the sun," but then again, they are not meant to be. Rather they arise through the bodiless and yet embodied form of language itself, which looks past the transcendent myths of Keats's urn, or Donne's, and toward a poetry that recognizes its own mortality.

I

From the beginning of his career, Hart Crane based his poetics on a belief in formalism. This belief was more than poetic, however, for Crane also intended it to be therapeutic. He meant to live a formalist life, if such a thing is possible. In this, he was in accord with New Critics, including Cleanth Brooks, who wrote in 1947, providing both text and subtext to the New Critical creed: "[The poet's] task is finally to unify experience. He must return to us the unity of the experience itself as man knows it in his own experience" (quoted in Kalaidjian 6). Along the same lines, though more presciently, Crane wrote to his father from New York, when he was seventeen years old: "There is only one harmony, that is the equilibrium maintained by two opposite forces, equally strong. When I perceive one emotion growing overpowering to a fact, or statement of reason, then the only manly, worthy, sensible thing to do, is build up the logical side, and attain balance, and in art,—formal expression" (*Land* 10). Balance in one's life, then, is tantamount to artistic balance; the logic of the poet's life mirrors that of its metaphors. That Crane's letters to his father, as later to his patron Otto Kahn, are so often pleas for money, indicates that this declared ambition of attaining "formal expression" might also be a way for Crane to join the "materialism" of his father's business sense with the "Puritanical" artistic sense of his mother, and indeed of the critics he respected (see Hammer and Weber's *O My Land* 50 for an exposition of Crane's divisions along these lines).

Crane's letter, written in 1916, sounds very like John Crowe Ransom in the essay "Forms and Citizens," published in 1933, the year after Crane's death. Ransom directly addresses the relationship between poetic form and "real life," one that the New Critics' emphasis on the poem as a "well-wrought urn" often obscures. Art, in Ransom's terms, does not so much mirror life as slow it down, emphasizing mind over body, according to the familiar modernist dichotomy. Art—at least the art Ransom advocates—performs a moral purpose as an anti-Romantic system of checks and balances. He writes: "The aesthetic forms are a technique of restraint, not of efficiency. They do not butter our bread, and they delay the eating of it. They stand between the individual and his natural object and impose a check upon his action" (60). That Ransom means for his argument to apply to more than particular poets and particular poems is clear in what follows: "What I have in mind is an argument from aesthetics which will justify any formal art, even a formal literature" (61). He further intends for his argument to carry weight in social terms, in his claim that "the object of a proper society is to instruct its members how to transform instinctive experience into aesthetic experience" (67), to create Miltons, even if they be mute inglorious ones. That he may have had Crane in mind becomes clear when he talks about the specific, therapeutic, value of art: "the formal tradition intends to preserve the artist from the direct approach to his object. Behind the tradition is probably the sense that the direct approach is perilous to the artist, and may be fatal. It is feared that the artist who disregards the instruction may discover at length that he has only been artless; or, what is worse, that he will not make this important discovery, which will have to be made for him by the horrid way of autopsy" (61). This seconds Yvor Winters's famous assertion that any poet who follows Emerson must end his life by committing suicide. Hence the New Critics' attack on *The Bridge* for its formlessness, an argument that holds so little water it is surprising that it was effective for so long.[1] This poem, viewed through their critical lenses, had to be formless because its author was. What *The Bridge* shows best, perhaps, is Crane's desperate desire that poetic form *could* re-form a life, or a nation, suffering from what seems a chaotic loss of form. Form, in the New Critical philosophy, becomes quite literally (and literarily) a "code of conduct," an etiquette, one that Crane was eager to sign on to, because it promised a narrative of redemption.

In his 1952 essay, "Crane: The Poet as Hero," Allen Tate, like Ransom a Fugitive and political conservative, reads Crane's letters as formal exercises, seeing Crane's sexual life in formalist terms.[2] There is more than an implication in what he writes that the formalist poet, to be successful both as a poet and as a person (since he must be both, or none), must be heterosexual and lead an "ordered" life. He cites the letter by the seventeen-year-old Crane (noting well his age) as an impressive formal and moral document, reporting that "What astonishes me in the early letters—and what I had not got from Crane himself or from Mr. Philip Horton's excellent biography—is not only the intellectual precocity but the precocity of moral insight" (324–25). Tate then quotes a letter Crane wrote in 1926 to an anonymous friend (anonymity being a marker in the Weber edition of letters that the correspondent was a friend who knew of Crane's homosexuality, and probably was himself gay). In that letter,

Crane writes: " . . . with the sailor no faith or such is properly *expected,* and how jolly and cordial and warm . . . Let my lusts be my ruin, then, since all else is fake and mockery" (325). Tate immediately jumps forward in his argument, noting that Crane's "intellectual deterioration came more slowly," a remark that emphasizes the mind-body split that Tate accepts. Significantly, he fails to take into account the differences between Crane's correspondents—on the one hand, his father, and on the other a friend. Interesting that in 1968, in Tate's third published piece on Crane, he sees the poet—in 1926—as a precursor to the Beats (a point on which the Beats would agree). Perhaps Tate still thought of Crane as a last Romantic, attempting a solution for a problem that could not be solved. Or, more provocatively, Tate may have recognized that Crane was not the poet of a single tone, that he wrote both as the poet his father may have wanted him to be, and as another, in part homosexual audience, wished him to do.[3]

One can sense a crisis in the evolution, or re-formation, of Tate's view of Crane over time. The crisis is that of formalist criticism itself, as well as that of a man who was at once sympathetic to, and horrified by, a poet who had been his friend throughout the 1920s. Tate ends his 1952 essay with a sense of Crane's ambiguities that had escaped him and his colleagues in the 1920s and 1930s. There he presents the portrait of a man whose poetry was better than he was, whose poetic forms suggested a counterforce to his life's formlessness: "Out of the desperate conditions of his life—which included almost unimaginable horrors of depravity and perversity of will—he produced in the end a shining *exemplum* of uncompromising human dignity: his poetry" (327). The stern moralism of tone remains from the late 1930s, but what changes in Tate's vision of his old friend mirrors the changes in criticism over the thirty-some years Tate thought and wrote about Crane. The relationship between poetry and life becomes more ambiguous, less formal. By 1968, even the Beats have entered Tate's canon. The hegemony of New Criticism also wavered under the onslaught of the political events of the 1960s.

The Bridge, published in 1930 after nearly seven years of work, is as much a poem about form as it is about America; the bridge is the poem's inspiration, the site of its opening, and its central symbol and organizing principle; it is the poem's noun and verb, by a poet who believed that the poem created a "new word."[4] Crane's letters to his patron, Otto Kahn, which amount to the selling of *The Bridge* by a sometime advertising copy writer, foreground the poet's emphasis on form (something that might appeal to a businessman more accustomed to quantifiable than to quantitative judgments).[5] On March 18, 1926 Crane wrote to Kahn, for example: "Naturally I am encountering many unexpected **formal** difficulties" (*Land* 235); he continues with some shop talk, probably meaning for his jargon to impress: "The first and last sections are composed of blank verse with occasional rhyme for accentuation. The verbal dynamics used and the spacious periodicity of the rhythm result in an unusually symphonic **form.** What **forms** I shall use for the other sections will have to be determined when I come to grips with their respective themes" (236, boldface mine).

This last sentence alludes to the fact that Crane had determined the structure of the entire poem before he wrote much of it; he had "merely" to follow his blueprint, like the engineer whose bridge he praised. The certitude of the plan was, of course, to pose terrible problems for Crane toward the end of the poem's composition. To Kahn, however, he continued to write about formal problems, rather than philosophical ones. In September 1927, Crane wrote his patron in terms that suggested that the building of his bridge was tantamount to the building of an actual structure; Crane's famous logic of metaphor here comes in handy as a sales device. "It has taken a great deal of energy—which has not been so difficult to summon as the necessary patience to wait, simply wait much of the time—until my instincts assured me that I had assembled my materials in proper order for a final welding into their natural form." He tells Kahn of the difficulties of determining not just the forms of particular sections, "but also in relation to the other parts, *in series,* of the major design of the entire poem" (345). In so doing, he links technology with art, arguing that the best analogy to the poem as a series can be found in the Sistine Chapel. Perhaps the most telling of Crane's metaphors is the one that argues for the value of an epic as being "worth at least the expenditure necessary for merely the scenery and costumes of many a flashy and ephemeral play, or for a motor car" (349).

It should come as no surprise, then, that when Crane began to doubt the worth of his poem's architecture, he likewise expressed these doubts in formal terms. To Waldo Frank he wrote in June of 1926 (not long after the letter to Kahn, with all its official optimism): "The very idea of a bridge, of course, is a form peculiarly dependent on such spiritual convictions . . . By which I mean that however great their subjective significance to me is concerned—these forms, materials, dynamics are simply non-existent in the world" (258–59). Furthermore: "The form of my poem rises out of a past that so overwhelms the present with its worth and vision that I'm at a loss to explain my delusion that there exist any real links between that past and a future destiny worthy of it" (259). Crane's problem was, in his terms, insurmountable: he wished to make a platonic form out of a stone and steel structure, and to do so by way of a poem's strict forms. The many puns on "form" are telling, but as punsters know, they disintegrate form as much as they alert us to its existence.

In poems like "The Visible the Untrue" and "Tenderness and Resolution," written in the late 1920s, Crane mourns the loss of form both in his life and his work; these are elegies to *The Bridge*, specifically to the "Cape Hatteras" section where Crane seeks to join himself with Whitman. Where "Cape Hatteras" testifies to Crane's grand entrance into a poetic tradition of his own making, the two late poems are the work of a poet who possesses no confidence in himself or in his tradition. "The Visible the Untrue" is dedicated to E.O., or Emil Opffer, who inspired Crane to write "Voyages." In this poem Crane wonders what *The Bridge* was for, and considers the loss of his inspiration:

> I'm wearing badges
> that cancel all your kindness. Forthright
> I watch the silver Zeppelin
> destroy the sky. To
> stir your confidence?
> To rouse what sanctions—? toothaches?
>
> The silver strophe . . . the canto
> bright with myth . . . Such
> distances leap landward without
> evil smile. (198)

The "Zeppelin," the "silver strophe" and "the canto / bright with myth" all refer directly to "Cape Hatteras." That poem uses destruction to clear the way for affirmation. But here, Crane confesses to loss of faith, even as he remembers his earlier praise. The reference to "toothache" is new to the Simon edition, and suggests that the hurt is not merely psychic, but also physical. This passage follows immediately:

[evil smile.] And, as for me . . .

The window weight throbs in its blind
partition. To extinguish what I have of faith,
Yes, light. (198)

The grammar of the poem demands that we read a disjunction between the "silver strophe" of *The Bridge* and the poet who has been blinded: he is not related to that myth, those cantos. As if in the spirit of imitative fallacy, this poem, confessing as it does to the poet's diminished powers, records his inability to redeem loss: the last line reads: "And it is always the day, the farewell day unkind" (198). In making a subject rhyme between the imagery of this poem and that of an earlier, better, poem, Crane emphasizes how powerless is even his greatest poetry to give him faith. He is also reduced to writing poems about his own poems; the formalist trap closes around him, as poetry—or the loss of it—becomes the only fit subject *for* poetry. Self-quotation is not as powerful a muse as the quotations from Whitman that drive "Cape Hatteras" forward. He suffers more from what a belated Bloomian might call an "anxiety of self-influence" than from any attached to an earlier poet.

"Tenderness and Resolution" also deals with the possibility that the poet may die with his poems. Crane rewrites a famous passage from "Cape Hatteras," as if he were his own poetic follower. The following passage from *The Bridge* celebrates the aviator's power:

Remember, Falcon-Ace,
Thou hast there in thy wrist a Sanskrit charge
To conjugate infinity's dim marge—
Anew . . . !

Consider then the tone of "Tenderness and Resolution":

With desperate propriety, whose name is writ
   In wider letters than the alphabet,—
Who is now left to vary the Sanscrit
Pillowed by

My wrist in the vestibule of time—who
Will hold it—wear the keepsake, dear, of time—
Return the mirage on a coin that spells
Something of sand and sun the Nile defends . . . (217)

The "Sanskrit charge" of the aviator/poet's wrist, an image of great strength, has given way to a "sanscrit" pillowed by his wrist, not on "infinity's dim marge," but "in the vestibule of time," which sounds more like a cloakroom than a limitless frontier. If Crane had thought it possible to transform the world through the recovery of a reliquary language in "Cape Hatteras," in these later poems his marge has shrunken to the size of his doubt. The fear that no one will follow him reflects a profounder fear that he cannot follow himself.

Allen Grossman has written persuasively—though in some ways contrary to my argument—about Crane's "intense poetics," the way in which Crane sought to transcend history through historically marked poetic forms, those that came to him from "modern, Victorian, or Elizabethan poets" (234). According to Grossman, "his models, of structure and style, were bitter friends indeed, an enemy element, at the most intimate point of self-presence." They threatened at all times to swallow him up. Grossman's critique of Crane's poetics of self-denial, his tendency to write through old voices, is not one that would have particularly surprised the poet. For Crane was well aware of the strictures he had placed on his art by what he calls, in his "General Aims and Theories," an "absolute" poetry (*Complete Poems and Selected Letters and Prose* [*Complete Poems*] 220). In a famous letter to Yvor Winters in May 1927, he describes his narrow poetic field: "I write damned little because I am interested in recording certain sensations, very rigidly chosen, with an eye for what according to my taste and sum of prejudices seems suitable to—or intense enough—for verse" (Parkinson 91–92). He goes on to say that in prose he would likely reveal more about himself, but that he believes poetry's purpose is different (along the way, he had bought wholesale Eliot's notion of "impersonality"): "One should be somewhat satisfied if one's work comes to approximate a true record of such moments of 'illumination' as are occasionally possible." Poetry, he added, involved "[a] sharpening of reality accessible to the poet, to no such degree possible through other mediums." Again, Crane considers the poem to be important for its record (enactment) of illumination, not for its part in discovering such illumination.

As Crane wryly notes, it is difficult to write a lot of poetry of "illumination"; even Crane was not given a steady stream of such moments, and his efforts to re-create them in writing *The Bridge* from its pre-ordained blueprints became more and more difficult. He wrote very little in his last five years, a fact that critics have noted but not much discussed. Such inability to write was a recurring problem for Crane; as he wrote to his friend, Gorham Munson in January, 1921 in a passage I've already cited. Let me cite it once more. "Here is my sum poetic output for the last three months—two lines 'The everlasting eyes of Pierrot / And of Gargantua,—the laughter.' Maybe it is my epitaph, it is contradictory and wide enough to be. But I hope soon to make it into a poem and thereby, like Lazarus, return" (*Land* 58-59). He equates his inability to write with death, the ability to write poetry with resurrection. Later, after *The Bridge* had been published, his mood was similarly depressed. According to his Patterson, New York, friend Peter Blume: "*The Bridge* had been published and, for a book of poetry, widely reviewed. Hart was in a state of deep depression, declaring that he could never write a line of poetry again. The well had gone completely dry" (156). Edward Brunner, in a brief essay on the fragmentary poems of these last years, suggests—rightly, I think—that Crane "consciously set out to write a poetry of a kind new to him" (156). Brunner's example of this new poetry, "A Name for All," strikes a false chord to me, however; that poem, hardly as bad as Brunner suggests, seems to me consistent with Crane's formalist enterprise. More interesting to me are poems such as "Supplication to the Muses on a Trying Day," included in the Marc Simon edition of Crane's collected poems published in 1986; this poem *is* completely unlike any of Crane's published work. Brunner suggests that this new poetry contributed to the writing block, rather than freeing Crane to write more. "As it happened," he writes, "this poetry proved unusually difficult for him to compose, even though it was far less complex than any of his previous work, because it was at odds with so much in his life" (156). According to Brunner, this new poetry was more personal, and hence more dangerous to the poet. So dangerous that Brunner claims that, "[b]y imposing a set of poetics that prevented him from being himself even in his poetry, he had already guaranteed that a large part of him had died—clearly the most important part—before his own death" (170). But this new poetry, to my mind, was "unpublishable" because it so broke the forms that Crane had written by; no Otto Kahn would have patronized this poetry.

II

While I agree with Brunner that Crane was radically altering his poetics toward the end of the 1920s, I intend to argue, in contrary fashion, that he *was* on the verge of locating a way out of the formalist impasse that *The Bridge* had proved to be. Crane was becoming a "first postmodernist"; his experiments with what one might call "informal poetry" are more radical even than the free verse of the modernists, Pound and Eliot foremost among them. His "intense poetics" were giving way to modern conversation poems, though hardly ones that Coleridge and Wordsworth would recognize. Most interesting to me is the way in which poems like "Eternity," "Supplication to the Muses on a Trying Day," and "Havana Rose," written according to Simon between 1926 and 1931 (at about the same time as *The Bridge*, in other words), respond explicitly to the poet's problems in writing his formalist epic. These poems, to greater and lesser degrees, are self-parodies, which serve both to critique the poet's formalism and to suggest an alternate poetics. "Eternity," written in 1926–27, describes the hurricane Crane lived through during his Caribbean stay. ("Supplication," also written in 1926–27, responds to "The Hurricane" as well as to "To Brooklyn Bridge.") "The Hurricane," which Crane published in 1927, participates in Crane's high style, its sublimity and archaic language (two aspects of Crane's style that inevitably concur) matching that of "Atlantis" and of "Cape Hatteras." The hurricane's force destroys language as well as land, as "e'en boulders now out-leap / Rock sockets, levin-lathered!"

> Lo, Lord, Thou ridest!
> Lord, Lord, Thy swifting heart
>
> Naught stayeth, naught now bideth
> But's smithereened apart!
>
> Ay! Scripture flee'th stone! (124)

"Eternity," whose title promises such sublimity, enacts a radical deflation both of the hurricane's effects, and of the poem's grand reach. The poem is as purely descriptive as Crane gets, its language straightforward, at times humorous, its content directly autobiographical (and in this sense, Brunner is right about some of the late poetry):

After it was over, though still gusting balefully,
The old woman and I foraged some drier clothes
And left the house, or what was left of it;
Parts of the roof reached Yucatan, I suppose. (186)

The poem builds to a climax, the kind one expects from Crane: a "strange gratuity of horses" becomes symbolic—the Book of Revelations enters the poem, as does "Eternity," with its capital E: "And true, he stood / Like a vast phantom maned by all the memoried night / Of screaming rain—Eternity! (187)"

But what follows implies that this section is a near self-parody, for the last thirteen lines of the poem deflate Crane's allegory, return the poem to a banal world largely abandoned even in the most mimetic sections of *The Bridge:*

The morrow's dawn was dense with carrion hazes
Sliding everywhere. Bodies were rushed into graves
Without ceremony, while hammers pattered in town.
The roads were being cleared, injured brought in
And treated, it seemed. In due time
The President sent down a battleship that baked
Something like two thousand loaves on the way.
Doctors shot ahead from the deck in planes.
The fever was checked. I stood a long time in Mack's talking
New York with the gobs, Guantanamo, Norfolk,—
Drinking Bacardi and talking U.S.A. (187)

Eternity gives way to the quotidian; sublimity to the ordinary life of the poet.

Wilder both in its language and import, "Supplication to the Muses on a Trying Day" begins with a headnote from "To Brooklyn Bridge," the proem to Crane's epic: "*How many dawns, chill from his rippling rest, / The seagull's wings shall—,*" and thus engages Crane in a conversation with himself potentially more provocative than his ongoing discussions with Eliot (in "The Tunnel") and with Yvor Winters (in letters he exchanged with the poet-critic). The question that opens "To Brooklyn Bridge" itself concerns form: "how many[?]" suggests the poet's desire to order history as myth, to know quantity. "To Brooklyn Bridge" unfolds in quatrains, walks on steady metrical feet, fulfills its scheme of rhyme. Yet "Supplication's" first phrase suggests another possibility, a full stop to such ambitions: "*Hold* it in a high wind," the poet calls to himself. What follows is a cryptic and sometimes funny catalogue of the poet's difficulties with his long poem, and includes many allusions to it—not only to the first section, but to others as well. The tone, however, flies high over that of "The Visible the Untrue." Thus: "I watched to see the / river rise." ["The River"] "The forests had all given out their streams / and tributaries. When would the bones of De Soto come /down in the wild rinse?" [again, "The River"] "And when would Ponce de Leon / remember Hammerfest?" (184). Allusions to the first explorers, to whom Crane explicitly compares himself in *The Bridge,* give way to a long list of bodily complaints that liken the poet more to Job than to Ponce de Leon (remember that the headnote to *The Bridge* as a whole is from Job's book: "From going to and fro in the earth, / and from walking up and down in it").[6] In that sense, the poem *is* more personal than many. But confessional it is not—rather, it gestures toward a literary historical period past confessionalism. So:

> There were periods when the
> self-rising bread broke out all over me in heinous sores.
> If you can't abuse a machine, why have it! Machines
> are made for abuse. . . . Fool-proof! Human beings were
> never jetted, conceived, articulated, *e*jected, nursed,
> spanked, corrected, educated, harangued, married, divorced,
> petted, emasculated, loved and damned, jailed and liberated,
> besides being plastered, frightened and mangled, pickled
> and strangled—THEY were never meant to be abused! (184)

Quite a howl, indeed. Toward the end of this curious poem, Crane alludes to skin problems, caused by allergies that he suffered throughout his life, and—possibly—to the tremors caused by heavy drinking. The relative formlessness of this poem reflects the body's chaos; no longer does Crane attempt a formalist cure:

> These dermatologists of Mozambique have got hold of me since.
> They say my digits figit, that I'm but a follicle of my
> former fratricide. . . . What shall I do? I

masticate firmly and bite off all my nails. I practise invention / to the brink of intelligibility. (185)

The poem ends with what can only be a mention-by-displacement of
Crane's homosexuality in the reference to "Gomorrha" (rather than to
Sodom): "By all the mystery of Gomorrha, I ask, what can a / gaping
gastronomist gather in such a gulch of simulation?!!"

III

What is most astonishing about these lines, and about this poem, is the
way in which it prophesies certain practices of Language poetry, in particular those of Charles Bernstein. One need only read a few lines of
Bernstein's "Dark City"—for one—to notice the affinities; both poems
are generated by sound, travel great geographical distances, and both implicitly or explicitly criticize the notion of "intelligibility":

> He
> was the kind of guy who pushed
> my buttons but couldn't carry a
> tune from Kuala Lampur to
> Guadalajuara, like those zebras
> with cross hatchings, or the trapeze
> family with Venusian ventilators. (*Dark City* 141)

Here too, we see the momentum of the poet's mind in the creation of
poetry by the sounds of words—the "sound of non-sense," to mangle
Robert Frost (the second section of "Dark City" is entitled "Early Frost,"
and I wonder if it isn't the poet more than the climate to which Bernstein
alludes). Like Crane, in his supplication, Bernstein allows the sounds of
his words to carry him from mangled cliché to mangled cliché, from exotic name to exotic name (like Proust and Ashbery, they are more interested in the names of places than in the places themselves).

Bernstein's poem makes a fine counterpoint to Crane's because he has
embedded in it a couple of sections of subjective—even sentimental—
lyricism that he might otherwise attack as the product of "official verse
culture." The third section, "Endless Destination," concludes with an appeal to literalism that matches Stein's rosy assertions, and goes against
the frenetic wordplay of the first two. The poem bears extensive quotation:

If I should die
cut out my throat
and burn it on the pyre
of their indifference.
It means no more to me
than that, to take
your hand in my
hand and turn our backs
from the wreck
not of our lives
but where we have been given
to live them. (144)

Gone are the baroque buildups of puns, or the flippancy of a phrase such as *"Holy is as holy does,"* which comes toward the end of section two. Even when Bernstein does touch upon cliché here, he does so without any apparent desire to explode it: "Love's no more than that / a straw against the wind / that blows us to the ground / without submission" and "Come cast me / down 'gainst shore, where / sand enfolds us." He obviously is invoking song lyrics in these lines, but in such as way that they seem affecting, not distracting, or silly. The final part of this section invokes metaphor and simile for the most part to assert their truth, the conjunction of word and thing, sign and signified:

Love is like love, a baby
like a baby, meaning like
memory, light like light.
A journey's a detour
and a pocket a charm
in which deceits are borne.
A cloud is a cloud and
a story like a story,
song is a song, fury
like fury. (145)

So the sound and the fury that signify nothing in *Macbeth* here come to signify themselves, which is surely a recovery of meaning, rather than a dispersal of it. How are we meant to read this section of a poem writtcn in six sections, some of which are of such an opposing series of tones as to make these lines either signify too much or too little—too much if we greet them as meaning *something*, and hence take them to mean more than the other sections, where wordplay better matches Bernstein's claims that one should be always suspicious of "intelligibility." Too little if we assume that this section is nothing more than ventriloquism, Bernstein performing a cover version of free verse "authenticity." Whether the subjectivity of these passages is that of the poet himself matters less than that Bernstein—increasingly in recent years, I think—allows that subjectivity a role in his poetry. The last lines of this section are something of a benediction of the world as it is, its straightforward and somewhat "prosaic" rhetoric suggesting that the formal order of the sentence is matched by that of this relation to another person in the world. What we have then, is the kind of poem that Crane yearned to write, one in which form does mirror purported content (and contentment). Crane came closest in poems like "My Grandmother's Love Letters" and "Chaplinesque," but even in those poems there was always a profound gap between desire and its fulfillment in language. The poet is always, it would seem, attempting to communicate to people who cannot understand him. If anything, Bernstein usually attempts the opposite, beginning from an assumption that his audience may think it knows what poetry is and what it says, and then works hard to defeat those assumptions, create that gap between the reader's desire and his ability to "understand" the poem. Perhaps it's indicative of Bernstein's current success that he needs to challenge his reader by writing so straightforwardly; one feels a bit like someone schooled in Schoenberg who is given Chopin, and doesn't know what to make of it. We read these lines differently than we would lines by James Wright or Robert Lowell, from whom we expect "authenticity." But we are not obliged, even so, to dismiss them as "artificial" in the popular, negative, sense of the term.

What Bernstein's poem shows us, finally, is I suspect not that formalism, like God, is dead, but that it has been resurrected in new forms. For what Bernstein's poem does is to take its form not from "poetry"—a form that we have seen meant for Crane not just prosody, but also a whole series of assumptions about the relations between poetic form and life forms (as it were)—but from language, in its totality. By the time Crane had completed *The Bridge*, he had written a poem that was so tight formally, one in which every line in the seventy or so pages of text relates in some way to the central image of the bridge, and hence back to the poem itself, in particular to the "Atlantis" section, which he wrote first and put last, that its central relationship was to itself. Not America, but the poem, was the subject of the poem. And that poem was constructed of language so carefully purified of anything not related to itself that its ultimate triumph was its bridges between sections of text, rather than sections of America. Crane, by then, had discovered (as he probably already knew) that form did not a life make, and he rejected Winters's continued insistences that it did. What Bernstein discovers is a method by which to keep writing that is not unrelated to Crane's venture; but for Bernstein, the poem is not about itself, but about the forms (in the all-important plural) that language—all language, if it is possible to conceive of such a thing—takes. That is why he can write a poem like "Dark City," which is by turns nonsensical, sardonic, cliché-ridden, lyrical, and so on. Bernstein turns the inconsistency of language into form, a paradoxical attempt, for certain, but one that does justice to the way in which language works, in our time(s). And in so doing, oddly enough, he might seem to agree with Tate and Ransom; sure, he'd say, art is like life, so it had better be crazy.

IV

But let me return to Crane and thereby anticipate, again, his relationship to the mode for which Bernstein is best known, and which provides us with, if not an antiformal poetry, then poetry of a different form. In a later poem than the supplication to the muse, "Havana Rose," written in 1931 during Crane's ill-fated stay in Mexico, the poet returns to a discussion of the body, and then quotes the doctor's caution to him to renew his formalist contract as a way to save himself. As we shall see, however, the contextualizing of his statement in defense of formalism at the end of the poem suggests that Crane had lost the faith in it that he had expressed to his father and to Otto Kahn. "Havana Rose" can be read as an attack on Crane's metaphysical ambitions, even as they express ambivalence toward doctors (in these "fond remembrances of the great bacteriologist"). Crane's central concerns appear again, the conflicts between "antagonistic wills"; the desire for form; the poet's physical suffering. Again Crane alludes to an explorer, "*Cortez—Cortez—*," in his discussion of the doctor:

> Only the Mayans surely slept—
> whose references to typhus and whose records

spurred the Doctor into something nigh those
metaphysics that are typhoid plus—and had engaged
him once before to death's beyond and back again
—antagonistic will—into immunity. (200)

The doctor is a surprising metaphysician, caring as he did for his laboratory rats on the ship. His attitude toward typhus carries over to his "American" attitude (and perhaps the Christian Science attitude of Crane's mother) toward mental and physical distress. The caring words he offers Crane have already been deauthorized by what comes earlier in the poem:

And during the wait over dinner at La Diana,
the Doctor had said—who was American also—
"You cannot heed the negative—, so might go on
to undeserved doom . . . must therefore loose yourself
within a pattern's mastery that you can conceive, that
you can yield to—by which also you
win and gain that mastery and happiness which
is your own from birth." (201)

These have all along been words by and for Crane's fathers—Clarence Crane, Otto Kahn, Yvor Winters, and now the American doctor. But Crane's late poems in this mode—poems that "loose" him *from* a pattern's mastery—suggest a different shape to his career, given a too perfect shape by his last poem, "The Broken Tower." That poem is written in Crane's formalist mode, though its subject is the creation of form out of lack, a soul that is a "slip of pebbles," rather than anything more stable than that. No urn this. Instead, they introduce the concept of "shapelessness" into his career. The fragment, "I Rob My Breast," which Crane wrote in 1929, according to Simon, ends also with a discussion of form, but one that contradicts the doctor's words:

My countrymen,—give form and edict—
To the marrow. You shall know
The harvest as you have known the spring
But I believe that such "wreckage" as I find
Remaining presents evidence of considerably more

Significance than do the cog-walk gestures
Of a beetle in a sand pit. (219)

The "wreckage" here alludes to the dead from French wars—Foch, Napolean—but also to the poet, who robs his breast "to reach those altitudes," but whose "vision is a grandiose dilemma—" (219).

For Tate and Winters, such a loss of formal shape would have denoted an unfortunate lack of control—the poet as an "incomplete man" (to paraphrase Winters; see "A Letter to Yvor Winters" from Hart Crane 5/29/1927, in *Complete Poems* 241)—but for us such a loss can be seen as gain. For what Crane does in these poems, unpublished in his own lifetime, is to propose another narrative for the history of postmodernist poetry in our age. That narrative would show us the ways in which postmodernist writing emerges out of formalism, and provides a way through or around the formalist impasse that blocked Crane and other like-minded poets. In that sense, Crane would be a figure like Montaigne, whom Jean-François Lyotard describes curiously as both a modern and postmodern figure in his essay "What is Postmodernism?" That Montaigne was neither only serves to make Lyotard's argument more provocative.

Lyotard describes modern aesthetics as "an aesthetic of the sublime, though a nostalgic one," which "allows the unpresentable to be put forward only as the missing contents; but the form, because of its recognizable consistency, continues to offer to the reader or viewer matter for solace and pleasure" (81). This is an aesthetic of "intensity" according to Grossman's (and Crane's) use of the term, one that tries to achieve, out of the chaos of the modern, a "new word" that will reorganize the world. Eliot's "shantih," not a new word, but one new to western literature, aims to create this binding effect at the end of "The Waste Land." What Crane does in his late unpublished poems is to approximate another kind of intensity, described by Fredric Jameson, which is that of postmodern affect. According to Jameson, postmodernism does not so much introduce a world without affect as one in which emotions come to be redefined, following Lyotard, as "intensities," or feelings that are "free-floating and impersonal and tend to be dominated by a peculiar kind of euphoria" (16). This is a euphoria without solace, according to the French philosopher of postmodernity, one that looks to the future rather than to the modernists' safe haven of the past. "The artist and the writer, then, are working without rules in order to formulate the rules of what *will have been done*" (16). What follows, in Lyotard's argument, are words that apply to Crane in a literal as well as a speculative sense, to a poet whose "Supplication," for example, is a late poem that comes too early to be recognized or published. "Hence the fact that work and text have the characters of an event, hence also, they always come too late for their author, or, what amounts to the same thing, their being put into work, their realization . . . always begin too soon. *Post modern* would have to be understood according to the paradox of the future *(post)* anterior *(modo)*" (81).

It only makes sense that Crane's pre-latedness, as one might call it belatedly, relates not just to his poetics, but also to the formalist criticism of his era. While his letters are full of examples of his formalist poetics, they also contain radical statements directed against New Critical assumptions, especially those that were radically anti-Romantic, anti-"sentimental." For example, he joined forces with Gorham Munson and Waldo Frank to reintroduce the "barbaric yawp" of Whitman into the modernist 1920s and 1930s. And his later letters to Yvor Winters indicate his great resistance to Winters's description of the poet as a "complete man." He was fighting the New Critical hegemony even as it was being put into place, and became a scapegoat figure in its ongoing narrative, as the contemporary reviews of *The Bridge* attest.

In this sense the late Crane was more a member of the avant-garde than of modernism, according to Andreas Huyssen's definitions: "modernism always remained bound up with the more traditional notion of the autonomous art work, with the construction of form and meaning . . . and with the specialized status of the aesthetic" (192). Furthermore, according to Huyssen, the avant-garde "presupposed a society in which high art played an essential role in legitimizing hegemony, or, to put it in more neutral terms, to support a cultural establishment and its claims to aesthetic knowledge" (192). That is, it presupposed the hegemony in order to oppose it. The "cultural establishment" that Crane opposed from within, and to a greater degree than he himself may have realized, was gaining its ascendancy in the late 1920s and 1930s—a position of dominance it would not surrender until at least the 1960s. Crane's late poems speak to us out of our own moment, though his formalist poems could just as easily be taken as arguments against that moment.

2

Laura Riding's Essentialism
and the Absent Muse

There is a man of me that sows.
There is a woman of me that reaps.
—Riding, "Mortal"

Poetry is not contemporary poetry. It is not philosophy. It is not
even literature. As between literature and life, it is closer to life. But
life invents time rather than poetry, a sanctimonious comment on
itself, a selflessness. Poetry invents itself. It is nearly a repudiation of
life, a selfness. Unless it is this, it is a comment on a comment, ster-
ile scholasticism.
—Riding, "Poetry and the Literary Universe"

LAURA RIDING WAS TORN between essentialist and cultural explanations
for a division between what she perceived to be the "masculine" and
"feminine" sides of her character—between the sower and the reaper of
my headnote from her poem "Mortal." This internal and, to some extent,
unconscious conflict presaged a more recent debate between essentialist
and cultural feminist critics, although the "feminine" is no longer assumed to be silent, the "masculine" loquacious. Riding's belief in sexual
essentialism—which assigned her the role of reaper rather than sower—
proved fatal to her career as a poet, and she renounced poetry in 1939,
but that essentialism was itself determined by her position as a woman
poet in her culture.[1] The essentialism of Riding's time, as well as that of
ours, is not itself an ungrounded phenomenon, but has a cultural basis;
Victorian ideas of the exclusive capability of men and women have given
way to contemporary notions that a woman's essential qualities distinguish her work, such as writing, from that of men.

Both of these arguments are troubling, and some critics have com-
mented on parallels between them. In her 1985 survey of feminist theory,
Toril Moi argues that, "to define 'woman' is necessarily to essentialize
her" (139); she attacks Sandra Gilbert and Susan Gubar for subscribing
to the very patriarchal assumptions that they argue against. Moi's odd

bedfellow, Frank Lentricchia, makes a similar point about Gilbert and Gubar in *Ariel and the Police,* and argues for historical rather than essentialist readings of literature.[2] Both of them argue that men and women (or at least the masculine and the feminine) are not so much born as made by their social and cultural contexts. I mean to show that the argument over an essentialist construction of gender sheds light on modernist, as well as current, critical praxis. For modernism was defined by way of essentialist categories, as Gilbert and Gubar have shown. James Joyce's response to *The Waste Land* that it "ends [the] idea of poetry for ladies" is merely symptomatic, according to them, of a larger modernist tendency to define good poetry as "masculine," bad poetry as "feminine."[3]

This essay argues not only that Riding's internal argument over her role as woman and poet was ultimately self-defeating for her as a poet, but also that there is a necessary relationship between her belief in sexual essentialism and her renunciation of poetry. Riding's rigid belief in ahistorical formalism prevented her from recognizing the historical forces that contributed to her self-silencing. The prime historical force was Victorian essentialism, perpetuated early in this century by critics such as John Crowe Ransom and even by Riding's longtime companion, Robert Graves. It was Graves who declared that "woman is not a poet: she is either a Muse or she is nothing" (446). Riding became, in effect, both nothing and a muse because, as the purest of the formalists, she rejected the muse as something outside of poetry and irrelevant to it.[4]

I

Riding, who published her collected poems in 1938, took both sides of the argument that I've described above, at times asserting that "woman" was a construct, and at other times that she herself possessed a "masculine" and a "feminine" aspect.[5] Considered within the context of her time, we can see the way in which these two arguments are related; Riding's essentialism merely replicates a culturally enforced distinction between masculine and feminine modes of writing. According to the perhaps unreliable T. S. Matthews, who knew Riding, she thought that her "masculine" or "sun-side" wrote poetry, and that "[h]er 'moon-side,' the brooding, all-knowing feminine part of her nature, to which she seldom referred and then only in hushed hints, was the essential Laura, the true core of the sage and prophetess who would change the world" (288).

Much later in her life, Riding was to write in her intellectual memoir, *The Telling*, published under her married name, Laura (Riding) Jackson, that women are essentially better than men. To the question of how "the woman-part" of ourselves can "become free," she answers: "Through an instant readiness, eternized by the woman-part in itself, to pass beyond kindship to oneship (to eternal humanship) when the man-part, knowing itself at last its own prisoner, ceases to love the half-world formed of its self-doubling—in which both parts huddle—and calls for the whole" (46). Women, therefore, are better formalists than men; it is they who can "transcend" life, who can "unify" existence: the very jargon is that of the New Critics. This sense of wholeness as a quality existing outside, and before, poetry is one she shared with Hart Crane, to the detriment of them both.

The New Critics made Riding welcome, even as at least one among them lashed out against women poets. For, despite their insistence on the clean break between the poet and his or her poem, they more than once indulged in *ad hominem* attacks. Riding was for a time part of the southern Fugitive group, whose members included Allen Tate, John Crowe Ransom, and Robert Penn Warren; the Fugitives awarded her their annual prize in 1924.[6] In that year, Allen Tate wrote: "Her intelligence is persuasive. It is in every inflexion of her voice, every gesture" (Cowan 147). Riding was not a typical "female lyric poet of the 1920s," as Alicia Ostriker describes that poet, "[m]odest as her grandmothers when it came to self-promotion" (46). Rather, as Allen Tate describes her, "Laura's successes drive on apace. That young lady has more energy than a phalanx of dynamos, with seven billy-goats thrown in" (Cowan 217). According to Tate, that is, Riding was a typical lyrical poet—as masculine as a billy-goat, as voracious as a dynamo.

But the bias by some of the Fugitives against women poets was evident in 1938, the very year that Riding renounced poetry, when John Crowe Ransom published *The World's Body*. Ransom was a poet-critic whose work in both genres was weighty, influential. In an essay from that book, "The Poet as Woman," he indulged in some old distinctions between male and female poets, declaring that, "A woman lives for love, if we will but project that term to cover all her tender fixations upon natural objects of sense, some of them more innocent and far less reciprocal than men" (77). His notions are Victorian, his vocabulary Freudian; we should remember that it was Freud who asserted that beautiful women wcre model narcissists. Ransom is here attacking, among other things, Romantic poetry, which fixed its attentions "upon natural objects of sense," but he sublimates his attack on the Romantics into the attack on women poets generally, perhaps because there were more women poets than Romantics to aim at in 1938. Or perhaps because, as Sandra Gilbert argues in an essay on Sylvia Plath, "Women and Romantic poets are, after all, alike in certain interesting respects" (*Shakespeare's Sisters* 260). But Gilbert's statement is as dubious as Ransom's, because she argues for an essential Romantic and an essential woman poet. Gilbert merely flips the essentialist coin, finding good rather than bad in the romantic/woman complex.

To follow Ransom's line (or swerve) of argument for a moment, women such as Edna St. Vincent Millay are not good poets because they cannot achieve the intellectual distance that the male writer gains through poetic form, the mechanics of poetry. "The minds of man and woman," Ransom writes, "grow apart, and how shall we express their differentiation? In this way, I think—man, at best, is an intellectualized woman. Or, man distinguishes himself from woman by intellect, but he should keep it feminized" (77), a backhanded compliment of the "feminine" component of the male poet's mind. This last phrase shows that Ransom's own neat division of poetic labor cannot survive the rigors of his own intellection: he ends up asserting that only a *man* with a mind at once intellectual and emotive can be a poet. Certainly Ransom makes no room for the poet that his friend Tate considered to be intellectual; his very phraseology goes a long way toward showing the hostility of the environment in which Riding worked.

Riding may have been the Fugitives' darling precisely because she seemed to them to provide an exception to Ransom's rule: her poetry is difficult and obscure only to the extent that it is abstract and intellectually rigorous. According to Deborah Baker, Allen Tate told Riding that she would save America from the Edna St. Vincent Millays (11). Riding's poetry was radically different from what they considered "modern," as well as from what Ransom described as "feminine." Where Allen Tate considered modern poetry difficult because it was metaphorically dense, and Cleanth Brooks thought it difficult because of its imagery (3), the difficulty of Riding's poetry derives from its very lack of these devices. As Riding puts it, her poetry is obscure paradoxically because it says what it means, and because it refers to nothing (such as Ransom's "natural objects of sense") outside of itself. In their remarkable book of criticism, *A Survey of Modernist Poetry,* published in 1928, Riding and Graves describe the modernist poem in a way that may be unfamiliar to readers raised on Pound's and Eliot's versions of the modernist creed: "The ideal modernist poem is its own clearest, fullest and most accurate meaning. Therefore the modernist poet does not have to talk about the use of image 'to render particulars exactly', since the poem does not give a rendering of a poetical picture or idea existing outside the poem, but presents the literal substance of poetry, a newly created thought-activity: the poem has the character of a creature by itself" (118). According to Riding and Graves, the poet who abides by this definition of a modern poem, and so "means what he says," is thought to evade meaning rather than to state it. To mean what one says is, of course, not to follow one of the prime tenets of Eliot's modernism, that the poem must be ironic.

What is at stake, then, is not just the modernists' definition of "women's" poetry, but also their definition of "modern" poetry. Understandably, Riding's explanation of the difficulty of modern poetry is quite different from the explanations of her fellow Fugitive critics. For Riding, as she does at every juncture of her criticism, lays the full burden of misunderstanding squarely on the reader's shoulders, not the writer's. If the reader finds the modernist obscure, then that obscurity originates in the reader, not in the poet. Hence the poet-critic Riding's inconsistent hatred of the craft of criticism, the business of reading and mediating literature for a larger audience. The audience should not provide a mirror to the poet; the poet ought instead to be her own audience, be not a reflection but a form, in the platonic sense. In "Poetry and the Literary Universe" she writes: "The only individual, then, whom it is safe to presume as a reader for poetry is that poet himself" (*Contemporaries and Snobs* [*CS*] 47).

II

Poets traditionally write for their muses, so Riding's quarrel with her audience is equally a quarrel with the muse. The muse is, on one level at least, an idealized audience, the poet's mirror of himself (himself, because the muse is traditionally a woman, like Petrarch's Laura). To be the poet's mirror is, of course, not to be the poet; Robert Graves, the man with whom Riding lived during her most productive years, writes as much in *The White Goddess.* In renouncing the muse/mirror, and in coming close to renouncing the very concept of an audience, Riding was a poet who deliberately chose not to have an external, or extrapoetic, muse of her own. Her strategy matches the one Mary K. DeShazer describes when she writes that, "One tactic of the woman poet has been to evade the problem of the muse altogether, to insist on writing poetry without invoking any superior or exterior force" (27). But there are also problems attendant on a poet's having no muse. Some women, such as Dorothy Wordsworth, who might otherwise have been poets, renounced poetry almost before they began to write. Margaret Homans argues that Dorothy Wordsworth denied herself the feminine muse of nature on which her brother William relied because she could not separate herself from it (her). "Dorothy leaves herself out of every center she proposes," writes Margaret Homans. "She experiences an imposed separation from origins that her brother does not experience in the same way and that deprives her of the strong sense of identity necessary to writing Romantic poetry" (*Women Writers* 70). Identity, even for a Romantic solitary, is a social construct.

Riding, living in an age when fragmented identities seemed more the norm, desires the strong Romantic identity at the same time that she fears it. We can see this in her dominant (perhaps domineering) personality, as T. S. Matthews and others have described it, and we see it also in her poems and stories. Like Dorothy Wordsworth, she has no muse outside herself, although she aims to make a virtue of that fact. The extreme intellection of her poetry, noted by Tate, may be due to the fact that abstract thinking is an activity that requires no muse; Riding's poetic persona thinks because thinking makes her self-sufficient.

The muse came to represent for Riding not just the deified female figure (like Petrarch's own Laura) but also images, metaphors, the very substance of poetry itself, which she believed to be extrapoetic. In the original 1938 preface to her collected poems, Riding attacks male poets whose muses, according to her, are false: "Thus W. H. Auden, unwilling to conceive that a large-scale compulsion may originate in the poet, has told me that I am 'the only living philosophical poet'—my muse is, presumably, Philosophy, as his is Politics" (410). She goes on to attack Eliot for his "tailor's-dummy muse of Religion" and (without naming him) Hart Crane for his use of "Red Indians or Columbus . . . or Brooklyn Bridge." The problem with Auden and his fellows is that they evade the muses within themselves, and hence invite the same mistake in their readers. Poets become the muses of poetry: "The trouble is that as poets have transferred the compulsion of poetry to forces outside themselves, so readers have been encouraged to transfer their compulsion to the poet: the poet in turn serves as muse to them" (*Poems* 411). Any inspiration that the poet locates apart from himself objectifies him. We can see here the consequences of Riding's extreme formalism: the poem, not the poet, is important; therefore, the less a poet intrudes on the poem the better. As Riding and Graves phrased it: "Language in poetry should not be treated as if it were a paint-box, or the poem something to be hung on the wall, so to speak" (123). They mean, of course, to argue that poems are more important than pictures, but in saying it in so many words they attack the Imagist theory of poetry, which argued for poems that recorded images, not sentiment—pictures, not modes of thought.

Riding and Graves considered Imagism to be a "dead movement"—one for which language was, in some sense, a paint-box.[7] "It had the look of a movement of pure experimentalism and reformation in poetry," they write. "But the issuing of a public manifesto of Imagism, its massed organization as literary party with a defined political programme, the war it carried on with reviewers, the annual appearance of an Imagist anthology—all this revealed it as a stunt of commercial advertisers of poetry to whom poetic results meant a popular demand for their work, not the discovery of new values in poetry with an indifference to the recognition they received" (116).

Ironies are at work here; Imagism, as Hugh Kenner writes, "was named for a component of the poem, not a state of the poet, and . . . its three principles establish technical, not psychic, criteria" (179). But most important for Riding and Graves is the fact that the Imagist movement became its own muse; poets were inspired by its manifesto, and they wrote in order to fulfill its tenets rather than to "tell the truth." Riding and Graves abhorred the poet who looked outside of himself for a muse because in doing so he became a member of a poetic guild; poetic movements justified poets in writing poems that were more professional than truthful. Poetry had, according to Riding, become a big business and, for that reason, she and Graves also disdained Marianne Moore, who included the language of business in her verse; "it is bad for both poetry and business," they concluded (*Survey* 186). The net result of the professionalization of poetry was to make the poet conform to "literature" rather than to make literature subservient to the poet (*CS* 10).

Among the foremost Imagists were two women, Amy Lowell and H.D., but Riding ignores this fact in the attack on the professional and masculine poetical establishment: all of her metaphors for movements associate them with male dress. In one of the few instances of savage humor in Riding's work, she writes of modernist movements in "Poetry and the Literary Universe": "Can it be that the social backing of contemporary poetic gentlemanliness is only, after all, a gloomy medley of scholastic anthropology, spaded Freudianism, Baroque Baedeckerism, sentimental antiquarianism, slum-and-boudoir philology, mystical Bradleyism, tortoise-shell spectacled natural history, topee'd comparative religion and Arrow-collared Aristotelianism?" (*CS* 119). This is reverse Ransomism. Nearly all of these movements are associated with "gentlemen," more specifically with gentlemen's clothing, as if these ways of thinking were not essential (as "Laura" was) but a kind of fashionable covering that was intended more to conceal than to reveal. Riding's response is to assert that, "we must, so to speak, undress man's mind, in order to find out what actually happens in it beneath the layers of habitual thought" (*Word "Woman"* [*WW*] 36). As I will argue later in this book, the language of fashion is crucial to the work of Charles Bernstein, who adopts "layers" as his own particular mode of poetic dress. Riding's critique of poetry as a profession is one she shares with nearly all the poets discussed here; an abhorrence of "mammon" characterizes at least some of the moods of Gertrude Stein, Susan Howe, and Ronald Johnson, especially.

In her much-anthologized poem, "Because of Clothes,"[8] Riding proposes a woman's garb which, she claims, unites rather than divides the self, denies the binary worldview that masculine poetry demands. The dressmaker unites mind and body:

> Without dressmakers to connect
> The good-will of the body
> With the purpose of the head,
> We should be two worlds
> Instead of a world and its shadow
> The flesh. (*CP* 285)

These clothes do not so much cover the body as enable a neat reversal between inner and outer realms, between thought and the world: "But putting on the cloak and cap / With only the hands and the face showing, / We turn the gloom in and the glow forth / Softly" (285). Finally, the needle's "neutral grace" balances the opposition of triumph and defeat, allowing us quite simply to "live." Yet all clothes, whether masculine or feminine, are images, and images are what Riding writes against; this helps explain why this is an unusual poem in her oeuvre. In response to elaborate poetic disguises, Riding finally performs a literary striptease that aims to undo poetry's sartorial splendor.

The problem of disguise has not only to do with the gentlemen's dress of professional poetry, but also with the audience for Riding's poetry; just as women are defined by their appearances, so is a woman's poem judged by male readers. Thus we can juxtapose Riding's argument about the way in which women's roles are defined by men, in "Difference of Appearance," with her comments on the fate of her own poems, in "On Having a Poem Accepted by a Magazine." In the essay, as in other essays later collected in *The Word "Woman" and Other Related Writings,* Riding concentrates on woman's outward appearance and its effect on man (she usually resorts to the universals, man and woman, rather than their individual instances): "Woman appears to man in the clothes, the form, indeed, the very flesh, with which he endues her—no more than an appearance until man inquires, instead of imagining, her meaning. And all this time she is the different appearance rather than, actively, the different person. She is silent, neither resisting nor accepting the meaning man gives her; until man actually asks her meaning—asks it of her" (5). When a woman poet puts forth her meaning, goes Riding's argument in her poem, "On Having a Poem Accepted by a Magazine," that meaning is mistaken for appearance. This is very like the style that Riding so detests in the poetry profession:

Now it goes to a boutonniere to
Some fine gentleman all
Tidied for to-day's brief gallantries, and
I am wondering if
Some fair passing flirt will pluck my nosegay
Coyly from his coat and
Let its wilted petals shower into
An old lovers' scrapbook,
Fittingly forgotten. (*FA* 52)

That Riding sees her audience as masculine may help us to understand the particular form of hostility she bears toward it. In her 1928 book, *Anarchism Is Not Enough,* she writes, "but as to loathing: I feel an intense intimacy with those who have this loathing interest in me. Further than this, I know what they mean, I sympathize with them, I understand them" (308). She describes this relationship as one more intimate even than love: "There should be a name (as poetic as love) for this relationship between loather and loathed; it is of the closest and more full of passion than incest" (308). A less violent—and more directly literary—expression of this loathing sense of audience emerges in her early poem, "Unforfeited":

> It's true I have disdained
> All their attempts to read me. I am written
> In strange tongues, if they read, they would be smitten
> With fear of me much worse than their dislike.
> I'd rather slowly die behind my blind
> Than let them know how much I hate their kind. (*FA* 85).

The word "blind," in the penultimate line of the poem, evokes not only Riding's desire to conceal herself, to wear her woman's mask, but also suggests the violence of her emotion, if we are to think of "blinds" as places where hunters lurk in order to see their prey close-up. In fact, the sublimated violence of this passage resembles Dickinson's poem about her life as a loaded gun. The trap (another sense of "blind") that's sprung on the poet is due to her necessary desire for the very audience she must despise. Like Dickinson, she is at once the gun and the "object" (unnamed) the gun shoots. The only way for Riding to write, then, is blindly, ignoring the perverse dynamic that operates between poet and reader. It is this blindness that Riding ultimately refuses to put on (as one of the disguises she herself sees through).

Deborah Baker asserts that Riding's poetry was suicidal from the beginning (176); whether or not this is true (and I believe it is), Riding repeatedly expressed a desire for her poems to be silent. Unlike Dickinson, who wrote and then submitted to the silence of non-reception, Riding means for her very poems to be quiet. This is doubtless a different kind of silence from the one she describes as operating between men and women who allow themselves to be defined by men. But it is, nonetheless, silence. She describes it rather gently in "The Quietest Song":

> Be judged better in your silences,
> Vain songster.
> Night and a nest
> Contrive a common peace,
> A reverence and rendering
> Of each to each.
> The quietest song is sleep
> Where self allows the strings and wings
> The humble grace
> Of dreaming other things. (*FA* 221)

With its Romantic evocations of "sleep" and "dreaming," this passage resembles Yeats's occasional nods to Maid Quiet, or one of Keats's odes, translated so as to render the bird's song futile. But Riding is much more aggressive in her poem, "Last Women," where she asserts the futility of childbirth, even as she makes clear its (traditional) connection to the writing of poetry. The "murdered men" here might well be war dead, but the poet's response is to favor an infertility that has explicitly to do with her own voice, even if the word "still" expresses an ambiguous feeling in regards to her self-silencing:

> Now, delight the end with indifference!
> Sister us with the childless skies
> And show our breasts
> That will never spill for a child
> Merrily from the broad hills with mother-pride
>
> Now, gather as many flowers as women may
> Who leave no children to gather the rest of them,
> And heap them wastefully on our murdered men.
>
> Still, voices, still. (*FA* 176)

If, as she writes in "Definitions and Generalizations," "women are strangers in the country of man" (*WW* 19), then she will exile herself from this country. Riding's paradoxical obscurity, due more to her straightforwardness than to the density of her language, seems a reaction to the very fact that readers are free to interpret poems. The question of interpretation becomes especially vexed when men "interpret" women; that interpretation is also judgment is by now a critical given. For John Crowe Ransom, the connection between an interpretation of Edna St. Vincent Millay's work and a judgment of it, was not so clear— and his voice was more typical than not.

In response to such misinterpretations, Riding attempts to create a wedge between the poem and its interpreters. As she writes in *Anarchism Is Not Enough* (1928), "Poetry is . . . not concentrated on an audience but on itself" (35). The poem, like a woman, is; it cannot be changed by its interpreter. This is the truth of the matter, for a poet obsessed with capital-T Truth. As we shall see, however, this wedge also creates the option—or necessity—of Riding's conceiving of silence as better than language. Silence, at least, cannot be so easily interpreted. In "Being a Woman," Riding describes woman as being like the moon, which though it has been interpreted by men, refuses to become that interpretation: "woman does not become what man variously 'makes' of her. So when a certain imaginative interpretation is put upon the moon's movements and prevails as a convention by which conveniently to describe the moon, the moon and its movements do not adapt itself to the interpretation; a new lunar manifestation would change the interpretation, but no new idea about the moon changes the moon" (*WW* 47).

But what is the moon, then, without interpretations of it? By conceding the role of interpreter here to men, the role of moon to women, Riding creates an impasse in her own argument. Poems need interpreters, poets readers. To deny this fact is indeed to silence oneself—and Riding's lack of a sense of feminine community suggests that she is not reaching toward an audience of women to counterbalance the loss of a male audience. The word "woman," as she defines it, "comes to represent . . . man's power over his own fortuitousness; woman is the symbol for the conquered, or conquerable, enemy" (*WW* 50). So woman has little choice but to present a mask to men (*WW* 120), and the woman poet has no choice but to aggressively silence herself.

The fissures created between woman and man's interpretation of her, and between the poem and the audience's interpretation of it, lead Riding into a further, temporal, bind. A poem without an audience has no history, just as a woman (speaking here in historical generalities) requires a man's presence to become a historical figure. This split shows up radically in Riding's curious prose antihistory, *Lives of Wives,* which sets out to tell the story of famous ancient men from the perspective of their lives as husbands. As she explains this from a woman's point of view: "But we must see how the age of Aristotle looks by the light of the age of Alexander. And we must also take into account the lives of the various wives whose husbands gave this period their name: for the way in which women live their lives is an eloquent commentary on the circumstances with which men fill them" (78). This mention of "commentary," and of "circumstances," suggests that Riding, perhaps because prose is a liberating genre for her, will consider women's roles as historically circumscribed, and that interpretation is an act that changes through time. In fact, Riding's interpretations of the history she tells attempt to change that time, to render it comprehensible to a contemporary readership. That many of the women in the book are fierce or downright murderous is due to their relative powerlessness: "The frighteningly ungentle women of history are eloquent memorials of the desolation of the times through which they lived—more so than any stories of men descended to us from the horrors or poverties of the past" (103). Here, it would seem, is a territory where there are truths rather than a single Truth. Riding's sense of history—a history she is quite evidently making up as she goes—is suitably "poetic." "The shape of history—the living shape—is a haze," she writes; "we must be careful not to make the light too clear—or the things we try to see by it will vanish" (283). Riding gives life to the histories she recounts precisely because she is willing to forgo traditional conceptions of history as "having happened." A woman's history, as later poets such as Susan Howe make even clearer throughout her work, must be fabricated paradoxically from the gaps left by male historians and editors.

Yet in her afterward, composed in 1988, Riding returns to her preoccupation with the truth that lies outside of history, and which cannot be explained by it. She describes the period of her life when she wrote *Lives of Wives* as being "one of crisis" (325), in which she sought to work through "the essential factors of the story of human existence; its historical reality, the poetic promise, part-implicit, part-explicit, in it, of a reality transcending the historical identity-limits of human nature, and the coherencies of language in relation to this" (325). The conundrum she worked through had to do with the difference between human beings as historical creatures, and "as an essence of a living universal immediate" (327). In short, she wondered if there could be a conjunction between human being's living in history and the essential human being who transcended it. Her solution, which I would argue was hers both in 1938 and in 1988, though more so at the later date, was to side with essence over circumstance, to create a vision of human identity as being very like that of a formalist poem. Just as the New Critic argued for the ability of a poem to transcend its time, Riding argues for the human ability to transcend individual identity: "I could not have written the book without knowledge of what the human was-is. The nature of the form of life we are, as I understand it, is indwelling, knowable only inwardly, not taxonomically: human identity is not distributive, collective, a sum—its detail is its general, its general its detail, it spells not a kind but encompasses the unities of living being" (327). While the lives of the wives she chronicles in her book do not represent any unity "of living being," Riding—stepping outside of her own history—claims knowledge of a singular human nature, which is separated from that, or any, history.

Riding's later prose (from the 1960s until her death in 1992) is largely devoted to explanations of her abandonment of the poetic muse. This prose is every bit as ahistorical as was her poetry. Where prose seemed to make an alternative view of history possible to Riding in the 1930s, it assumes the role of the poems in the last thirty years of her life. That is, the prose assumes a vatic, transhistorical, tone. Despite the many years between that renunciation and her later defenses of it, Riding's reasons are consistent, and stem largely from her belief that poetry is corrupt because it is professional, and thus cannot be an exercise in truth-telling. In the 1963 postscript to *Four Unposted Letters to Catherine,* originally published in 1930, she explains her conversion out of poetry with the by now familiar metaphors of clothes: "you will see, in the letters, that I held a poem to be an achievement of the highest worth. But in the days of my second understanding of things I became aware that a poem resembles an eternal good only as Sunday-best (in clothes, dinner, behavior) resembles Best" (75). Riding's retrospective critique of modernism is in many ways apt; the era of modernism, as Louis Menand and others have shown, was one in which literature became a profession, was institutionalized within the academy, and created the atmosphere in which poets could become professional teachers of poetry. As professionals, poets and critics dispensed advice not so much on what Riding continually refers to as "Truth," but on the craft of poetry. Riding's attack on the profession of poetry is thus equally an attack on craft: "The liberty of word that poetry confers," she writes in *The Telling* (1972), "is poetry's technique, not truth's" (66). Technique is institutionalized as a kind of poetic authority, with "power-using, authority-imposing, devices" (66). *The Telling*, which is Riding's scripture concerning wisdom, and an extended explanation of how one can arrive at truth, depends (as all of her work does) on the un-telling of poetry; Truth, it seems, comes as a result of the renunciation of poetry. (It would often seem that she made her profession of renouncing poetry.) So she writes: "Late in my own poetic professionalism I renounced the satisfaction of poetry success in words. *The Telling* is descended from that renunciation. I speak in it at the common risks of language, where failure stalks in every word" (66). Deborah Baker sees this kind of renunciation in Riding's life as well: "Sex for Riding quickly became a metaphor for the corrupt mythohistorical imagination that she found in [Robert] Graves, while her more poetic celibacy revealed the way to truth" (243).

Poetry's failure, and its concomitant seductiveness for Riding, came in the immediacy of its effect; language was the problem, for words seemed to communicate meaning when, in fact, they did nothing but convey the poet's artfulness. "But only a problem of art is solved in poetry," she writes. "Art, whose honesty must work through artifice, cannot avoid cheating truth. Poetic art cheats truth to further and finer degrees than art of any other kind because the spoken word is its exclusive medium; the product, reaching mind at instant quickness, scarcely leaves time for questioning of its entitlement to welcome as truth-natured utterance—as to the actuality, truth nature" (*Telling* 67). This is why Riding, on the one hand, declares herself a writer who aims to interrupt "the reading way-of-things" (61)—what Charles Bernstein calls writing nonabsorptively, or what Ron Silliman courts in his New Sentence—and, on the other, thinks of herself as the most pellucid and literal of writers. In her 1938 preface "to the reader" of her collected poems, she writes, after St. Francis of Assisi, that she writes "literally, literally, without gloss, without gloss, without gloss" (*Poems* 413). In excerpts from a recording of her work done in 1972, she says: "Nowhere should I be taken as speak-

ing by what are called 'symbols'. If, for instance, I say 'the sun which mul-
tiplied' or 'the moon which singled', as I do in one poem, I am endeav-
ouring to indicate actualities of physical circumstance in which our
inner crucialities of human circumstance are set" (*Poems* 417). Riding's
attempt, then, is to make poetry at once direct and free of art's ornamen-
tation, even as she tries to separate poetry from the ordinary world,
which is one of artifice and "clothing." She claims to aim at "human"
and not "literary" value, and insists that the two need be divorced from
each other. As she writes in her 1980 introduction to the poems, the "de-
generation" of the language of poetry is due to its style of incorporating
"'everyday speech' in the poetic expression-mode" (10).

III

To attain "human" truth, then, is to require a language not ordinarily
considered human. In order to communicate that truth the writer must
avoid art's outer clothing, as well as the profession of poetry. These paradoxes are not generative, but create an impasse at the level of the poet's
production of her work. Riding's frequent turn toward prose, whether in
her rewriting of ancient history and myth (in *A Trojan Ending* and *Lives
of Wives*) or truth-narratives (like *A Telling*) suggests that she found
prose less obstacle-ridden than poetry. But, as we shall see, although her
efforts at fiction are often more overtly playful than is her poetry, she
did not find fiction to be a suitable alternative.

Riding's book, *Progress of Stories,* originally published in 1935, is as
much a book about storytelling as it is a book of fictions. Her preface to
the second edition (1982) is full of the same rhetoric as are the prefaces
to her poems, for her ambition is not to tell stories, but to tell *the* story
that unifies human experience: "the pleasure that I took in writing them,
and that I hoped they would excite in the reading of them, was pleasure
of an order related to the unities of human concern that I describe in
the original preface as resting on the principle that (ultimately) there is
only one subject[,] . . . the principle that (ultimately) all conversation is
the same conversation" (xxxi). The stories in this collection are especially revealing about Riding's conception of the relationship between
teller and audience, one fraught not only with the gender problems I've
discussed above, but with further ambivalences for a writer who wants
to communicate truth without using the language of ordinary life. Thus,

in the first story, "Socialist Pleasures," she tells of a woman "who studied the mental disorders of professional entertainers, from circus people to musicians" (5–6). Her thought is that entertainers are victims of their public; she attempts to organize groups of people who will cooperate in their entertainment.

This gesture toward cooperation is not necessarily a gesture toward truth, as Riding makes clear in "Reality as Port Huntlady." Here fiction masquerades as fiction: "It is, of course, obvious that to tell a story is to persuade people of something almost false. We are aware that there is no such place as Port Huntlady" (96). The humor of this passage rests on the narrator's telling us something we know, but often suspend our belief in, while we read stories. This is serious humor, as one might imagine. And soon enough it's directed at the audience, accused of actively evading the very truths that Riding wants to communicate; she writes of "the nature of this transaction, which is, after all, a cold exchange between your desire, on the one hand, to pay your respects to the really important things without getting actually involved, so to speak in their family life, and, on the other hand, my desire . . . to make somewhat light of the really important things before visitors, or at any rate, not to urge anyone to stay longer than he wishes" (97). The story serves "as a substitute for any more profound experience of each other, an emotion-screen in whose making we both co-operate" (98). Cooperation, then, does not lead us to truth, but to the charming evasion of it.

Throughout these stories Riding struggles with the apparent fact that we read stories not so much for what they tell us (or what she keeps announcing in the midst of her stories) but for what they allow us not to tell each other. The story, then, is "just a piece of verbal luggage, belonging to anybody who cares to be bothered with it" (132). They must, as she writes in "A Crown for Hans Andersen," be "just a little pleasant" (269), despite the fact that "nothing new ever happens" (274).

Over thirty years after her renunciation of poetry, Riding still actively defended that renunciation, and in the same terms, noting her argument that poetry did not get at human truth, but was instead a profession whose only truth-value was in its art. Art was as much a disguise as she thought a woman's appearance to be; the only way to break through that disguise was to destroy appearance, or image, in poetry and to stop writing. *The Telling*, published in 1972, proposes a prose solution to the twin gender and genre problem. Riding's tone in this book, which one might term a philosophical treatise or a prose poem (or both), is in some ways more moderate than one might expect from a writer who wanted a new word for the loathing she had for her audience. But the problem remains the same: man is a divisive creature, what one might call the ultimate professional in Riding's lexicon. Woman unifies, reaches toward Truth (which is never quite defined), and yet she is objectified into part of man's division by his gaze. And so women are still silent: "Most mute, as rememberers of First Things and perceivers of Last Things, and knowers of ourselves as that in which First and Last are bound together, are women" (45). It is the man who, in a reversal of Milton's sexual politics, "speeds and delays," and finally only talks. Juxtaposed to that man is "the woman-part of ourselves, harborer of the force of kindship (I use this old word to go beyond the softer, lighter, meaning of *kindness* to a meaning of making-one-kind-with, by the painful work of feeling the likeness of the different" (46). Only if woman is allowed to become the truth-teller that she is (in this book, "telling" is not so much storytelling as an attempt at an exquisitely abstract truth-telling, shed of its always fictive contexts), will human beings "pass beyond kindship to oneship (to eternal humanship)" (46). And this will only occur "when the manpart, knowing itself at last its own prisoner, ceases to love the half-world formed of its self-doubling" (46).

Yet Riding, despite the abstractions, resorts to the metaphor of storytelling to explain herself and so brings back the possibility of audience. Her tone has moderated, because her words sound more like an invitation to audience (in the most active sense of the word) than an assertion of solitary self-sufficiency. Note the move toward rapprochement in the following passages: "Our truth cannot be all-told, from the beginning told, unless we tell it to one another" (21); "Thus, in the very telling of our story to one another is the crux of salvation: as we speak it true, we *have* new being, and are in the new time" (37); and finally, in one of the codas to her text: "As to this, we are one another's record: we must read one another" (107).

Because Riding's words are (of necessity) so abstract, the terms of this conversation remain obscure. What is this conversation to be about? How can one talk of truth without defining it in and through language? And how can one talk while avoiding Riding's strongest critiques of talking, such as the one she utters in "The Talking World"?

And talk in talk like time in time vanishes.
Ringing changes on dumb supposition,
Conversation succeeds conversation,
Until there's nothing left to talk about
Except truth, the perennial monologue,
And no talker to dispute it but itself.
The pleasure of talk is the pleasure of weakness. (*CP* 192)

Riding's move toward conversation suggests an uncharacteristic flexibleness; it also seems doomed to failure because empty of content. Despite Riding's assertion that her book "can seem, by the temper of the reading-matter of the time, not of the time" (60), the gesture toward talking that occurs between speakers (rather than from poet to a silent audience) amounts to a brief connection with that new time. If modernism put us under "the spell of pseudo-myth" (78), then Riding's myth casts part of that spell. *The Telling* more resembles Yeats's *A Vision* or Lawrence's mythical imaginings of gender roles than it does John Ashbery's *Three Poems* (published in the same year as Riding's book), a wisdom text that takes apart the very wisdom it imparts, and whose ironies aren't so much scaffolding as trapdoors. Ashbery's conversation with himself, a solitary creature who has at least himselves to circulate among, is more of the age than Riding's pseudoconversation, or mere suggestion of one. The difference is not, I would suggest, between modernist formalism and postmodernist contextualization, between the pure text of the New Critic and the endlessly muddy one of the poet after (or during) poststructuralism. It is a difference between formalisms, for Ashbery's world is every bit as textual as is Riding's; but where Riding's intense formalism always endeavored to use the poem to transcend the poem, then Ashbery's uses the poem to generate more poem, even as he writes on spiritual matters. Ashbery revels in the poem as artifice, and in himself as a "poetry professional"; Riding remains, to the end, a seeker of a truth that cannot be arrived at in poems.

IV

But let me return to the poems, for it is there that Riding made her strongest case for solitude and silence, without—if not within—poetry. To write poetry that is true to poetry and not to the literary marketplace, then, is to go naked and without a muse: "When . . . bare, undressed ideas are found in poetry instead of the rhetorical devices by which poets try to 'put over' their ideas, such poetry is naturally accused of being didactic . . . As a matter of fact all that has happened is that he has made the poem out of the poem itself" (*Survey* 142). Here we see Riding begin to elaborate her essentialist poetics. If masculine poets dress up for an audience, then Riding's feminine verse is stripped to the bone; she describes the idea itself. Insofar as Riding claims to eschew the pretensions of male poetics, she argues for a feminist poetics. Such a poetics, we gather, is not professionalized or worldly but strictly idealist and rigorously intellectual. (This emphasis turns Ransom's essentialist beliefs on their head, but does not question the notion that there are "essentials.")

Quite obviously, Riding's preoccupation with ridding poetry of the muse, as well as her insistence on naked poetry, have profound implications for the poet's sense of her own identity; identity is rarely, if ever, acquired apart from the images and the objects (or subjects) of the world. One reads Riding's poetry often with the sense that there is no one identity behind it. This no-identity paradoxically might be that of a God, who is everything, or the "nobody" of Dickinson's famous poem; opposites ever define each other. One of the pieces included in *Progress of Stories* (1935, reprinted 1982) exemplifies the poet's double, and divided, sense that she is whole—a God—and that she is fragmented. This story, "Miss Banquett, or the Populating of Cosmania," points toward a possible solution to the problem of the muse: God is self-sufficient and therefore needs no muse. But it also reminds us of the problem of identity that faces the poet: Laura Riding changed her last name from Reichenthal to Riding to Gottschalk to Riding and, finally, to (Riding) Jackson. This negative uncapability of the name has plagued not just Riding but also women generally. And, as Suzanne Juhasz reminds us, while self-assertiveness is a poetic virtue, it has not traditionally been considered a "feminine" one, something that the poet who is also a woman must face.[9]

One side of the poet's identity is to be found in a story that was told about Riding during her tenure in Majorca with Graves: she was reputed to have hanging on her wall a sign that read, "God is a woman." (For what it's worth, she denied the rumor.) But "Miss Banquett, or The Populating of Cosmania" takes up the theme emblematized by the apocryphal sign on the wall. The protagonist is God and, like the Riding of the poems and the biography, at once a supreme egoist and a woman with precious little sense of her own identity—so little, in fact, that "she [Miss Banquett] decided that she would for seven days be as one of her own instruments; to be something definite" (152). She decides, that is, to live in the world of images, and to be judged by an audience; as Riding writes in the first paragraph: "Miss Banquett had not only to be beautiful, but to make herself known as beautiful" (134).

Because Riding's short stories are not widely read, I will briefly summarize the plot of "Miss Banquett, Or the Populating of Cosmania." Miss Banquett undertakes a voyage in order to make herself better known. She is shipwrecked in an uninhabited country and knows that it must soon be populated "if her memory that in the place she came from she had been beautiful was not fast to disappear, and so herself" (135). So she populates Cosmania in the space of seven days; or more poetically, "out of her beauty she made a world of self" (136). At the end of the seven days, she goes out to meet her people: black, yellow, tawny-faced, blue (these last are authors). These blue people "went on, hoping to write something that would not disappoint them, but growing continually more and more disappointed and therefore more and more blue-in-the-face" (150). These authors call Miss Banquett their Muse; she gives them prizes. After some time, "the authors no longer cared what they wrote"—their work becomes professionalized. Miss Banquett is still not content, and so she decides "to be something definite" (152); she goes among the white people incognito. When things do not go well, she comes forward and claims that she is Miss Banquett, which the white women refuse to believe; they kill her. She again becomes a figurehead. "'For their sake as much as for my own,' she comforted herself, 'for the sake of those who I so uniquely am. We must not be afraid of the truth, however metaphysical it may seem. After all, one is not metaphysical *one-self*'" (155). Still not content, Miss Banquett goes among the fire-people. She has a child who finally swallows her: "And so it was a relief to be swallowed. 'Why,' she said, 'what a pig I am!' For she had swallowed herself (hence, perhaps, her name). She felt herself solidly inside herself" (158). The story ends with the narrator's first appearance; she first states her identity with Miss Banquett, then denies it: "I live in a splendid house . . . The people are not too intelligent. They are even more inaccessible . . . I am not Miss Banquett; I do not wish to find peace or not find it. Let my beauty do for itself. Let my beauty do for me, if it wishes. Let it become me. I am undertaking this voyage for a holiday, not because I am beautiful. Miss Banquett undertook this voyage because she was beautiful, not for a holiday" (164–65).

Miss Banquett seems at first to be something of an antitype for Riding herself; where Riding dismisses her audience, Miss Banquett seeks one out; where Riding defies the muse, Miss Banquett becomes the muse. But Riding is closer to Miss Banquett than she would perhaps care to be. The story seems to fulfill the dreamwork necessary for Riding to rid herself of the desire to be what her (male) audience wants her to be. It does this at the same time as it helps Riding explore her own desire to be a literary goddess. Miss Banquett embarks on a voyage because, although she is beautiful, she needs to make her beauty known, rather as a poet usually needs not just to write, but also to publish her work. The world of the self and the world of knowledge are for Miss Banquett separate realms, and they only meet in the region of paradox: "And this was the difference between the world of self and the world of knowledge: that the world of knowledge was only an endless prolongation of uncertainty, while the world of self was a prolongation of fear of uncertainty" (136). The world that Miss Banquett enters is, therefore, not the perfect mirror to her beauty that she thinks and hopes it will be.

Mirroring, as I have already shown, is something that Riding wants to avoid; she will not be "the mirror dawdling down a lane" that Stendhal wished the artist to be. For the "mirror of nature" in which the Romantics read themselves was a mirror of feminine nature, as Margaret Homans has shown. To reject the muse is, then, to reject one's mirror image and to yearn for dispersal rather than for a totalizing image of the self. Riding writes of her desire to wreck a mirror world in her poem, "Life-Size Is Too Large":

> To the microscopy of thinking small
> (To have room enough to think at all)
> I said, 'Cramped mirror, faithful constriction,
> Break, be large as I.' (*CP* 86)

Here we see Riding at her most radical. By challenging the primacy of human identity, she precedes by several decades theorists such as Julia Kristeva, who writes: "I therefore understand by 'woman' that which remains outside naming and ideologies" (Moi 163), or a kind of negative capability that cannot be defined. And yet by breaking the mirror, which shows its "audience" the outward image that represents identity, Riding again participates in an inevitable Catch-22. For, in wishing to break her own mirror, she wants at the same time to disappear—a death wish that denies, rather than gives her, poetic power. Rather than re-forming her identity so as not to conform to the social pressures that the mirror represents, Riding deconstructs the very concept of identity. The poem, as it must, ends with nothing rather than everything:

> Then I heard little leaves in my ears rustling
> And a little wind like a leaf blowing
> My mind into a corner of my mind,
> Where wind over empty ground went blowing
> And a large dwarf picked and picked up nothing. (*CP* 86)

This is an ending, but not a conclusion; the "large dwarf" of consciousness embodies the problem without suggesting a solution. Miss Banquett, like the poet of "Life-Size is Too Large," creates order, but she is also reduced to mind: "So out of her beauty she made a world of self. Or it might be put in this way: that having (all because of the magnitude of her beauty) got beyond knowledge, there was nothing to do—if she was not to disappear—but think" (136). To think or to disappear, that is the burden of Riding's work, as it is of Descartes'. But, as we've seen above, thinking and disappearing can be synonymous, rather than mutually exclusive. And so Miss Banquett becomes the muse, falls from godhead into human divinity. Playing the role that Riding so consciously detested, she awards prizes, "as if to say: 'It is well to regret that the last word has not been written, and it is well that the last word has not been written'" (150–51). These are the words of the godlike creator to her minions, of one who can and will have the last word—as Riding eventually tries to have it by declaring the death of poetry. Miss Banquett is like a writer who seeks an audience, and then realizes that it is better not to have one. She believes in a radical self-sufficiency, which most resembles Emerson's ideal: "I must not be ashamed to admit that I am a thoroughly selfish character—in the best sense of the word. That is, I am a thoroughly unselfish character: myself is enough for me. I have no wish to be more than I am. I am thoroughly satisfied with what I am: beautiful. Anything more would be—others" (158). In this she is like one of Riding's ideal poems, divorced from any connection with an audience.

V

Images are problematic for Riding, as I have suggested, because they invite the gaze of an audience. The very word "gaze" ushers in a whole new world of feminist thinking for, as Toril Moi explains its origin in Freud: "The *gaze* [is] a phallic activity linked to the anal desire for sadistic mastery of the object" (134).[10] In pointing out the importance of the male gaze in objectifying women—in making them into muses—Riding anticipates feminist theory by many years. That is part of the reason for her hatred of the image, her insistence on presenting the inside rather than the outside. As she writes in "I Am":

> I am an indicated other . . .
> I am a such-and-such appearance
> Listed among the furnitures
> Of the proprietary epoch[.] (*CP* 196)

But not only do images objectify us, so do names: to *say* oneself is to invite objectification by an audience. Again, in "I Am," she writes:

> You, spent kingdom of the senses,
> Have laid hands on the unseeable,
> Shadows' seeming fellow:
> And all together we
> A population of names only
> Inhabiting the hypothetic street,
> Where no one can be found
> Ever at home. (*CP* 196)

She refuses the easy option of creating a male muse, and of writing a mirror-poetry that reverses the masculine idiom into a feminine one. At the same time she more radically refuses to be part of the *king*dom of the senses, or the worldliness that Riding associates with the masculinity she associates with images. Masculinity is merely a stepping-stone to the feminine "unseeable," or the world radically deconstructed. Part of Riding's deconstructive project, however, amounts to the unraveling of her own work; later poems unsay earlier ones, as Riding moves toward silence. This is the point at which Riding's triumph is also her shortcoming: her attempt to rid poetry of images is so radical that it threatens to destroy her poems by ridding them of a subject, except insofar as they are about the impossibility of having one. So in "Divestment of Beauty," Riding argues against the feminine clothing metaphors that she appropriates in "Because of Clothes" and, more radically, against the definition of women as "women." Here it is that language itself, even when stripped of outside reference, proves dangerous:

> She, she and she and she—
> Which of these is not lovely?
> In her long robe of glamour now
> And her beauty like a ribbon tied
> The wisdom of her head round?
>
> To call these 'women'
> Is homage of the eye:
> Such sights to greet as natural,
> Such beings to proclaim
> Companion to expectance. (*CP* 267)

To say something's name, Riding posits, is to see it and hence seek mastery over it. What she does to reclaim the self from this false and unnatural homage of the eye, which expects something for its gaze, is to rid the self of its clothing and to find more enterprise, as Yeats put it, in going naked:

> But were they now who take
> This gaudy franchise from
> The accolade of stilted vision
> Their lady-swaddlings to unwrap
> And shed the timorous scales of nakedness— (*CP* 267)

Here she pulls away yet another layer from the image of the clothed woman, that of the religious value placed on the adored female muse. Lady-swaddlings at once signify suppression and the image of the infant Christ in swaddling clothes:

It were a loathsome spectacle, you think?
Eventual entrails of deity
Worshipful eye offending?
It were the sign, man,
To pluck the loathsome eye,

Forswear the imbecile
Theology of loveliness[.] (*CP* 267)

This undoing of the image will "[fell] the patriarchal leer" to disclose the "she, she and she and she—" or the self behind the image. The "divestment" of beauty is an appropriate phrase, for it contains within it a suggestion that the culture invests in the idea of beauty, and that there is poetic capital to be gained from it. She also comments on the connection between religion and the position of women: the muse is a religious as well as a poetic construct.

Riding's reaction to the force of the gaze is, like that of some poststructuralists, antihumanist; she prefers the annihilation of the poetic subject to its objectification by an audience. Riding's terror of being defined from the outside is so great that she believes personification to be another form of objectification. In the anti-Whitmanian "Disclaimer of the Person," which begins, "I say myself," she writes: "I am personified, / Of being caught in that pressed confluence / And proved look-substantial" (233). Where Whitman's cosmic ego frees him to gaze upon others, Riding feels herself looked at, made substantial rather than a Kosmos.

Riding's refusal to name herself is a refusal to play into the game that the gaze represents, but also a more disturbing return to the game in which women have no names, in which they are at once everything and nothing, as Miss Banquett was. "Divestment of Beauty" thus seems an apt companion to the earlier "Postponement of Self," in which the speaker reports that she first defined herself through her mother and then through her father because, as she puts it sarcastically, remembering her Freud: "At six little girls in love with fathers." But what she discovers past the age of twenty is that neither means of self-definition can be true to her self, in part because each comes out of a mirroring (which is the imaging of the parent in the child) and out of language, which is itself of course a mirror:

At twenty I say She.
Her face is like a flower.
In a city we have no flower-names, forgive me.
But flower-names not necessary
To diary of identity. (59)

The perfect resemblance is also perfect counterfeit (100), a quality that engenders love in the poet, but which takes her away from her self-imposed quest for the naked truth. Or, to continue with the metaphor of clothing and unclothing:

Under apparel, apparel lies
The recurring body:
O multiple innocence, O fleshfold dress.

One self, one manyness,
Is first confusion, then simplicity. (*CP* 77)

One might ascribe Riding's obscurity to this "manyness," or to this refusal by the poet to speak in her own voice: many of the most difficult passages in her poetry can be made easier through the insertion of a first-person pronoun. Yet even in such a poem as "Advertisement" (one thinks of Mailer's *Advertisements for Myself,* or Whitman's), Riding—even when she tells the reader at what exact moment she is writing the poem—refuses even the fiction of mastery that the personal pronoun offers poets such as Whitman:

For twenty-six years, six months, seventeen days,
Have studied what for what,
Spoken of what to what
And known not what
For all the what have read or written
Since was who. (*CP* 117)

Riding then parodies "personals" precisely for dropping all that is personal about her self-description: abstraction at once universalizes and diminishes the self:

Have quantity guaranteed self
Willing affiliate with private party. (*CP* 117)

VI

The great irony of Riding's work is that in attempting to create herself
on paper as a subject rather than an image, she objectifies herself. The
word is an image for Riding, and her record of the ways in which words
use the writer make her an important precursor of the Language poets.
(One of her later essays was published in *Sulfur,* which had ties with the
contemporary avant-garde.[11]) Through words is she made and unmade,
reduced to singleness, expanded to manyness, but never for an instant
still. "Disclaimer of the Person" is the best example of Riding's attempt
at once to explain and to dismantle herself, and to show the ways in
which language (as image) lies rather than tells the truth:

I am I.
I am my name.
My name is not my name.
It is the name of what I say.
My name is what is said.
I alone say.
I alone am not I. (*CP* 229)

The poem grows by diminishment, saying then unsaying the poet's identity until she herself wonders, "But is this I interior"? The point at which
this very long poem collapses is that at which the poet realizes that the
interior I perhaps cannot be represented in words:

If I my words am,
If the footed head which frowns them
And the handed heart which smiles them
Are the very writing, table, chair,
The paper, pen, self, taut community
Wherein enigma's orb is word-constrained. (*CP* 235–36)

Instead of freeing the self from the world, language objectifies it. The
poem ends with a question, an indication of the gravity of Riding's cri-

sis, for she can no longer claim either personhood or the concomitant authority over language that the person possesses:

And what think I?
The world in me which fleet to disavow
Ordains perpetual reiteration?
And these the words ensuing? (*CP* 236)

In other words, the poet, in attempting to disavow the world, merely re-iterates its presence, and all that ensues is language, which represents not abstract thought but the material needed to counterfeit it—paper, pen, and self are on a level. The poet asks if "this I [is] interior," knowing that it is not. In this poetry so radically stripped of outward description there is no way, finally, to avoid the self's image.

Riding's stance is at once heroic and troubling. Heroic, because she pursued the implications of her thought to their necessary end; troubling because these implications have not only to do with the interior spaces of poetry as Riding thought they had, but also with powerful external forces, such as those represented by John Crowe Ransom—and eventually by Riding herself. T. S. Matthews includes a disturbing—if perhaps apocryphal—anecdote in his memoir of Riding, Graves, and Schuyler Jackson.[12] The story dramatizes the results of the essentialism perpetrated by John Crowe Ransom and others. Matthews, who knew all the parties, speculates that Jackson, the man Riding married, forced her to stop writing poetry, as he himself had done years before: "And Frank Baisden, who had endured the Schuyler-Laura establishment [in Florida] almost as long as the boy who stood on the burning deck, had told me of a scene he had witnessed in his own house: Schuyler grim-faced and Laura in tears but obediently burning an armful of papers—presumably her poems!" (319).

Although the metaphorical relation between suicide and silence is never exact, it bears telling that Riding had, in 1929, attempted suicide over an Irishman without whom "she could not work," according to Joyce Wexler (53). Certainly there is a relation between her two attempts to silence herself. Riding has always claimed that she stopped writing poetry because poetry failed to arrive at Truth. "My kind of seriousness, in my looking to poetry for the rescue of human life from the indignities it was capable of visiting upon itself," she writes in the 1980 preface to

her collected poems, "led me to an eventual turning away from it as fail-
ing my kind of seriousness" (9). She meant to transcend language by way
of language—to follow through, after all, with the modernist and New
Critical poetics with which she sometimes took such issue.

Whatever the reason, personal or philosophical, for her extended and
complete reticence in poetry, both explanations point to one of the weaknesses of formalism (even as her brilliant poems also show us formalism's strengths). For the bottom line in both instances is that one cannot
mix "real life" and "art." The story of Riding's silence may be inscribed
in her later poetry as well. Knowing that Riding had once declared herself divided between the male sun (the poet) and the female moon (a
silent goddess), I am troubled when I read her late poem, "Nothing So
Far." In "Nothing So Far" Riding speaks as one for whom the essential
feminine has won out: the words are lovely, but their implications, at the
same time, are terrible. The poem, considered by itself (as Riding would
have us do), is a beautiful prophecy of the future "swell curved round /
To all that was"—the future feminine:

> Nothing so far but moonlight
> Where the mind is;
> Nothing in that place, this hold,
> To hold[.]
>
> Yet here, all that remains
> When each has been the universe:
> No universe, but each, or nothing.
> Here is the future swell curved round
> To all there was. (*CP* 318)

And finally:

> It makes a loving promise to itself,
> Womanly, that there
> More presences are promised
> Than by the difficult light appear.
> Nothing appears but moonlight's morning—
> By which to count were as to strew
> The look of day with last night's rid of moths. (*CP* 318)

A poetry nearly without images yields finally to one without sounds. It is significant that this is the penultimate poem in Riding's collected work, for, as I've shown, she had associated her masculine self with the writer, her feminine self with silence. Riding's equation of feminine power with silence is a dangerous one, for it can only mean transcendent and hence abstract, rather than actualized, power. From the outside it seems to represent the self's power to repress itself, the artist's to take away her only real means to attain.

Riding's vaunting of the feminine in this poem, then, is prelude to the renunciation of her art. The image of moonlight, Romantic image for the imagination, Riding's image for the feminine, is but a beautiful veil that Riding puts finally over her poetic self (though this metaphor reverses that of unclothing). It may come from that "matriarchal age" when, as Graves writes, "[p]oetry began . . . and derives its magic from the moon, not from the sun" (448), when the "Naked King" was crucified by women. But, as Graves points out, that age is gone; in years since, he writes, "Truth has been represented by poets as a naked woman: a woman divested of all garments or ornaments that will commit her to any particular position in time and space." In stripping her poetry first of images, and then of words, Riding gets closer, rather than farther away from, the muse. She has divested herself of any power except that of silence. Graves likely is thinking of himself when he writes: "Determined to escape from the dilemma, the Apollonian teaches himself to despise woman, and teaches woman to despise herself" (448). Yet his words have resonance in relation to Laura Riding, whose rigorous poetic logic sentenced her to the fate of Orpheus, to self-sacrifice on the altar of poetry. Riding's formalism, like that of her onetime friend, Hart Crane (who called her "Laura-Riding-roughshod"), finally demanded not a poetry that had worked its way through contradiction, but one that fell into silence. Like the Victorian woman described by Gilbert and Gubar, she "died to her own desires, her own self, [and] leads a posthumous existence in her own lifetime" (*Madwoman* 25).

Clearly, Riding did not recognize the political implications of her poetry, much of which sounds feminist to the later twentieth-century ear; although she recognizes the dangers of "the patriarchal leer," she ultimately fails to "break out of the snare of silence," as Cixous puts it (285). That she never broke through the snare to write more poetry is, I think, a tragic loss to the literature of our time. But new readings of Riding's poetry (of which there are now many) should restore her work to its rightful place among that of the pioneering modernists, Eliot, Pound, Crane, Moore, and others. More significantly, we need to recover Riding as one of the founders of a tradition that is only now coming to the fore, one whose proponents include John Ashbery and Language poets, all of whom—like her—relinquish the muse.

3
Gertrude Stein and Self-Advertisement

I often think how celebrated I am.
It is difficult not to think how celebrated I am.
And if I think how celebrated I am
They know who know that I am new
That is I knew I know how celebrated I am
And after all it astonishes even me.
—Stein, *Stanzas in Meditation*

All this is to be for me.
—Stein, *Stanzas in
Meditation*

What you say has nothing to do with what you write.
—Stein, *The Geographical History of America or
The Relation of Human Nature To the Human Mind*

I HAVE THUS FAR suggested speculatively that the end of modernism can be located in the quite literal silences of two of its strongest poets, Hart Crane and Laura Riding. These poets rode out the implications of formalist notions of poetry as a self-contained genre that answers only to itself. In so doing, they exhausted poetry's resources: the poem about the poem has a limited shelf life. Also, and somewhat paradoxically, they participated in modernism's absolute belief *in* poems and their power to put back together a world that came to them in shreds. Such absolute belief, in their view, could not sustain itself in language; Crane, shortly before his death, began to write poems that fruitfully evaded this impasse, poems that were very much of and about the world, and that talked more than they were "written." Riding simply (though that is to put it too simply) renounced her art and turned her attentions away from poems and onto words, in a dictionary project that, in allegorical fashion perhaps, was never completed. Her interest in language prefigures that of later poets, although her utter belief in its singularities may not. While she believed in the possibility of a language that meant what it said, she did not believe in poetry as the medium for saying it. Furthermore, as I hope I have shown, the medium was itself defined by social and cultural forces that encouraged women to think of themselves as silent.

I

Now I move to the part of my presentation in which "silence" becomes less literal, more figurative in its connotations, where the word itself acquires a complexity that renders it problematic. Part of the layering of complexity has to do with the way in which silence has been validated as a positive; a poetry of silences, for example, can be read as liberation rather than confinement, as expression rather than suppression. The word "silence" has come to stand in for crucial ideas about gender and genre, especially in arguments about women's writing, which many critics argue contains such silences within it. The word, defined through context, comes to mean "rupture," "unintelligibility," and any number of other concepts that describe obstacles that experimental writers put in the way of their readers. These obstacles, contemporary critics often argue, paradoxically free the reader to assist in "writing" the poem. Or, as Susan Howe would argue, such gaps or spaces in the text allow voices that had been suppressed to emerge again from holes in the historical record. By recovering the holes, as it were, the poet can create the possibility for filling them productively, but she cannot do all the work herself. Silence, then, permits the poet to work without "authority," to set up the conditions for, if not subversions of, old texts or old ideas of them, then for fresh perspectives on them.

In ":RE:THINKING:LITERARY:FEMINISM:(three essays onto shaky grounds)," poet Joan Retallack argues for an equation between experimental and feminist writing, and contends that such writing is characterized by its silences. She hinges her argument on the assumption that "woman" and "silence" go together. She uses the word "silence" to denote other words such as "rupture," "disturbance," "obstacle," and so on. Her definitions depend, then, on an essential sleight of hand that resembles Gertrude Stein's definitions by evasion, the most famous of which involves the rose that is a rose. "In our silence," she begins, "out of docile bodies and silent minds—out of multiple silences more and more audible—we've constructed theories and accounts of a historical endurance and power we call 'woman's silence'" (344). Retallack expands the field to include male experimental writers whose silences she hears participating in the "genre trouble" that she associates with "gender trouble" (346). As Marianne DeKoven writes in her study of Stein, "Experimental writers do not *become* women, they locate themselves *in the position of* woman: the opposite of, and antidote to, patriarchal modes of signification" (xx). In their challenge to "the conventions of language itself," these writers create "a culturally alternative language" (xiii). Among the writers who attend to silence Retallack includes Gertrude Stein, whose "silences [are] of depunctuation and repetition" (345).

To talk of repetition and depunctuation as silence—or to speak of Stein as in any way silent—seems on the face of it quite a stretch. Stein was, after all, one of the century's most prolific writers; whatever silences she experienced were either brief or metaphorical. Such quick shifts of definition as Retallack's have the virtue—and the weakness—of reclaiming a concept from the very word that has confined it. In somewhat the same manner of argument, Stein, responding to questions from University of Chicago students about her redundant rose, said that hers was the first red rose in recent poetry. The insistent rose, then, recovers its blush, just as Retallack's insistence on the term "silence" for "repetition" and "depunctuation," opens the concept to a host of meanings other than those we anticipate when we come to the word "silence." Retallack defines the term rather broadly as "nothing more or less than what lies outside the radius of interest and comprehension at any given time" (345). Later in her essay she builds on ideas gleaned from Judith Butler: "What I want to suggest . . . is that to make really productive and useful gender/genre trouble is not to repeat old forms with a difference (parodic or not) but to open up radical explorations into silence—the currently unintelligible—in which our future may make sense" (358).

The word "unintelligible" does as much work as the word "silence"; one might argue that to use it this way is to make *it* unintelligible. That may, of course, be the point, but I would venture to suggest that there are as many versions of unintelligibility as there are of silence, and that not all of them are liberating. I will have more to say about the subject later, but for now let me suggest that the silences Retallack would have us attend to are silences in the narratives that we already know. Charles Bernstein, in hyper-Orwellian fashion, would say that these narratives are built into the very syntax of the language. So that Stein, when she disrupts that syntax, or when she fails to provide her reader with the expected word—the expected idea—is calling on that reader to question her assumptions, not just about the sentence, but about the world that that sentence represents. The sentence, then, is synecdoche for the culture that it upholds. To disrupt the sentence is to disrupt the culture, to challenge its continuous narrative of itself. Marianne DeKoven describes Stein's larger project when she writes of *How to Write:* "she was pursuing the literally opposite goal of destroying continuity utterly by writing one word at a time, in such a way that it is virtually impossible for the reader to move from word to word" (120). Or, as Stein said it, rather more concisely, "A sentence should not be familiar" (*How To Write* 166–67).

Thus are Stein's silences obviously different from the silences of Hart Crane and Laura Riding, which were more literal, though Riding ultimately conflated "silence" with her own search for truth. Where Crane and Riding retained the modernist belief in intelligibility, even as an idea more alive in nostalgia than in fact, Stein, in her more experimental work, courts the ruptures that unintelligibility provides. These ruptures are based not so much in the text as they are in the reader; DeKoven describes this as the "obstruction of normal reading" that characterizes experimental writing. Stein's prime follower, Charles Bernstein, calls this process the writing of "non-absorptiveness," or writing that refuses to carry the reader along, reminding her at every juncture that language is material, not metaphysical, that meaning arises out of verbal habits that have installed themselves in the language we speak, falsely imagining our own free will with it. But, like Bernstein, Stein writes extremely intelligible works in defense of her unintelligible ones, betraying a profound ambivalence about audience. Her essays and lectures, not in journalistic or academic language, are eminently readable pieces. The violence of her vacillations between intelligible and unintelligible texts betrays Stein's mixed desire to write for herself and for strangers, audiences that she considers incompatible. Stein's relationship with her audience merits a long look, as it has as much to do with "silencing" as it does with "silence"; Stein's silences, while they are often liberating, can also be stifling.

II

The point at which we can approach Stein's paradoxical thinking on this issue of silence, however, comes out of her brief, and uncharacteristic, experience of writer's block in the early 1930s. This block apparently resulted from her acquisition of an audience and sudden arrival as a celebrity, although these are not necessarily related; as Stein herself knew, she was famous not so much for what she'd written as for who she was. The who she was threatened to become what she wrote, as public Stein took precedence over private Stein and readers picked up the Toklas autobiography rather than *Tender Buttons*. She explains this period best in her extremely accessible *Everybody's Autobiography* (1937): "And I was not writing. I began to worry about identity. I had always been I because I had words that had to be written inside me and now any word I had inside could be spoken it did not need to be written" (64–65). In other words, the fact that Stein had an audience meant paradoxically that she no longer needed to write. I disagree with Alan R. Knight, who describes her emergence from the block as a need to reach this audience on a more profound level: "She had to break through her block and begin writing again and she had to convince her large new audience that they should actually read her and not just 'about' her" (Neuman 151). To read her, on Stein's terms, was not to read her; she wanted this audience to know about her work, but not so that the audience could more easily read it. Bob Perelman is closer to my view in his contention that Stein used her obscurities in a literary public relations campaign meant to install her as a "genius."[1] The success of *The Autobiography of Alice B. Toklas* resulted in a period of sterility (Dydo, "Reading the Hand Writing" 85); her shift back to an experimental mode of writing she described as a "difficult return from 'outside' or 'audience' writing for success to serious 'inside' writing of literature." Dydo quotes Stein: "I have come back to write the way I used to write and this is because now everything that is happening is once more happening inside, there is no use in the outside" (86). What might seem a triumph in the life of a writer, in other words, created a crisis for Stein. By reading her work, Stein seemed to feel, readers were silencing her, forcing her to change her identity; only their not-reading would insure her privacy.

Stein's dilemma over audience is more like the one posed by Emily Dickinson than we might expect. Stein's "solution" to the problem was more complicated than Dickinson's; she could not choose not to publish, but she could choose obscurity—silence—as her method to be at once read and unread. What Stein does, then, to write again, is to transfer her writing block back to her reader, in the guise of what one might call a "reader's block." This reader's block transfers power back to the writer who, in controlling her text, also controls those who read it. At the same time that she creates these obstacles, however, Stein continues to write and talk persuasively and clearly about that work, thus attempting to create in her readers the desire to read—or at least to know about—her experiments in language. The real problem with audience, for Stein, is that the relationship that develops between the writer and her audience changes both of them; the writer loses her work when it is received. Reception, for Stein, is not receptive, but prescriptive, necessarily a distortion of the author's intention, to which Stein held fiercely as an idea. Paradoxically, she does so most strongly when she seems to let go of the idea of the author. It's as if the vaunted "death of the author" were simply the author's final revenge on her public, that their reader's grief (if such can be proposed as a possible response to her silences) simply reinstates her presence after all.

Stein lays out her problems with audience in, among other brief essays, "What are Master-pieces and why are there so few of them," (in Meyerowitz) which was published originally in 1936, after the period of blockage and readjustment. Toward the beginning of this essay she describes what she learned about "the question of a writer to his audience" in giving lectures. Her exploration of this relationship leads her to investigate the differences between writing and speaking: "One of the things that I discovered in lecturing was that gradually one ceased to hear what one said one heard what the audience hears one say, that is the reason that oratory is practically never a master-piece very rarely and very rarely history, because history deals with people who are orators who hear not what they are not what they say but what their audience hears them say" (Meyerowitz 147). Thus, the moment when a work of art enters into this relation between artist and audience, "it is common knowledge and anybody can feel and know it and it is not a master-piece" (149).

What Stein reaches here is the idea that great art cannot have an audience; she does so in language that is paradoxically accessible. Where most writers use essays or lectures to create an audience for their work, Stein uses her works of self-criticism to alert the audience to its own superfluousness. Such is the nature of her self-advertisement that, while they can read her criticism, they cannot read her masterpieces. In much the manner of the Groucho Marx joke, great art cannot join the club that would have it as a member. Or, as she puts it in *The Geographical History of America or the Relation of Human Nature to the Human Mind* (1936), "The words spoken are spoken to somebody, the words written are except in the case of master-pieces written to somebody, somebody somebody there is the identity that of somebody" (199). To write a master-piece, then, requires the lack of an audience, not the cultivation of one. To write about a masterpiece, as Stein does here, paradoxically requires an audience. One way to express in shorthand this ambivalence is to cite the title of one of her autobiographies, *Everybody's Autobiography,* with its conflation of outside (everybody) and inside (autobiography).

The conclusion to Stein's essay on masterpieces makes it clear that the stakes in this matter are even greater. The issue is not just the question of what is or is not a masterpiece, but also who is or is not a great writer; a writer who has readers cannot create masterpieces because that writer is changed by her audience. The great writer must be as unchangeable as her work: "When you are writing before there is an audience anything written is as important as any other thing and you cherish anything and everything that you have written. After the audience begins, naturally they create something that is they create you, and so not everything is so important, something is more important than another thing, which was not true when you were you that is when you were not you as your little dog knows you" (153–54).

The identity of the work, then, is identical with the identity of the writer of that work; Stein fears that if she is known and read and understood, then she will no longer exist as herself. Or she will no longer exist as the writer she is; Stein, as I shall soon show, provides an opening for a profound difference between the person who lives in relation with others, and the writer who does not, the person who speaks and the writer who does not.

There's another, contrary, way to explain Stein's hostility toward her audience, however, than to say she doesn't want to have one. That is to say that Stein wanted (however ambivalently) to be her own sole audience, rather in the way that she is Toklas in the *Autobiography.* According to this reading, the word "audience" does not "[spell] everything that was corrupt" for Stein, as Ulla Dydo claims ("Reading"). Instead, the *Autobiography* can be read as a plea for audience, as well as an extended complaint about the misconceptions of the as-yet-uneducated audience. Thus Stein/Toklas describes Stein's bewilderment in the face of Matisse's nonacceptance by others: "It bothered her and angered her because she did not understand why because to her it was so alright, just as later she did not understand why since the writing was all so clear and natural they mocked at and were enraged by her work" (32–33). Or, as Thornton Wilder quotes her: "But what's the difficulty? Just read the words on the paper. They're in English. Just read them. Be simple and you'll understand these things" (25).

Stein's ideal audience, then, is either herself or Toklas, whose very identity she usurps in the *Autobiography.* Just as she denies the difference between herself and Toklas in that book, she asserts control over the reception of her texts through the operation of her reader's block. While this control is veiled in the *Autobiography,* at least until the final page when Stein removes her Toklas mask, it is more evident in her long poem of 1932, *Stanzas in Meditation* (in Kostelanetz 316–464), whose surfaces are far less welcoming, and whose subject is Stein's desire to manage her text's reception. This poem, perhaps more than any of Stein's other works, asks the following crucial questions: for whom is Stein writing, herself or someone else? To what extent can she become her own audience? To what extent does the equation of the artist with her audience obviate or exacerbate the modern artist's problem with audience?

She asks these same questions in the more accessible *Autobiography,* written in the same year as *Stanzas,* but her strategies are more radical in the long poem, whose title suggests a Romantic artist's search for herself. Stein deconstructs the Romantic landscape, however, and moves toward a purely linguistic one, which cannot be described because it is a landscape of words, not a place. A closer look at this poem will help us to understand the unresolved conflict over audience that became the generating principle behind the poem. Her block is cleared when she makes the subject of that block her subject—and when her refusal to resolve the conflict keeps the issue, and the text, alive. In that sense, she operates according to Kenneth Burke's "situation strategy," except that hers is a strategy of repeated blocking. For Stein, repetition is refusal, and refusal is the engine of her work. But, for Stein more than for any other writer, perhaps, refusal is a fertile strategy, for repetitions create variations, if not new themes. Stein is, above all, the poet of variations, and these variations are in their own ways wise, especially in the pragmatic sense that they allow Stein to continue. Riding, one might say, refused repetition. For all its admirable certitude, this choice was her undoing as a poet.

Yet too much refusal can confuse, and ultimately, alienate an audience. And audiences are desirable in part because they can be influenced; the artist who influences others takes power from them, or so they might hope. Thus part of Stein's business as an explicator of her own work and career is her claim to having such an audience, to participating in a tradition of which she is both origin and end. Thus Stein/Toklas claims, in the *Autobiography,* that she has an audience, and has molded a generation of younger writers. Stein establishes this claim over and again, with her usual persuasive vagueness:

> Gertrude Stein had written the story of Melanctha the negress, the second story of Three Lives which was the first definite step away from the nineteenth century and into the twentieth century in literature. (50)

> She realizes that in english literature in her time she is the only one. She has always known it and now she says it. (72)

> [*Tender Buttons*] as everyone knows, had an enormous influence on all young writers. . . . (147)

> It was in Saint-Remy and during this winter that she wrote the poetry that has so greatly influenced the younger generation. (197)

But Stein could not admit that this influence influenced her in any way. Her mirror works in but one direction. Stein is, if anything, even less obscure about her position in *Stanzas,* where she chides herself for wishing too desperately for an audience. The very circularity of the passage that follows, in which she listens to herself think about the problem of audience, insures that the work matters because it is hers, but is hers only insofar as it examines its relation to its audience. *Stanzas* is so long, then, at least in part because it forms a loop. After Robert Bridgman, I take the "they" here to be her audience, earned through the accessibility of the *Autobiography,* and potentially lost by their as yet hypothetical encounter with *Stanzas.* From Stanza VII of Part II:

When they were not only laden with best wishes
But indeed not inclined for them to be careless
Might they be often more than ever especially
Made to be thought carelessly a vacation
That they will like this less.
Let me listen to me and not to them
Can I be very well and happy
Can I be whichever they can thrive
Or just can they not.
They do not think not only only
But always with prefer
And therefore I like what is mine
For which not only willing but willingly
Because which it matters. (343)

The last line ends her thought ambiguously; whether she likes her work because it matters, or whether it matters because she likes it, is not clear. The making of "material" is obviously important to Stein—an enormously prolific writer—as a sign that matter matters. And, by extension, her material will insure that she, the mother of the text, will also matter. This is to jump ahead of things; Stein identifies her problems with audience from the onset of the 150-odd page poem. That this audience includes Toklas is clear; the danger is that this audience/lover will separate from the author and then recreate her in its own image:

They like it as well as they ever did
But it is very often just by the time
That they are able to separate
In which case in effect they could
Not only be very often present perfectly
In each way which ever they chose.
All of this never matters in authority
But this which they need as they are alike
Or in an especial case they will fulfill
Not only what they have at their instigation
Made for it as a decision in its entirety. (316)

Stein's particular anxiety is revealed in the line, "All of this never matters in authority"; if she, as writer, wielded authority over her audience, in other words, none of this would be a problem. The problem has to do not with the audience's particular likes or dislikes, but with its attendant separation from the writer: "But it is very often just by the time / That they are able to separate." Separation denotes a kind of refusal that Stein fears, because separation creates, or is born out of, another authority. In her author-centered view, such authority is hers by right.

One final example of Stein's treatment of audience in *Stanzas* (and there are dozens more) should complete the picture of a writer who cared so desperately not to care what her audience thought of her:

> I have been worried I will be worried again
> And if again is again is it
> Not to be interested in how they think
> Oh yes not to be interested in how they think
> Oh oh yes not to be interested in how they think. (421)

The only means which Stein finds to persuade her audience is to incorporate or to absorb it into herself, as she claims to do in Stanza XIV of Part II, playing on an ambiguity in the word *absorb*. The Romantic context of her meditations plays itself out in references to nightingale and robin, though Stein appears not so much as a perceiver of a landscape that offers itself up as a mirror, but *as* a landscape in which she sees herself. Where a Romantic poet might "be absorbed" in a landscape, the verb denoting an abstraction of the act of perceiving through self-loss, Stein's audience is quite literally absorbed into the subject of its meditations, the poet herself. It may be that Stein's insistence on conflating poet and subject, poet and audience, is no more than a repetition (with a difference) of Keats's conflation of himself with the nightingale, or Shelley's insistence on a bird "that never wert," but Stein's insistence is wholly modern. Or perhaps wholly American, rather like Whitman's ego insistence that he knows exactly what the bird says to him.[2]

> It is not only early that they make no mistake
> A nightingale and a robin.
> Or rather that which can which

Can which he which they can choose which
They know or not like that
They make this be once or not alike
Not by this time only when they like
To have been very much absorbed.
And so they find it so
And so they are
There
There which is not only here but here as well as there.
They like whatever I like. (350)

III

Stein's recurring discussions of authority have everything to do with the names that are given to objects in the world, objects that are seen through the names we give to them; later in the poem, she will claim to "look" without describing, to regard the landscape without giving it the old names. As she comments in "Poetry and Grammar," "So as I say poetry is essentially the discovery, the love, the passion for the name of anything" (*Lectures* 235). The way in which Stein names her landscape is the focus of this section of the chapter, because names have value to her—not simply her own name, which increasingly had monetary value on the lecture circuit, but new names for the objects of the world insured both her work's difficulty and its power. Stein means to create her own authority through her name(s), unlike those persons described in Stanza X of Part I who "call a pail a pail and make a mountain cover / Not only their clouds but their own authority" (*Stanzas* 327). Stein wants clear weather always. In this stanza she parodies Keats, an old authority.

It might be very well that lilies of the valley have a fragrance
And that they ripen soon
And that they are gathered in great abundance
And that they will not be refreshing but only
Very lovely with green leaves
Or managed just the same when payed or offered
Even if they do. (328)

The last two lines sound a discordant note; surely even bad gardeners don't usually think of paying off their flowers. But in conflating a

Romantic-sounding description of flowers with a reference to payment, Stein ushers in a difference between what she terms "god" and "mammon" in her lecture "What is English Literature," published in 1935. In that piece, she distinguishes between writing that sounds like old writing and writing that does not, and also between the stuff that sells and the stuff that does not: "If you write the way it has already been written the way writing has already been written then you are serving mammon, because you are living by something someone has already been earning or earned. If you write as you are to be writing then you are serving as a writer god because you are not earning anything. . . . But really there is no choice" (*Lectures* 54).

There is humor in her assertion that "writer gods" don't earn anything. But there's also a good deal of puritanical nervousness about the relationship between art and commerce, a puritanism that informs the work of many an American writer, including that of Crane and Riding. She also shares in the drive toward originality that informs American Romantics from Emerson to Harold Bloom. Originality, as she knows, typically earns no money.

Like Riding, Stein felt that there was an intense split between writers who wrote for god and those who wrote for mammon. As a writer who had for decades not been recognized, her sudden accession to fame and modest fortune seemed to intensify her ambivalence on the matter. For mammon meant, inevitably, that the writer had an audience—even, in Stein's case, one that paid more attention to Stein as artist than to what that artist produced. And, as we have seen, having an audience meant inevitably writing for that audience's expectations rather than for one's own, which were the only pure ones. In her lecture, "What is English Literature," originally published in 1935, she wrote about poets in a tone resembling Riding's: "The minute they all begin to think what they want to say and how they want to say it they no longer choose. And when they no longer choose then as far as writing goes they are no longer serving god they are serving mammon" (32). Contrariwise, "If you write as you are to be writing then you are serving as writer god because you are not earning anything" (54). In *Everybody's Autobiography,* Stein describes the sea change she went through when people began to buy her work and the work changed value. "Value," in this case—as in medieval drama— must be contrasted with "goods." That is, value changes from inherent to monetary value, from the value of the inside to that of the outside:

"because suddenly it was all different, what I did had a value that made people ready to pay, up to that time everything I did had a value because nobody was ready to pay" (44).

The question of monetary value, like that of audience, hinges on Stein's strong sense that her identity would be altered by it. Where Wallace Stevens proposes that money and poetry are one and the same, Stein (rather less surprisingly) suggests the opposite, that poetry and money are incompatible. "It is funny about money," she writes in *Everybody's Autobiography*. "And it is funny about identity. You are you because your little dog knows you, but when your public knows you and does not want to pay for you and when your public knows you and does want to pay for you, you are not the same you" (44). Yet there remains the question of Stein's evident love of her own celebrity; her autobiography of everybody positively radiates satisfaction that she has been recognized, and rewarded for, her public identity. Stein surely realized that the opposition she created between god and mammon, or more accurately the opposition she inherits and perpetuates, was reductive and inadequate to the complexities of her own identity. For her sense of herself was necessarily stronger than the one her dog had of her; her reiteration of the notion that she was because her dog knew her became an affectation that contained more than a little irony. (Although, if quotation equals one kind of literary value, then this quotation was valuable to Stein, because so often repeated.) Instead of exploding this opposition, however, she established it even more strongly in her discussions of the writer's identity. She simply established herself as both a talker (who had an audience and relished it) and a writer (who, to some extent, reveled in her lack of one). The identities of talker and writer are then identified with those of one who has a "human nature" and one who is solely "mind." The very languages that these parts of herself speak or write are opposed, just as the language of the newspaper is necessarily different from that found in "master-pieces." Rather than collapse her oppositions, then, Stein piles them on end, until their very absurdities call them into question—or would, perhaps, if one were not to compare *Everybody's Autobiography*, say, with *Stanzas in Meditation*, "What is English literature" to *Tender Buttons*.

Writing, according to this scheme, amounts to refusal; immediately following her description of the effect of payment on the writer's work in *Everybody's Autobiography*, she writes: "And that is because talking

and writing have gotten more and more separated. Talking is not thinking or feeling at all any more, it used to be but it is not now but writing
is, and so writing naturally needs more refusing" (46).

The refusing that is writing is a refusal of audience, of sound, of feeling (if not always of thinking), and ultimately, it would seem, of communication in the sense we usually mean it. Unless, of course, communication operates on the inside rather than the outside, to an audience
of one, the writer herself. So, she writes, in a book that sounds spoken:
"When I write I write and when I talk I talk and the two are not one, no
not for any one and when they come near being one, then the inside is
not inside and the outside is not outside and I like the inside to be inside
and the outside to be outside, it makes it more necessary to be one" (264).
To a question addressed to her at Berkeley about why she did not write
as she spoke, Stein answered that were they talking to Keats they would
not expect him to answer them with his "Ode to the Nightingale" (292).
The politics of plain speech in poetry, from Wordsworth to Walt Whitman to Robert Frost, was not her politics; if plain speech is "common,"
then the writer of masterpieces refuses commonality. And, if the ordinary person, like the Romantic poet, has and expresses feeling, then in
her writing she will obscure feeling, concentrate on mind, much as Eliot
does in his essay about impersonality.

Yet Stein's position is more extreme than Eliot's; where Eliot means to
use tradition as a vehicle for human emotion to purify itself into art, and
where he acknowledges that the desire for impersonality rests on an intense experience of personality,[3] Stein insists that art is essentially other
than life. "And now," she asks in "Pictures" (in *Lectures*), "why does the
representation of things that being painted do not look at all like the
things look to me from which they are painted why does such a representation give me pleasure and hold my attention." Having asked herself
this question, she answers as follows: "it has achieved an existence in and
for itself, it exists on as being an oil painting on a flat surface and it has
its own life and like it or not there it is and I can look at it and it does
hold my attention" (61). That is why, she remarks later on, that "one
comes to any oil painting through any other oil painting" (72).

Part of what drew Stein to art was its stasis. Her feeling on looking at
a painting of Waterloo was that art was deathly: "I remember standing
on the little platform in the center and almost consciously knowing that
there was no air. There was no air, there was no feeling of air. . . . It the

oil painting showed it as an oil painting. That is what an oil painting is" (63). In fact, good paintings stop movement, though the painter's first desire is to make the painting move. This resistance to movement that she finds in painting, and which has an appropriate internal logic, since painting is spatial, is a resistance she attempts to transfer into language, which moves—like it or not—in time. She shares with Wyndham Lewis the desire to stop language, render it spatial, kill it productively.[4] But she also means to get at the way in which art operates apart from life; in this view she is not so far removed from a New Critical view of art as occupying a privileged and separate place. Art is about art, and that is its virtue.

Thus art has its own language, separate from the language of the real. In *Everybody's Autobiography,* Stein recounts a conversation with an Egyptian man in which he describes the difference between spoken language and the language of art in Arabic; she tells him that this separation will soon be true for English:

> That is very interesting I said, now the English language I said has gone just the other way, they always tried to write like anybody talked and it is only comparatively lately that it is true that the written language knows that that is of no interest and cannot be done that is to write as anybody talks because what anybody talks because everybody talks as the newspapers and movies and radios tell them to talk the spoken language is no longer interesting and so gradually the written language says something and says it differently than the spoken language (13).

Stein best develops the line of (pseudo)argument about the split between speaking and writing, human nature and mind, in her geographical history of America. Early on she trots out her dog metaphor to do more work for her: "So then human nature can talk but so can any dog." What dogs cannot do, according to Stein, is write; that is what humans do, and therefore what distinguishes their minds from their nature. This metaphor follows on another exercise in playful (and specious) logic in which she wonders: "is writing a different thing, oh yes . . . it makes everything everything writing has nothing to do with the human speech with human nature and therefore and therefore it has something to do with the human mind" (68–69). In fact, she later claims, the human mind *is* writing and nothing else (97). Herein another paradox: Stein's claim that the problem with audiences is that they force the writer to change her identity, and therefore should be at best ignored, would seem to assert the desirability of identity, her need to stay fixed. Yet in her essay about masterpieces, Stein describes the process of creation as one in which identity is lost: "The thing one gradually comes to find out is that one has no identity that is when one is in the act of doing anything. Identity is recognition, you know who you are because you and another remember anything about yourself but essentially you are not that when you are doing anything" (Meyerowitz 146).

There is no reason, of course, why these two possibilities need be exclusive; certainly Stein's fear of losing her identity to others helps to drive her sole desire to hold onto that identity. Self-recognition, then, can be seen to be other than recognition, pure and simple (and the monetary value that often accrues from it). Writing may, in fact, be the sole process Stein recognizes for remembering herself, and for creating that self anew. In this sense, as in many others, she is a Romantic, akin to Whitman and Dickinson. But she is not democratic in the way Whitman is, because she cannot afford to be. Whitman's expansiveness and Stein's are very different creatures; Stein's expansiveness is also a shrinking. She enables herself to continue writing, where Crane and Riding did not, by depending on that expansiveness to defend her core sense of identity; Riding, in particular, required a profound asceticism to uphold her sense of herself. Between profligacy and self-denial there are, of course, many parallels, as many a saint's life can testify.

Yet there is, after all, in her writing a silence not so dissimilar from that of other modernists, whose credo on impersonality was spelled out by Eliot in his "Tradition and the Individual Talent," an essay much stronger on tradition than on the individual. This silence is an abstraction of self into language; if the language of art is to be other than the language of life, then any representation of the self in art is bound not to resemble a personality, even in an autobiography like *Stanzas*. The identity one creates is not the identity that one is; it is at least separate from that identity. As "Toklas" writes in her autobiography, which does contain a multitude of personalities:

> Gertrude Stein, in her work, has always been possessed by the intellectual passion for exactitude in the description of inner and

outer reality. She has produced a simplification by this concentration, and as a result the destruction of associational emotion in poetry and prose. She knows that beauty, music, decoration, the result of emotion should never be the cause, even event should not be the cause of emotion nor should they be the material of poetry and prose. Nor should emotion itself be the cause of poetry or prose. (198–99)

Thus the language of art, as distinct from the language of life (or the written language as opposed to the spoken one), requires a move from particularity to abstraction, from the language of resemblance or likeness to that of unlikeness. Stein comes to distinguish between the descriptiveness that appeals to an audience and the abstraction that loses it. As if to counter Wallace Stevens's "Description without Place," Stein asserts, "I can look at a landscape without describing it." The task of renouncing a Romantic relationship between the self and the landscape, Stein avers, is not an easy one.

> It is not easy to turn away from delight in moon-light.
> Nor indeed to deny that some heat comes
> But only now they know that in each way
> Not whether better or either to like
> Or plan whichever whether they will plan to share
> Their which indeed which can they care
> Or rather whether well and whether.
> Can it not be after all their share.
> This which is why they will be better than before
> Makes it most readily more than readily mine. (*Stanzas* 429)

Stein's language turns rapidly from particular reference, which in the first instance ("moon-light") is also a symbolic, Romantic trope, to a language emptied of direct reference ("they," "theirs," "this," "which"), which is *hers* and yet also impersonal. This emptying of reference is also an emptying of tradition, paradoxically in the name of it; Stein's belief in art is precisely what drives her to create such large silences within it. To create a hole in the tradition, or between the twin facts of speaking and writing, enables Stein to "make it most readily more than readily" hers.

Stein's renunciation of landscape description had come earlier than her expression of the difficulty of renouncing Romantic images, however. In Stanza II of Part III of *Stanzas,* she explicitly denudes the landscape of content before turning her attention back to the stanzas themselves. This is a classic statement of refusal; she sings of what she has refused to sing about:

> It is not only that I have not described
> A lake in trees only there are not trees
> Just not there where they do not like not having these
> Trees.
> It is a lake so and so or oh
> Which if it is could it does it for it
> Not make any do or do or it
> By this it is a chance inclined.
> They did not come from there to stay they were hired
> They will originally will do
> It is not only mind but also
> They will three often do it.
> Not now.
> Do I mind
> Went one.
> I wish to remain to remember that stanzas go on. (358–59)

Stein questions her own presence in the stanza's last line; if the landscape is denuded of everything, including description, then where is the author? But what she proposes is that this act of not describing the world is what makes art.

This process accrues throughout the poem; Stein's language steadily loses mimetic value; in Stanza LXVI of Part V, she deliberately conflates a "plain" with plainness. A word for a feature of landscape is deliberately used as a pun for writing; a plain is plain talk (or writing), not a distinguishable bluff. It is here that language becomes the landscape rather than a means of describing it.

> Once in a while as they did not go again
> They felt that it would be plain
> A plain would be a plain

And in between
There would be that would be plain
And in between
There would be that would be plain
That there would be as plain
It would be as it would be plain
Plain it is and it is a plain
And addition to as plain
Plainly not only not a plain
But well a plain.
A plain is a mountain not made round
And so a plain is a plain as found (454–55)

And yet, at the end of this poem about a poet's renunciation of her audience, and the very images that poets use to reach their audience, Stein ushers her audience back in, and her language once again becomes instrumental. One cannot but think, however, that her invitation to the audience comes too late, is too much an afterthought.

No what I wish to say is this.
Fifty percent of the roses should be cut
The rest should bloom upon their branch
Because because there is very little wind here
Enough of rain sometimes too much
But even so it is a pleasure that whether
Will they remain or will they go even so. (462)

And, apparently to Toklas: "I can I wish I do love none but you." The final stanza is worthy of the inconclusive conclusion to Whitman's "Song of Myself" and announces Stein's presence in the poetic world, much as his "Preface" to *Leaves of Grass* had some seventy years previously.

I call carelessly that the door is open
Which if they can refuse to open
No one can rush to close.
Let them be mine therefor.
Everybody knows that I chose.
Therefor if therefor before I close.

I will therefor offer therefor I offer this.
Which if I refuse to miss can be miss is mine.
I will be well welcome when I come.
Because I am coming.
Certainly I come having come.
　　These stanzas are done. (464)

Stein's final choice seems a conservative one; she writes, finally, for an audience, and in so doing her poetry becomes more lyrical, more Romantic—
especially in its obvious bow to Whitman. Yet this conclusion seems less
earned than imposed, as if in the turning of Stein's mind toward and
then away from her audience, she merely happened upon these concilia-
tory lines.

IV

It should by now be clear that Stein, despite her current reputation, especially among Language writers, is not always a precocious postmodernist, someone thoroughly out of step with her time, but not with ours.
Her reliance on oppositions—between god and mammon, writer and
audience, writing and speaking, identity and the lack thereof—is more
modernist than post-. The traps she lays for herself, then, are potentially
every bit as lethal to the writing process as were those set by Crane and
Riding. Why then was she able to keep generating work? Why and how
did she turn away from the writer's block she suffered in the early 1930s?
How could she create work that seems so distinctly postmodernist in its
form and content, while holding to the reductive oppositions that inform her critical work about herself?

The answer, I think, lies in her almost Emersonian ability to believe
in polar opposites at the same time. Unlike Riding, Stein was not a firm
believer in one term of her opposed categories; she did not find truth
apart from literature, nor did she quite believe in either god or mammon.
She quite openly wanted both. Rather, what happens increasingly in the
1930s is that Stein writes from two sides of herself, the talking as well as
the writing side, the seeker of fortune as well as the quasi-religious as-
cetic. Stein, more than most, and at least sometimes, refuses the very pu-
rities of spirit and philosophies of writing that she often expounds.

The central silence in Stein is the one that would entertain consideration of the very paradoxes she trots out in her lectures and essays. On

her own inconsistencies Stein is ever reticent. But it is this reticence that keeps Stein writing—and which insures that her several autobiographies will have different names and different contents, even different subjects. In her position paper about geography, Stein speculates on the question of titles and autobiographies: "think how many different titles have been invented for autobiographies . . . it is astonishing always astonishing how many people can think of a new title for an autobiography" (80–81). Yet she answers her own astonishment with what follows, in what is itself an astonishing distinction between the human mind and the genre she discusses: "And yet autobiographies have nothing to do with the human mind, and they really have nothing to do with tears and reading" (81). If autobiographies do not have to do with the human mind or with audiences that shed tears, then with what do they have to do? Stein's surprising answer, which she all but states here, is that autobiographies have, plainly and simply, to do with writing autobiographies.

This logic, which amounts to saying that the purpose of autobiographies is the writing of them, is—of course—circular. Here, as elsewhere, what is Stein's insistence is our repetition; the rose that is a rose is, at the least, a redundant flower. But the very circularity of Stein's thinking, which we find most excessively displayed in the experimental work, is precisely the key that unlocks modernism's trap and springs her clear to write and write again. For Stein, the verbal material that is a word (which is a word) can be used not so much to transcend itself but to put back in place the world that language lost through overuse. Her declaration that her rose is the first red one in centuries is not without justice, even if what strikes this reader as equally important is that Stein is pointing to the absence of redness in the word "rose," and to the status of words as players in the larger game of writing them into her mind (which is not nature or outside identity).

Stein discovers her own postmodernism (or, better to say, she discovers *our* postmodernism) in her evident belief that both elements of her oppositions can be true concurrently, and in the notion that logic is circular rather than linear. But she does so by indulging in the aspects of modernism that, according to my speculative narrative, condemned it to end. Rather than explaining modernism's flaws, however, and moving on from them, she reifies them, puts them all into play. Modernism's myth-making drive becomes her self-advertisement. Modernism's attempts to systematize become her offbeat critical essays and lectures. And its persistent categorizing of ideas about art and culture become elements in her game of words, a game whose purpose is both to win and to keep on playing. Her postmodernism is the intensest form of modernism. As I will argue later, this modernism (and its excesses) still lives on strongly in the work of later poets such as Charles Bernstein, who position themselves in a self-consciously postmodern moment, but who stay there by adopting and adapting Stein's technique of circularity.

4
"Returning to Bloom"

John Ashbery's Critique of Harold Bloom

In the struggle of the reader both with and against a strong poem, more than an interpretation of a poem becomes the prize. What instruction is more valuable than that which shows us how to distinguish real or illusory dangers to the self's survival, and how to ward off the real menaces?
   —Harold Bloom, *Agon: Towards a Theory of Revisionism*

I shall keep to myself.
I shall not repeat others' comments about me.
   —John Ashbery, "Wet Casements"

As I NOTED IN THE introduction, the instigator of an impasse in writing is often an "enemy" agent; in the case of local writers in Hawai'i, that agent has often come in from the outside, considering itself a "civilizing" mechanism, and advised writers to write in "better English." But what happens when the blocking agent is a friend, when the critic is not an enemy but the writer's strongest ally in the world of literary reputation? What if the writer is John Ashbery, and his antagonist is Harold Bloom, who has done more to support Ashbery's career than any other critic?

   That critics write about poets is no surprise; what is surprising are those moments when a poet directly confronts and addresses his critics and the content of their work. One of these moments—attenuated, most certainly—occurs in John Ashbery's *Flow Chart* (1991), the book that comes closest to being an autobiography of the poet's career. In this book-length poem, Ashbery takes on the critic most responsible for elevating him into the canon, at some times comically and at others caustically; his critique of his foremost critic is, to steal one of Harold Bloom's favorite words, "strong." This criticism is so strong, and comes so late in the professional relationship between the two men, because—even as

Ashbery possesses evident staying power in the twentieth-century canon of American poets—the bloom on Bloom's reputation has, over the past couple of decades, faded. As Marjorie Perloff puts it, rather more dramatically, "Then suddenly the bubble seems to have burst. By the mid-1980s, younger poets were no longer lining up to receive the Bloomian accolade, and graduate students seemed barely to know who Bloom was" ("Modernist Studies" 161).

Yet however much critics cultural, feminist, New Historicist, and otherwise (those he refers to in his book *The Western Canon* as "The School of Resentment" and a "rabblement of lemmings" (4) have come to displace Bloom, he cannot so easily be dismissed from the very history he often elides. And his influence, if not on Ashbery's writing (though there is that), then on the trajectory of his career as poet, means Ashbery confronts the impasse of an approving critic who tries to lock his favorite poet into one mode of writing, the one of which he approves. Conversely, as is sometimes the case with Bloom and Ashbery, a hostile critic may turn against the poet and work to undermine his reputation. Bloom's rather straightforward Freudian theory of the "anxiety of poetic influence," bolstered by arcane vocabularies borrowed from mystical religious texts, may sound to the ear of today's critics tinny and out of touch with social and historical concerns. But the reputations of Wallace Stevens and John Ashbery, while they would likely have ascended of their own luminosity without Bloom, would not have done so as quickly without his agency.

Among contemporaries, John Ashbery has been the foremost beneficiary of Bloom's marketing strategy. Ashbery, who represents the end of literary history (at least thus far) for Bloom, became one of the unwitting agents of Bloom's own rise in his profession. Bloom's career within the academy has been virtually unparalleled: he has his own department at Yale University and also teaches at New York University; he won the coveted, if mysteriously proffered, MacArthur Award in 1985; he was, in 1987–88, the Charles Eliot Norton professor of Poetry at Harvard University (Allen xvii). His books, if you include the Chelsea House collections of essays on writers, which he edits and introduces, number over one hundred. He has been featured in national news magazines and in *The New York Times Magazine.* This is not to say that Bloom could not have achieved such prominence without Ashbery. But Bloom, like the prophet he sometimes proclaims himself to be, needed a contemporary hero, and Ashbery, often in conjunction with A. R. Ammons and Elizabeth Bishop, just happened to fill those shoes.

This dual career history becomes more interesting if we consider that Bloom and Ashbery are nearly exact contemporaries (Ashbery was born in 1927, Bloom in 1930) and that Ashbery's career has occasionally dovetailed with that of his critic. Ashbery, for example, also won a MacArthur Award in 1985 and was the Norton Lecturer at Harvard in 1989–90, right after Bloom's stint there ended.[1] The dovetailing of their career paths illustrates the way in which critics and poets have come to play on the same field with one another. This does not mean that the poets are the players and critics the referees; Bloom makes it clear that he, too, is a player. Asked why he had embarked on the outrageously ambitious (or at least extensive) Chelsea House project of editing and introducing over eight hundred critical anthologies about writers, he told David Lehman, abiding by the strictures of his own theory of influence: "It makes me feel like Milton's Satan. You know, the authors are God, and what keeps me going is this feeling that it's a kind of hopeless struggle with them" (56). Bloom has claimed repeatedly that criticism is creative rather than parasitical, a notion that puts Bloom directly into competition with his poet-hero and renders their relationship more problematic than that of a father-critic and son-poet, as Bloom seems often to portray them, despite their similar ages.

If you believe Bloom's theory, which owes its force to Freudian notions of the oedipal complex, there can be no relationship more problematic than that between fathers and sons; that "complex" is in fact the governing trope for the relationship between poets and their precursors, as Bloom tells it. In Blooms' theory, every "strong" or "great" poet is forced to confront his strong precursors (as Ashbery confronts Stevens, or Stevens, Emerson) and find a way to avoid falling into imitation. How this happens is that the younger poet "misreads" his precursor, in a process that Bloom labels "misprision." His task grows increasingly difficult over time, since poets are more and more the "belated" members of an old tradition: less and less material is original; more and more of it depends on prior poems. Since the publication of *The Anxiety of Influence* in 1973, Bloom has used his theory to map out American literary history, always emphasizing the romantic strain of that literature. His canon moves from Emerson to Whitman to Stevens, not from Eliot (though Eliot has recently moved into the Whitman tradition in Bloom's revision of his own earlier work) and Pound to Charles Olson and Charles Bernstein, as many critics—notably Marjorie Perloff and Jerome J. McGann—would have it. Like Oswald Spengler, Bloom sees history as the repetition of pattern rather than the elaboration of accidents or differences. In that sense, it can be—and has been—argued that his theory is ahistorical.[2]

Bloom's theory allows him to build a very personal canon and to give it the credence of a system, even as he admits to its idiosyncrasies. In a November 1975 review in *The New Republic,* entitled "Harold Bloom on Poetry," Bloom suggests that all canons directly reflect the critic's tastes; he denies the possibility of objectivity in criticism. And so he writes that, were Hugh Kenner writing the review, Kenner would choose to include books by George Oppen, Louis Zukofsky, and Charles Olson, since his "central American poets of the century" were Pound, Eliot, and Williams (24). "I myself prefer E. A. Robinson, Frost, Stevens, and Hart Crane, who seem to me the rightful inheritors of Emerson, Whitman, and Dickinson," Bloom continues. Then this intense admirer of poets curiously distinguishes between himself and "[i]dealizers of poetry, of teaching and of criticism" who say that "*they* read accurately and selflessly," for "such an assertion is always a self-deception" (24). Within the space of a few sentences, he turns this confession of subjectivity into a global rule, placing America in the context of his own theory of belatedness: "America is the Evening Land, or the last phase of Mediterranean culture, and this late in tradition all reading (and writing) is heavily shadowed by the past" (24). By this point, he has mustered a sweeping generalization about world culture as a defense for his own admitted defensiveness: "Where the shadow is so long and so dark, reading and writing inevitably manifest defensive patterns, whatever the overt intentions and ideals of readers or writers" (24). In the 1980s and 1990s, Bloom has positioned himself as a guardian of aestheticism, besieged by what, in conversation, he calls "a rabblement of lemmings" (Begley 34) whose work is governed more by ideology than by a pure love of literature, which love Bloom would claim, contra his critics, has no ideology at all.

Bloom himself writes in *A Map of Misreading* (1975), "As literary history lengthens, all poetry necessarily becomes verse-criticism, just as all criticism becomes prose-poetry" (3). In *Agon: Towards a Theory of Revisionism* (1982), Bloom suggests that strong poems are ones that engender strong critics: "A strong poem, which alone can become canonical for more than a single generation, can be defined as a text that must engender strong misreadings, both as other poems and as literary criticism" (285). Bloom himself acknowledges that his narrative of Ashbery's importance likely differs from Ashbery's own sense of himself; at the same time, he suggests that poets cannot do without their critics, just as they cannot do without their precursors. Ashbery's crucial precursor, for Bloom, is Wallace Stevens, whose poetic fathers (hence one-sided sparring partners) were Emerson and Whitman. In *Figures of Capable Imagination* (1976), Bloom notes Ashbery's likely disapproval of his reading of his work and then goes on nonetheless to assert the truth of that reading, a truth that is also a genealogy: "Ashbery (who is not likely to be pleased by this observation) is at his best when he is neither revitalizing proverbial wisdom nor barely evading an ellipsis, but when he dares to write most directly in the idiom of Stevens" (172). The poet, then, is at his best not when he is most himself (and his use of proverbial clichés does distinguish Ashbery from other poets, including Stevens), but when he fits neatly into Bloom's scheme of influence—when he is most like Stevens. Bloom's argument has had ramifications in the popular press and in literary journals, as well as in academe. Paul Gray's brief 1976 review of *Self-Portrait in a Convex Mirror* in *Time* magazine includes the following comment, which mirrors Bloom's: "This is the gaudy tightrope mode of Wallace Stevens, and few poets since Stevens have been able to escape the pit of arrant gibberish that yawns below" (96). In his review of the book for *Poetry*, Richard Howard invokes Stevens and Bloom, albeit dismissively, noting that "Harold Bloom was so quick to seize upon it ["As You Came from the Holy Land"], exhibit A in the endless catalogue of belatedness which for him constitutes poetry's knowledge of itself" (350). Gray's connection between Stevens and Bloom, as well as Howard's very anxiety about Bloom's interpretation of Ashbery's poem, speaks to the influence of Bloom's theory on discussions of the poet's work in 1976.

Again and again, Bloom aims to *correct* Ashbery's attempts to position himself in ways different from Bloom's. For the poet, according to Bloom's definition of him, necessarily misunderstands his own motivations: "To live as a poet," he writes in *Figures of Capable Imagination*, "a poet needs the illusive mist about him that shields him from the light that first kindled him" (174). To be a critic is, by extension, to penetrate that mist, clarify the situation, or misread the misreadings. Bloom's strategy is notable for its being so personal, as if literary history were

Bloom's reading of it. Aside from his characteristic opening anecdote about the first time he encountered a poet's work (most notable in this genre is his story about reading Hart Crane at the age of ten),[3] Bloom goes to great pains to separate his own interpretations from Ashbery's, and then to proclaim the truth of his own reading, in contrast to the relative mistiness of the poet's. A poet's value is located in the fact that he compels Bloom to read and reread his work: "But this I think is part of Ashbery's true value; only he and Ammons among poets since Stevens compel me to re-read so often, and then reward such labor" (*Figures* 200). Then, in commenting on thirteen pages in *Three Poems* (1972), Bloom writes, and the emphasis is his, not mine: "I suspect that these [pp.73–86] are, *for Ashbery,* the most important pages in his book, but except for the lovely pathos of a dreamer's defense, they are too much the work of a poet who wishes to be more of an anomaly than he is, rather than the 'central' kind of a poet he is fated to become, in the line of Emerson, Whitman, Stevens" (206).[4] Ashbery, according to this narrative, is a weak reader of his own work, whereas Bloom's reading represents nothing less than "fate." Bloom's theory depends on a poet's being both an anomaly (a solitary figure caught in a life-and-death tussle with his "fathers") and a predictable part of a chain of being. He would, I suspect, be the last to deny that this chain includes Bloom. The critic poses a further resistance to the poet by making his work more difficult, thus acting like another precursor figure, someone prior to—not contemporary with—the poet: "One of the functions of criticism, as I understand it, is to make a good poet's work even more difficult for him to perform, since only the overcoming of genuine difficulties can result in poems wholly adequate to an age consciously as late as our own. All that a critic, as critic, can give poets is the deadly encouragement that never ceases to remind them of how heavy their inheritance is" (*Map* 10).

There is evidence within Ashbery's poems that he has read or listened to Bloom, that he knows the role he is meant to play in Bloom's theory, and that his attitude toward the theory, and the visionary tradition from which it springs, is one of extreme ambivalence. Much of the direct evidence comes from Ashbery's work of the 1970s, when Bloom's theories carried the most professional—and cultural—weight. Consider Ashbery's "And *Ut Pictura Poesis* Is Her Name," from *Houseboat Days* (1977), which opens with what could be quotation from Bloom: "You can't say it that way any more," and the poet's subsequent swerve away from the critic, whose primary interest is in agon, not relaxation: "Bothered about beauty you have to / Come out into the open, into a clearing, / And rest" (*Selected* 235). Or, take the aptly named poem from *As We Know* (1979), "Late Echo," which takes Bloom's theory and suggests a way around it in simple repetitions of old poems:

> Alone with our madness and favorite flower
> We see that there really is nothing left to write about.
> Or rather, it is necessary to write about the same old things
> In the same way, repeating the same things over and over
> For love to continue and be gradually different. (88)

Again, Ashbery deflates the agon, by writing in the second stanza about "it get[ting] slowed down to the pace of an authentic / Saraband and huddle there, alive and resting" (267).

Ashbery's feelings about Bloom are mixed, I presume, because he may at one time have relied on the critic, consciously or not, to make his reputation, at the same time that he wanted to avoid seeming to write his poetry so that it would fit into the critic's preordained scheme of things. A strong poet would never submit to a strong theory; even Bloom would concede that point and, in so doing, emphasize the inherent competition between poets and critics. (Unlike A. R. Ammons, for example, Ashbery has dedicated no poems to Bloom.[5] Nor—and this is doubtless deliberate—does he speak very cogently in interviews about his and Bloom's work. But, as Bloom will tell you, poets are the first to lie about such things.) In a 1977 interview with Sue Gangel, which he edited in 1980, Ashbery claimed that having an audience had not changed his work, because "After I gained a certain amount of recognition, I realized that this recognition had arrived precisely because of this work which I felt was never going to achieve any, and therefore if I were to continue to get recognition, I would have to continue in the same way" (Interview 13). In other words, if your success depends on writing as if you were in a vacuum, you must keep doing so even if spectators appear; your success depends upon your lack of an expectation of success. In *Flow Chart,* Ashbery rephrases this sentiment as follows: "Surely, in my younger / days people acted differently about it. There was no barnstorming, just quiet / people going about their business and not worrying too much about / being rewarded at the end when it came down to that" (14). Furthermore, he reports in the 1977 interview: "I rarely discuss my poetry. I find it distasteful. I'd rather not know much about it myself" (14).

Ashbery's strategy during the 1970s when, not coincidentally, both his and Bloom's reputations were made, was one of entertaining Bloomian ideas (often wittily) even as his notion of literary history—any history—obviously diverged from Bloom's. Most notably, Ashbery argues against theory as an ahistorical reading of historical (specifically art historical) events. This split emerges most clearly in "Self-Portrait in a Convex Mirror" (1975), where Ashbery writes less about the portrait itself than about the ongoingness of the daily activities surrounding it. Such a notion of time, which has obvious effects on one's conception of "works" of art, links him with certain of his contemporaries, including Elizabeth Bishop who, in her valedictory "Poem," from *Geography III*, argues against momentary "visions," or those which are lifted out of time. Instead, she is most interested in "looks," which are best represented for her in what might otherwise be termed "bad art." An earlier poem, "Large Bad Painting," also bears out this revision of the romantic/modernist notion of art as something that organizes, and hence redeems, history.[6] Like Bishop's, however, Ashbery's "looks" are often redemptive, if not, strictly speaking, visionary.

In "Litany," published in the 1979 collection *As We Know*, Ashbery's own literary criticism appears in the form of a "verse epistle," after Alexander Pope. Better yet, it is an "essay on criticism," or an essay *of* criticism. It may in some ways be as old-fashioned as Pope, for Ashbery suggests that the critic ought not to consider himself more than a handmaiden to the poet:

> *Therefore a new school of criticism must be developed.*
> *First of all, the new*
> *Criticism should take into account that it is we*
> *Who made it, and therefore*
> *Not to be too eager to criticize us: we*
> *Could do that for ourselves, and have done so.* (34)

Ashbery emphasizes the importance of the critic's work to bringing forth poetry's "*enchant[ment]*" (33), and the (tongue-in-cheek) need for critics to address themselves to "*your average baker or cheerleader.*"

What follows Ashbery's emphasis on the relative importance of poetry and criticism is an attempt completely to de-authorize the very genre of criticism:

Nor
Should it take itself as a fitting subject
For critical analysis, since it knows
Itself only through us, and us
Only through being part of ourselves, the bark
Of the tree of our intellect. (34–35)

The critic ought to confine himself to barking rather than to biting, Ashbery more than implies. But he does not go so far as to name his critics; in these passages he attacks the genre more than any specific perpetrator of it.

In his poems of the 1960s and 1970s, Ashbery distinguishes between ways of organizing time. Bloom knows that the critic's function is to stop time—chart it—in order to tell it better: "Criticism may not always be an act of judging, but it is always an act of deciding, and what it tries to decide is meaning" (*Map* 3). One of his books is, of course, a "map" of misreading. Ashbery, on the other hand, often emphasizes the waywardness of the compass, preferring the journal to its end, the murkiness of daily experience to its apotheosis in masterpieces. In "Soonest Mended," published in the late 1960s in *The Double Dream of Spring,* he writes:

Night after night this message returns, repeated
In the flickering bulbs of the sky, raised past us, taken away from
   us,
Yet ours over and over until the end that is past truth,
The being of our sentences, in the climate that fostered them,
Not ours to own, like a book, but to be with, and sometimes
To be without, alone and desperate.
But the fantasy makes it ours, a kind of fence-sitting
Raised to the level of an aesthetic ideal. (18)

Fence-sitting is not an option that Robert Frost considered; his wall required mending, even if that mending was a convenient fiction for an awkward and ambivalent sense of community. Ashbery here decides not to decide; and his refusal "to grow up," in this poem and others, is equally a refusal to buy fully into a "visionary company," even as the lines also echo that company: "Yet ours over and over until the end that is past truth" retains the visionary sweep of Keats and Crane. Perhaps, he seems to suggest, such vision requires that the poet never (as happened literally in the case of Crane) graduate:

> Better, you said, to stay cowering
> Like this in the early lessons, since the promise of learning
> Is a delusion, and I agreed, adding that
> Tomorrow would alter the sense of what had already been
>   learned,
> That the learning process is extended in this way, so that from
>   this standpoint
> None of us ever graduates from college[.] (18–19)

Yet Ashbery's debunking of that tradition is constant. In "Self-Portrait in a Convex Mirror," Ashbery is more interested in what gets lost than in what gets captured; he is less taken by theory than by what escapes it:

> Each person
> Has one big theory to explain the universe
> But it doesn't tell the whole story
> And in the end it is what is outside him
> That matters, to him and especially to us
> Who have been given no help whatever
> In decoding our own man-size quotient and must rely
> On second-hand knowledge. Yet I know
> That no one else's taste is going to be
> Any help, and might as well be ignored. (81–92)

This is as antitheoretical a statement of theory as one might want to locate, and it finds its most apt response in Bloom, for whom such statements are anathema, as when he writes about "Ashbery's zeal in tacitly rejecting a poetry of privileged moments or privileged phrases." This zeal, it is clear to Bloom, is a waste of energy: "But this zeal is misplaced, and almost impossible to sustain, as will be seen in his later development" (*Figures* 177). Ashbery, in other words, came to his senses, which meant that he came to Bloom's senses.

Ashbery's "later development" can be read as a continuation of this antitheoretical line of argument—not so much development as Steinian repetition. Temporal reality in Ashbery is always an "emulsion" rather than a "negative" or a "print" or "portrait" in the conventional sense of the term (another way of saying this is that his portraits are more like Gertrude Stein's than like Parmigianino's). Early in *Flow Chart*, Ashbery describes the painting as something potentially moving, not fixed: "the point is one was going to do to it / what mattered to us, and all would be correct as in a painting / that would never ache for a frame but dream on as nonchalantly as we did" (8).

Yet memoirs generally rely on frames rather than nonchalance as their organizing principles, and the notion of a career (great or otherwise) depends on there being development and progress in a person's work. So Ashbery's task in *Three Poems* and *Flow Chart*, his most "autobiographical" books, is a difficult one; he needs to chart his career without fixing it, and he needs to counter Bloom's theoretical description of that career without offering up a counter system. As can be expected of him, Ashbery performs this act of distancing in large measure through parody, both of his "precursors" and of his critic, who has set himself up as a kind of contemporary precursor.[7]

What we have, then, are competing portraits of a poet's career.[8] The stakes behind these portraits are high. Bloom needs to delineate the form of the strong poet's career as a constant and predictable struggle between sons and fathers, a struggle that threatens to annihilate the son if he does not adequately misread his precursors. Ashbery's self-described career plan is less fraught with oedipal overtones, less easily fixed or mapped. He wants to see it implicated in his ordinary life, not just in the struggle to ascend Parnassus. Ashbery discusses the concept of career in *Three Poems* (1972), a book that he wrote at about the time Bloom was thinking through his notion of anxiety, which he would publish in *The Anxiety of Influence* (1973). Ashbery inaugurates a section of "The System" with the following question: "The great careers are like that: a slow burst that narrows to a final release, pointed but not acute, a life of suffering redeemed and annihilated at the end, and for what? For a casual moment of knowing that is here one minute and gone the next, almost before you were aware of it?" (69). An odd passage, this one; the poet destroys himself for a "casual" and not an apocalyptic moment. It is also a profoundly un-Bloomian moment, denuded of "crisis" and sublimity.

What follows in this prose poem "The System" is an argument against reading poetry theoretically, nay, even critically, an argument that shows Ashbery's keen awareness of the power held by the reader of texts: "Besides the obvious question of who knows whether it will still be there, there is the even more urgent one of whose life are we taking into our hands? Is there no way in which these things may be done for themselves, so that others may enjoy them?" (69). The very notion of "career" strikes the speaker as a dangerous one for the way in which it separates the individual from his own activities. The "career" idea is fraught insofar as it milks "lessons" out of ordinary human experience; to understand a poet's career is very different from understanding his life, or his poems' recounting of that life. To have a career is to have a theory, just as in literary studies having a theory often means having a career.

> But still the "career" notion intervenes. It is impossible for us at the present time not to think of these people as separate entities, each with his development and aim to be achieved, careers which will "peak" after a while and then go back to being ordinary lives that fade quite naturally into air as they are used up, and are as though they never were, except for the "lesson" which has added an iota to the sum of all human understanding. And this way of speaking has trapped each one of us. (70)

In his development of this idea, Ashbery goes on to suggest that the "career" idea is a fetish, which "hardens it [the object of contemplation] into a husk around its own being" (70). To talk about life as a ritual strikes Ashbery as a better idea, but one also fraught with dangers, including the destructiveness welcomed by Bloom in his tracing of the poet's career. "[T]he ritual is by definition something impersonal, and can only move further in that direction. It was born without a knowledge of the past. And any attempt to hybridize it can only result in destruction and even death" (70). Theories, like rituals, are impersonal; Bloom's theory, more than many, is ahistorical, lacking in the "knowledge of the past" that might personalize it.

But *Three Poems* is ultimately not the narrative of a secular career but one that traces the possibilities for spiritual development.[9] The speaker of these poems places himself inside and outside of the game, participating in a spectacle in which he also plays a central role. It becomes impossible to fetishize a self that cannot be extricated from its situation either as participant/poet or as spectator/critic, or so Ashbery seems to hope. Twenty years later, *Flow Chart* tells Ashbery's career narrative in language that tries at all moments not to be fetishistic. And since "tradition" in criticism from T. S. Eliot to Harold Bloom has become fetishized (and so merchandised), Ashbery necessarily avoids expressing reverence for that tradition, even as his poem obsessively engages with it.

By the late 1980s and early 1990s, Ashbery began to stress his independence from Bloom, and it is here that I can begin to unpack the narrative in the nonnarrative of *Flow Chart*. To play with Bloom's notion that great poets misread their precursors, the book might as well be called "Flaw Chart." The title, which offers us both the possibility of organizing history—charting it—and that of refusing to do so—allowing it to flow—can be read as a miniature description of the relationship of poet to critic, as Ashbery sees it. Early on, the speaker wonders when he can meet a friend who is "uncertain where to locate" him (27) and then abruptly enters into a meditation haunted by Stevens and by Bloom (who is included here as a verb). He suggests a movement away from them both:

> I see.
> I'll try another ticket. Meanwhile thanks for the harmonium: its
> inoffensive chords swept me right off my feet near the railroad
> and—nice—are returning to bloom tomorrow and each day after
>   that. (28)

Any reader of Stevens can tell you that "harmonium" was a crucial word for him; his first book bore it as a title, and he wanted to title his collected poems "The whole of Harmonium."[10] That the chords from the harmonium might be "returning to bloom" suggests that Ashbery is sending the theory of his having been influenced back to its sender. This leads to a meditation on the relationship between a poet and his "confessor": "I thought nobody needed a confessor any more, but I was wrong I guess, / so, old stump, I'm off until tomorrow or some day early next week, I mean / how much more can I say," which returns him to an "elementary precept" of (again using the natural metaphor) "how we flowered, and lost, and rose up thin again with our thoughts" (28).

In the next section, Ashbery turns more explicitly to a concern with his reputation, particularly with his place in the canon, wondering if he is "the ghost this time" and "wringing his hands" over the question:

> And if I am to be cast off, then
> *where*? There has to be a space, even a negative one, a slot
> for me, or does there? But if all space is contained within me,
>   then
> there is no place for me to go, I am not even here, and now, and
>   can join
> no choir or club, indeed I am the sawdust of what's around but
>   nobody can
> even authorize that either. (29)

Here Ashbery worries over what seems clearly to be an Emersonian principle, that "all space is contained within me," one that he must associate with Bloom, whose use of Emerson is legendary. But the problem with this metaphysical principle is an intensely practical and personal one for Ashbery; if he's merely "the sawdust of what's around," or if he's one of the background singers and not the lead, then no one can "authorize" his place in the canon. Thus Ashbery at once perceives a problem with Bloom's theorizing, which attempts to make history out of metaphysical pronouncements, and expresses a desire for there to be an "authority" like Bloom's for his authorship. Recognizing the illusory nature of present fame, he worries further about "some day several centuries from now / when they open a time capsule" (29). He imagines that no one will want to hear the old stories, yet imagining them reminds him of his own future as part of that history: "Its job is done. We all live in the past now. And so the children / must still hang on somewhere, though no one is quite sure where or how many / or what paths there are to be taken in darkness. Only the fools, the severed heads, know" (30). Severed Orphic heads are one of Bloom's favorite images for the poet; he frames his criticism of Hart Crane (a poet dearer to him even than Stevens) with a discussion of Orphism.[11]

The romantic vision of the poet as a beheaded singer can hardly rest

easily with Ashbery, who has spent so much of his career in print finding ways in which to survive the assault of images that his mind generates. Ashbery's famous (or notorious) passivity, it could be argued, defends him against the aggressive mutilation, self and otherwise, that his
primary critic glorifies. He wishes, rather, "[t]o pass through pain and
not know it," as he writes at the beginning of his long poem "A Wave"
(*Wave* 68).

The smallest common denominator of Ashbery's deflation of the importance of tradition and the individual talent is his frequent punning
on that tradition; *Flow Chart* is replete with echoes of the *Norton Anthology* poets from Whitman to Eliot to Stevens. The poem opens in "the
published city," which quickly harkens back to Baudelaire's "fourmil-
lante cité" and to Eliot's waste land: "Sad grows the river god as he oars
past us / downstream without our knowing him: for if, he reasons, / he
can be overlooked, then to know him would be to eat him, / ingest the
name he carries through time to set down finally, on a strand of rotted
hulks"[12] (3). This is an Eliotic world, most certainly, but the speaker
knows that he is reading a text rather than a sanctified tradition; furthermore, he forgets what the big deal is: "*It seems I was reading something; /
I have forgotten the sense of it or what the small / role of the central
poem made me want to feel*" (3). The "central poem," we scavengers of
tradition's echoes will quickly note, belongs to the vocabulary of Stevens, one bandied about liberally by Bloom. So in a book that, from its
very girth and weight, appears to be an epic, we are advised from the
get-go to look not for the poem's centrality but for its eccentricities.
The subtle syntax of this quotation shows Ashbery at once debunking
the central poem and wishing that the poem (or poetry) were more central. He is dealing, for better and for worse, with a vision of language that
has diminished considerably even since Stevens tried to make a heaven
out of it: "the Logos alone will have to suffice. / A pity, since no one has
seen it recently" (33–34). Among the book's other pointed puns: "I hear
America snowing" (141), rather than "singing," as Walt Whitman would
have it; "Another day we read the thunder its own prepared statement,"
which plays on the final section of *The Waste Land,* namely "What the
Thunder Said"; and "I will show you fear in a handful of specialists," a
play on Eliot's "dust." In the final item on this doubtless incomplete list,
Ashbery writes, "No use trying to cover your tracks using archaic words
like 'leman'; the sense / kills and you have the refrain to remind you"
(148). Here he recalls the moment when the speaker of *The Waste Land*

sits by the shores of Lake Leman and weeps; to adopt Eliot's vocabulary, he suggests, would be a way of "covering" his tracks, perhaps in order that others, like Bloom, might "uncover" them.[13] But there is no "sense" to this reference, and so Ashbery moves on: "Sure but I was just drifting / anyway, faintly out of tune, nothing scared could have happened to me" (148). The phrase "nothing scared could have happened to me" sounds odd, and is probably meant to. Surely Ashbery means to play on the similar sounding word "sacred" and, by revising it to "scared," to belittle the tradition (Bloom's) that he knows he could easily enter by aping.[14] That Ashbery pokes fun at tradition by misreading it bespeaks his ambivalent relationship to Bloom, who is one of the strongest defenders of (a) tradition since Eliot.

Ashbery attacks the messenger as well as the message, and it is here that he most directly addresses his central critic. I would argue, somewhat speculatively, that "the old guy" of the following passage is none other than Harold Bloom:

> an old guy comes up to you and tells you, reading your mind,
>   what a magnificent
> job you've done, chipping away at the noble experiment, and
>   then, abruptly,
> you change your plans, backtrack, cancel the rest of the trip
> that was going to promise so much good health and diversion for
>   you; you suddenly
> see yourself as others see you, and it's not such a pretty sight
>   either[.] (124)

Thus Ashbery suggests that the fact of being "seen" as a poet presents such an obstacle to him that he is forced to change direction, to go away from the vantage point at which he has been mapped or "charted." A page earlier, he remarks on his awareness of the way in which he could build his reputation — "All along I had known what buttons to press" (123) — (especially since "[r]epetition makes reputation" [133]), and how that awareness causes him to change direction. His repeated use of the image of a "train" is something I want to comment on.

> All along I had known what buttons to press, but don't
> you see, I had to experiment, not that my life
>   depended on it,

but as a corrective to taking the train to find out where it wanted
    to go.
Then when I did that anyway, I was not so much charmed as
    horrified
by the construction put upon it by even some quite close friends,
some of whom accused me of being the "leopard man" who had
    been terrorizing
the community by making howl-like sounds at night, out of
    earshot
of the dance floor. (123)

That Ashbery is not the poet who makes "howl-like sounds at night" is
quite evident. But his refusal to push the buttons he knew were there to
be pushed is especially interesting in light of Bloom's frequent, if not
usually noted, attacks on Ashbery.

Bloom is at least as strong a detractor of Ashbery's *The Tennis Court
Oath* (1962) as he is a happy advocate for the rest of Ashbery's oeuvre.
One of the poems that Bloom excoriates Ashbery for writing is the train-
related "Leaving the Atocha Station" (1962), a poem that Ashbery notably leaves out of his *Selected Poems* (1985). This collection of selected
poems is, in fact, very thin on the kind of poetry that Bloom disdains.
The poem, which *is* included in Paul Hoover's Norton anthology, *Postmodern American Poetry* (1994), sounds a lot like it might have been
written by Charles Bernstein; in other words, its value as "experimental,"
"avant-garde" writing sets it dramatically apart from Bloom's Romantic
tradition. In *Figures of Capable Imagination,* Bloom quotes from the
poem and then attacks it and its readers. The real burden of his criticism
is that neither Ashbery nor his readers have properly read Bloom's theory
of influence, nor do they recognize the enormous responsibility involved
in participating in his tradition. Those who don't are part of the "rabblement": "This is from the piece called "Leaving the Atocha Station," which
(I am told) has a certain reputation among the rabblement of poetasters
who proclaim themselves anti-academic while preaching in the acade-
mies, and who lack consciousness sufficient to feel the genuine (because
necessary) heaviness of the poetic past's burden of richness. *The Tennis Court Oath* has only one good poem, 'A Last World'" (173). In case
the poet dares to contest this tossing of his book on the dump, Bloom
quickly adds, "Poets, who congenitally lie about so many matters, *never*

tell the truth about poetic influence" (173). Leaving the Atocha station, it seems, was a dangerous thing for Ashbery to do; in Bloom's accounting, it nearly derailed his progress (a concept that Ashbery uses in describing his career as a "development / but not necessarily a resolution at the end" (*Flow Chart* 85).

Having dismissed Bloom (if I'm correct) as "an old guy" who admires some of his experiments, Ashbery entertains, but does not quite buy into, the notion that fame is less important than merely being understood:

> the hee-hawing ages in the time it takes to put an idea together
> from its unlikely components, package it, and go on being the
>   genius one was anyway
> but not for too long, or without general consent. It's enough if—
> my friend's mother is the one who believes in me and under-
>   stands me better
> than anybody, but I'm not going to let it delude me. There's a
>   world out there. (126)

The usual option for poets, that of "retreating into—or is it out of?—academia," simply means that they will be "beset by the / usual pit-bulls [critics?] and well-meaning little old ladies in tennis shoes [readers outside the academy?]" (133). That gives the poet very little room in which to work, especially one whose poetry doesn't necessarily appeal to a high percentage of the "world out there."

The narrowness, and perhaps nastiness, of these two alternatives, neither of which allows the poet much control over his own destiny, leads Ashbery, in one of the most unexpected passages in *Flow Chart,* to meditate on the Iran-Contra hearings and on Reagan administration underlings whose careers were so obviously at stake.[15] The hearings were noteworthy not simply for their concern with the Reagan administration's radical disrespect for the law, but also for the way in which they revolved around the control and dissemination of information, both within the administration and in Congress. Politics depends on reputations, and reputations on politics, as Ashbery well knows. And reputations are built, or lost, either on the uncovering of information or on its suppression.

Ashbery briefly imagines himself testifying about his own affairs:

> Those of us who did manage to keep control over our
>   personal affairs
> Before it was all over are obviously not going to testify anyway.
>   What would we have said?
> That we confronted the monster eyeball to eyeball and blinked
>   first but only
> after a decent interval had elapsed and were then excused from
>   completing the examination
> before defenestration became an issue? (176)

This passage could be deciphered several ways; one reading might see it as a defense of Oliver North, who according to his own estimation did not blink first. Ashbery's politics are not clear; he told one critic that he thought Nixon a great president, another that he was not sure he was opposed to the Vietnam War.[16] But in the passage prior to the one quoted above, Ashbery writes critically about Reagan: "but the Reagan / administration insists we cannot go to heaven without drinking caustic soda on the floor / of Death Valley as long as others pay their rent and have somewhere to go without thinking, / behind the curtain of closing down all operations" (175–76). It seems more interesting in the context of a discussion of careers, however, to consider that Ashbery (like his speaker) includes himself among the party of those who kept control over their personal affairs. He is, after all, someone who turned himself "from a / slightly unruly child into a sophisticated and cultivated adult with a number of books / to his credit and many more projects in the works" (177). While these passages say nothing directly about Ashbery's own role in managing his career, they do suggest that he *has* tried to manage it, and that he possesses a keen awareness of the effect of his work on others, even those who make "the old 'elaborate charade' accusation" (128). Oliver North then becomes an example of someone who controlled the narrative about the arms-for-hostages deal; no critic could touch that narrative because it was stronger than the truth (that the deal was illegal). Ashbery can only, albeit perhaps grudgingly, admire such control. Where reputations are concerned, control over narrative may ultimately be more important than the content of that narrative.

Ashbery has told one critic that he wrote *Flow Chart* after a friend suggested he compose a poem about his mother, who had recently died.[17] His magnificent elegy, a double sestina very close to the end of the book, comes after almost two hundred pages filled with brooding about his career; this is less surprising than appropriate in a book that helps to separate Ashbery from the theory of influence used both for and against him. That it is an elegy for his mother and not his father makes sense to a reading of the poem that takes into account its paradoxical reliance on Bloomian theories. As we will see throughout this book, the turn away from a masculine tradition and toward a feminine one will be a primary method for overcoming impasse among contemporary writers. This is not so surprising when one considers the work of Susan Howe, perhaps, but it is also true for male poets like Ronald Johnson and Charles Bernstein. While avoiding Bloom's oedipal model—writing not about his father but about his mother—Ashbery somehow still slips into it. That the poem has as one of its central images a sunflower, one of Blake's most famous images, also permits me to read it as a final song of separation to Harold Bloom, who has written extensively on Blake. It is "she" who inspires the poem, not the tradition. The final sestina ends with the speaker's assertion that his mother has been his central influence, and that that influence is fertile:

> The story that she told me simmers in me still, though
> she is dead
> these several months, lying as on a bed. The things we
> used to do, I to thee,
> thou to me, matter still, but the sun points the way
> inexorably to death,
> though it be but his, not our way. Funny the way the
> sun
> can bring you around to her. And as you pause for
> breath,
> remember it, now that it is done, and seeds flare
> in the sunflower. (193)

The poem's conclusion is profoundly ambivalent; Ashbery seems to concede that poets are the agents in a tradition, even as he wants it to be known that when he gets up to leave, he is that same person he was when he was writing (216).

As I've already suggested, one could easily read this conclusion as evidence for a Bloomian interpretation of the poem; Ashbery here reopens the bridge from which Hart Crane's bedlamite, "shrill shirt ballooning," threw himself. The bow to Crane might be read to reveal Ashbery's anxiety as he ends his career epic thinking about the earlier poet's American epic. The book is, after all, haunted by precursors of all manner and kind. Furthermore, because I have read the poem as (in part) a work of literary criticism, rather than merely as an epic poem, I can allow myself to submit to Bloom's notion that there is no real difference between poetry and criticism.[18]

This essay has not attempted to refute Bloom's theory, however, just as it hasn't defended Bloom's notions. The theory, despite Bloom's insistent self-parodying of the last couple of decades, is "strong" in the sense that it tells at least a partial truth about the history of literary influence; how partial that truth is depends on one's sense of allegiance to competing theories of reception, intertextuality, and historicism. The theory works well, however, when applied to the career of the man who marketed it and whose career grew out of it; Bloom stands in the line of succession of critics interested in the Romantic backgrounds of modern and contemporary poetry. His "anxiety of influence" theory, then, operates in somewhat the same way A Vision did for Yeats. As a system, it's highly flawed and incomplete; as autobiography of Bloom, it may just work.

Career is not history, according to Bloom, but a theoretical construct. Ashbery is brilliant in his realization that this theoretical construct can predetermine the moves that are open to the poet; and so he remarks that "all along" he knew "what buttons to press" but did not push them (123). In that sense, career is not just a theory but also a poem intent on "flowing." Ashbery, more than almost any poet I can think of, has survived his critics. But Ashbery himself, while he's always been attacked from the literary right (by critics like Mark Jarman and Mary Kinzie), has not seen his reputation diminish—and the very vociferousness of the continuing critiques speaks to his importance as a poet.[19] Many of the younger critics who dismiss Bloom find Ashbery every bit as interesting as Bloom does. The answer to this apparent conundrum can be found in lines from Ashbery's verse-criticism, from "Litany" (in As We Know). Or from "Self-Portrait in a Convex Mirror," where he shows himself less interested in the immortality of the work than in the hooting of horns that went on as the work was (and is) made. But even in what I take to be Ashbery's most explicit debunking of Bloom, the Flow Chart passages about "the old guy," Ashbery acknowledges that he's indebted to the deal, however rigged it is; the passage bears quoting at length for its appropriately intricate evasions. Watch for the reappearing blossoms, or blooms:

> you suddenly
> see yourself as others see you, and it's not such a
> pretty sight either, but at
> least you know now, and can do something to repair the
> damage, perhaps by
> looking deeper into the mirror, more thoroughly
> to evaluate the pros and cons of your success and
> smilingly refuse all
> offers of assistance, which would be the wrong kind
> anyway, no doubt, and set out
> on your own at the eleventh hour, into the vast yawn
> or cusp that sits
> always next door. And when we have succeeded, not
> know what to do with it
> except break it into shards that get more ravishing as
> you keep pounding them. See,
> I am now responsible though I didn't make it. And you
> can come back, I'm harmless now. Anyway, that's how it
> pleases me to
> detect myself. When the blossoms reappear, as they
> can, and the consumers,
> someone must pay to keep it poignant. Otherwise one of
> you will remain an outrider.
> Go finance the rigged deal then, and it can't hurt. (124–25)

5
"Grandmothers and Hunters"[1]

Ronald Johnson and Feminine Tradition

The rules of the menu are not in themselves more or less trivial than the rules of verse to which a poet submits.
—Mary Douglas

Invention, *we remember, really means* finding.
—Guy Davenport

To write about food is to write about the self as well.
—Anne Goldman (quoted in Campbell)

As WE HAVE SEEN, John Ashbery moves away from the potential impasse of an overbearing critic and his theory, at least in part, by claiming part of a feminine tradition rather than Bloom's overtly masculine lineage. When Ashbery elegizes his mother at the end of his poetic autobiography, *Flow Chart*, albeit through the language and imagery of William Blake, he performs an end-around reverse of Harold Bloom's theory. Ronald Johnson, as I'll soon point out, was a poet who desperately wanted to be part of the masculine tradition that included some of Bloom's heroes (John Milton among them) and some of his villains (among them Ezra Pound). Yet, the underlying and unacknowledged presence of a feminine tradition that begins with Emily Dickinson, becomes apparent only when one reads Ronald Johnson's cookbooks. The influence of the genre of recipe on Johnson's poetry, which is composed of gaps and erasures, bears scrutiny. But let me explain why I came to write on Johnson's poetry in the first place, as that story takes its place in the narrative I'm about to cobble together.

I was asked to write on Ronald Johnson's work because I am a woman and very few of Johnson's readers are women. The request was, in its own way, so odd—and honestly so—that I decided to look into his work, which I had not read. When I started looking at what has been written about the poetry, beginning with book jacket blurbs, I thought I understood why I hadn't found my own way there. Johnson is not simply a poet's poet, but, at least according to his commentators, sometimes including himself, he is a man's poet. In an introduction to Johnson's early book, *Valley of the Many-Colored Grasses,* Guy Davenport writes of Johnson's "special fascination with *men* [my emphasis] who have sharpened their eyesight: explorers, anatomists, botanists, painters, antiquarians, poets, microscopists, mathematicians, physicists" (192). In his article on Johnson, Eric Selinger writes about Emerson, Lincoln, Thoreau, and Charles Ives as American models for Johnson's work *(Dictionary of Literary Biography* 147). In a blurb to *ARK,* published in 1996, Robert Creeley comments that this epic belongs in the company of those "of its kind" that preceded it, namely Ezra Pound's *Cantos,* Louis Zukofsky's *'A',* Charles Olson's *Maximus,* and Robert Duncan's *Passages.* Look to Johnson himself for alternatives to this masculinist tradition (at once artistic and scientific) and you find no alternatives, save a mention here and there of "Emily" and Gertrude Stein. In "A Note" to *ARK,* published at the back of the book, Johnson presents as his "great obstacles" (namely, his exemplars), Pound, W. C. W., Zukofsky, Olson, and William Blake. At the bottom of the page, he quotes Gertrude Stein, but does not mention her as an *obstacle.* On the next page, Charles Ives is brought up for mention as "a major influence." I have abridged this rather unrelenting critical history for the sake of space, and to keep *my* women readers' attention. (Rachel Blau DuPlessis's "Echological Scales: On *ARK* of Ronald Johnson" is an important exception to the rule; hers is a sophisticated reading of Johnson, and gender in Johnson, but it's limited to the poems in *ARK.)*

Not until later did Guy Davenport's "Afterword" to *RADI OS* strike me as a way past this relentless consideration of Johnson as a *male* poet. For, what Davenport writes about Johnson's erasure of Milton's *Paradise Lost,* an erasure signaled by the title itself, reduced from Milton's, is the following: "The poem we are reading is still Milton's, but sifted" (200).

The world signified by the word *sifted* is what opened Johnson's work up for this woman reader (albeit one whose husband does most of the cooking). Yes, *sifting* has its scientific meanings, but it is also a term used in cooking. You will not find much mention of Ronald Johnson, cookbook writer, in his poetry books or in the commentaries about his work, although Guy Davenport finds evidence of Johnson's "objectivity" in his cookbook writing. During an interview with Johnson, published in *Chicago Review,* Peter O'Leary asked him, "Were you writing anything else while you were working on *ARK*?" Johnson responds that he was writing cookbooks. O'Leary ignores that statement and continues, "I guess I'm thinking about something like *RADI OS*" (43), completely eliding mention of Johnson's other genre. According to Eric Selinger, Johnson was sometimes complicit with this separation of the poet from the cookbook writer; when Selinger wrote his entry on Johnson for the *Dictionary of Literary Biography,* Johnson asked him not to mention the cookbooks. But you *will* find mention of Ronald Johnson, poet, on the jacket sleeves of his cookbooks. This writer of visionary poetry is presented on the back sleeve of *Company Fare* (1991), as "the author of the 1989 *Simple Fare* . . . an acclaimed presentation of inexpensive foods for the homemaker with taste but little money." This description continues: "He won a Tastemaker Award in 1985 for *The American Table.* A graduate of Columbia University, he has written nearly a dozen books of poetry, and has contributed to many literary magazines, earning several poetry awards. He lives in San Francisco." One yearns to do a close reading of this biographical blurb: surely, there is something to be made over the link between his fine sense of *taste* in food and in poetry, between the awards he has won as a poet and the quality of writing one will find in the cookbooks, to say nothing of his residence, San Francisco, known as much for its literary and gay communities as for the California cuisine that became famous in the 1980s and 1990s.

More to the point, however, is the blurb's mention of the rather less-than-wealthy "homemaker" as Johnson's audience in this blurb. As Mary Drake McFeely writes in *Can She Bake a Cherry Pie? American Women and the Kitchen in the Twentieth Century,* "middle class women remain the primary audience for cookbooks" (3). Sherrie A. Inness is more blunt; in a survey of juvenile cookbooks from the first half of the twentieth century, she finds that, "Whether directed at an audience of children or adults, cookbooks are one of the most strongly gendered forms of popular literature (along with romance novels). It is important to understand the process through which a cookbook becomes identified as reading material 'for women only' because this strong identification is one reason that domestic cooking remains women's work even today" (121). When boys are encouraged to cook, it's because they might have to; Ladd Plumley, writing in 1917, argued that boys should be taught to cook because that would prepare them for a future war when women might be missing (131). During the Depression, "The kitchen was 'women's sacred domain,' said a typical cookbook, the 'forbidden realm [to males] of the culinary arts'" (Levenstein 31). And the editor of *House and Garden* wrote in 1948: "Take cooking out of their [women's] hands is like telling them that they can't have children. Most women find cooking gives them a chance to use their imagination. Some of them even feel it's a way of holding a husband and making the kids happy" (Levenstein 103). At least in this genre, then, Ronald Johnson's audience, then, is largely female; that this audience is hidden from the purview of his poetry's readership seems no accident. "Women's subordination is locked into food," Sally Cline writes (Inness 6), but one might argue, by extension, that it is also locked into genres of writing and their intended, and extended, readerships.

From the point of view of some cookbook writers, poetry and recipes share a great deal in common.[2] "In telling the cook what to do," writes Sara Pitzer, in *How to Write a Cookbook and Get It Published* (1984), "how-to writing is like poetry in some ways. It compresses a lot of meaning into a few words." She goes on to point out that "layers of meaning" are missing from how-to writing, which should be "so clear that no one can possibly misunderstand" (73). Authorship implies recognition for one's work, and the sharing of recipes, according to Susan Leonardi, involves the ownership of authorship: to share recipes, she writes, "is an act of trust between women" (Inness 265). Certainly, the link between cookbooks and memoirs has been acknowledged often enough in print. According to Traci Marie Kelly, "The culinary autobiography is a complex pastiche of recipes, personal anecdotes, family history, public history, photographs, even family trees" (Inness 252). A tradition of culinary memoirs would include books by the following authors: M. F. K. Fisher, probably the best, and the best-known, of the memoirists; Alice B. Toklas, whose cookbook is a memoir of her time with Gertrude Stein, and Ruth Reichl. Their books tend to be more fragmentary than are standard narrative autobiographies. Estelle Jelinek argues that women's life stories often appear more fragmented than are men's (Inness 253). Some of that fragmentary sense of a life comes through in the disjunctions (which are also conjunctions) between narrative and recipe. Male writers of this form, such as James Beard and Ronald Johnson, whose

The American Table is as personally revealing a book as his poetry books are not, also tend to place themselves in a female tradition. James Beard's story, like his career choice, depends on a very vivid portrayal of his mother. ("When women were still subordinate and modest," he writes in *Delights and Prejudices,* "Mother was forceful and fearless. She swept through a room or down the street with an air of determination and authority, and she met men on their own terms". (9–10). Johnson's cookbooks also depend upon a female tradition of cooks, just as his poetry depends upon "dance," the art his mother performed.

> "like silver smiting silver"
> H.J. [Helen Johnson] on the harp
> behind order, Utopia cut figure (ARK 71, *Arches V*)

Poetry and form are also linked with food in the work of the anthropologist, Mary Douglas. In "Deciphering a Meal," she writes that a "more appropriate comparison for the interpretation of a meal" is "versification." The meal, which is a structured event, hence formal, "distinguishes order, bounds it, and separates it from disorder" (260). Douglas's examples come from Jewish and Chinese meals: "For Lu Chi, a third-century Chinese poet, poetry traffics in some way between the world and mankind. The poet is one who 'traps Heaven and Earth in a cage of form'" (261). Douglas, like the author of the how-to on writing cookbooks, finally subordinates meals to poems, asserting that "the cook may not be able to express the powerful things a poet can say" (261). But of course *saying* is not all there is to poetry, either. Consider Johnson's statement at the opening to *Songs of the Earth* (1970), a sequence based on Mahler's music. "Thoreau, as he walked year after year the Concord woods, was the first to record the musics of silence . . . 'As I leave the village, drawing nearer to the woods, I listen from time to time to hear the hounds of Silence baying the Moon. I hear the unspeakable'" (in *To Do As* 65). Johnson concludes his preface to the book by writing that "These translations and responses [to the Mahler] might properly be called 'strains'—as in a strain of music or poetry, but also those words & notes which strain their limits outward toward the unutterable" (65). Need this punster add that "straining" is equally a task ascribed to cooks and described in their books? Or that form is itself silent rather than spoken, that it contains language rather than voices it? Or that form, in recipes as in poems, was one of Johnson's evident obsessions?

This must have been a strange world for Ronald Johnson to inhabit, though he seems to have lived in them both—separately. On the one hand, he was obliged to be a kind of domestic mother-figure to women who had grown up without the family tradition of teaching cooking that he himself had enjoyed. He needed to be as reassuring as Anthony Bourdain's mother-in-law who "had no idea how magical, how reassuring, how pleasurable her simple meat loaf was for me, what a delight even lumpy mashed potatoes were—being, as they were, blessedly devoid of truffles or truffle oil" (Bourdain 75). On the other hand, he inhabited very macho worlds of poetry and cooking. Johnson's response, it seems to me, was to bury the terms by which he lived his own life in his poems, and only write (a little) more openly about the circumstances of his life in his recipe books. Even then he pulls up shy of talking about his life as a gay man, although he alludes to traveling and eating breakfast with Jonathan Williams, his companion of a decade. And, in his unpublished typed manuscript, *Up to Now* (1997), Johnson writes: "I learned quickly I was 'different', as well as how to assert my masculinity when necessary" (2), remembering being "pursued by yahoos in pickups" and running home away from them as a child in Kansas (3). In his writing *about* his poetry, Johnson fails to break free of the gendered terms according to which his poetry is read; in writing about cooking, however, Johnson shows us how to read the poetry differently, to read it as coming not merely from a tradition of mostly male writers, but from a more balanced tradition of male and female poets and writers. This reading is never overt, which is probably one reason why it has not yet been made. In its sub-version of the poetry, we see at once the force of the repression of a female tradition—and a female audience for the work—but also a way out, a way to read a female tradition in Johnson's work. That tradition is certainly there. The very origin of Johnson's interest in poetry was his reading of a woman poet, if only her letters. He writes of discovering himself as a gay man and a poet in college, and writing "rather flimsy poems, one which won a third prize in a school contest and was influenced by a two volume set of Emily Dickenson's [sic] Letters I found on my room's shelves" (*Up to Now* 5).

Johnson knew which of his genres had a larger audience, but he also knew that he was not the only poet to have been a cook. In *The American Table,* he links himself to Emily Dickinson—not by way of their poetry, but because she too *"seems to have taken an active pride in cooking,"* unlike other *"homegrown poets"* (340). According to Johnson, *"she constituted a whole family's active baker till infirm, and if her gingerbreads were more well known than her poems to the neighborhood, that seems to be the way of the world. I used to balk at being introduced as 'This is Ronald Johnson—he writes cookbooks,' but since there are more people who read cookbooks than poems, I now just shrug my shoulders"* (340). In this most American of books, Johnson begins by citing Thomas Jefferson as "our first noted gourmet," but most of his citations are to the work of women, including Alice B. Toklas, Irma Rombauer, whose *Joy of Cooking* he describes as *"the one indispensable tool of any American cook,"* and M. F. K. Fisher.[3] Johnson writes in recognition that cooking, like poetry, comes out of a tradition. "I am reminded, too," he writes in *Company Fare: Effortless Dishes for Intimate Gatherings* (1991), "how in debt I am to prior cooks, numberless through the ages, who have directed and refined perfections we take for granted. Like poets they are few in any generation" (139). Among the great cooks he numbers his mother and "Dorothy, who taught me the virtues of the simple," and whose name is a kind of subject rhyme with that of Dorothy Wordsworth and Judy Garland's character in *The Wizard of Oz,* a book and film that obsessed the Kansas poet throughout his writing life. Cooking and Oz took Johnson away from the prairie, as he writes in *Up to Now:* "I had an imaginary friend called Morris, and later when I discovered the Oz books believed until puberty there must be some way out of the prairie, some magical way I somehow associated with sitting in the middle of a huge lilac between my grandmother's house and ours" (2).

The country that spawned *Bartlett's Quotations* was founded on quotations from English philosophy, and its literature is built on a Watts Tower (see the cover of *ARK*) of quotations. If utter originality is considered a masculine virtue, then quotation might be seen as feminine. The cookbook is a genre based on (suppressed) quotation, as recipes are handed down from generation to generation, then transferred between women, often on scraps of paper that grow brown with age, spotted with use. It's no accident that *The Joy of Cooking* is described by its reviser, Marion Rombauer Becker, as "a family affair," and was originally printed privately in 1931 and distributed from the home.[4] Sara Pitzer writes that the passion to create cookbooks "has its roots in the generations of American women who essentially did write their own cookbooks. They collected and exchanged recipes, copying them carefully to pass from generation to generation, even including them [as did Emily Dickinson] in letters and diaries" (1). Traci Marie Kelly asserts that sharing "a recipe is to share a part of one's self and writing one's own name, signifying authorship or ownership, is an assertion on the part of the giver. She wants to be recognized for the dish" (Inness 265). And yet most recipes are anonymous in presentation. Open any cookbook at random and you'll find recipes whose only signatures are those of the book's editor, not the recipe's inventor. The creator of the recipe is, almost by default, the person who delivers it to the reader as an unattributed quotation, rather in the manner Johnson describes writing some of his early poems in Washington, D.C.: "I started 'writing' poems from clipped-out words and phrases from the daily news. These were my first experience making visual poems" (Up to Now 6). Johnson describes his own method of collecting thusly: "I've gathered recipes for twenty years in this manner, here and about, looked through every tiny spiral-bound cookbook put out by local church ladies that came my way, and it's surprising how many fine recipes turn up from our amateur cooks" (American Table xi). If Johnson's hunch is correct, that "our new [American] chefs have a culinary El Dorado all around them, just waiting to be mined, from sea to shining sea" (xii), then its discovery will have been a largely feminine one. As such, however, the discovery is anonymous: "For the most part . . . women's cooking remains an anonymous service to their families, while men's cooking tends to become a highly personal gift to a grateful audience," writes Laura Shapiro (222).

If Johnson's poetry is notable for its participation in a visionary company of men (if not of Harold Bloom's), then his cookbooks are notable for their emphasis on community, on family. The dust jacket to Johnson's aptly named Company Fare reads as follows: "ease and intimacy are the cornerstones of Ronald Johnson's entertaining philosophy. Believing that 'Conversation is always better than talk, and six is maximum, four better,' he presents an exquisite collection of recipes that are designed to be prepared ahead, or in a toss between courses." And this is not simply advertising copy. On page 11 of the book, from which I took the title to this chapter, Johnson writes that "Sharing food, from first campfire to day after tomorrow, *is* civilization. Its secrets have been passed from no end of grandmothers and hunters, ancestors who have grown and caught and sowed and cooked ingredients, to those nowadays in a city apartment." In his introduction to Laura Shapiro's *Perfection Salad: Women and Cooking at the Turn of the Century,* Michael Stern writes, "As much as the Sears or Victoria's Secret catalogues, cookbooks offer crystalline reflections of our communal hopes and dreams" (xv). That they are themselves historical texts is affirmed by Ruth Reichl in the first introduction to Shapiro's book. "I had only to open an old cookbook to find myself standing in some other place or time" (viii). An important part of this history, as Shapiro relates it, is a visionary community imagined by women "domestic scientists" at the turn of the 20th century, a community that would "transubstantiate food" (4) and change the very culture. Cooking, too, has a utopian history. Shapiro quotes an early twentieth-century clubwoman from Michigan: "To dignify the function of the humble kitchen until it becomes in the estimation of every woman a laboratory wherein God permits her to aid in fashioning human souls, is worthy of strenuous endeavor" (121). While Johnson's utopian vision does not seem to have extended to his cooking, his interest in the creation of community through food is one he shares with this tradition of ambitious (if wrong-headed, as Shapiro argues) women. And, as an earlier quotation from ARK indicates, Johnson associated the utopian impulse with his mother, the harpist: "Utopia cut figure."

According to Sara Pitzer's how-to book on writing a publishable cookbook, Strunk's *The Elements of Style* (1919) applies.

1. Use simple words.
2. Use short sentences.
3. Use the active voice.
4. Use strong verbs.
5. Arrange words in sentences . . . with nothing between them unless you have a good reason for deviating from this pattern. (73).

M. F. K. Fisher advises that "a good recipe, for modern convenience, should consist of three parts: name, ingredients, method" (quoted in Inness 162). That recipes should be exact is a truism that dates back only to Fannie Farmer's innovations around the turn of the twentieth century; she was called "the mother of the level measurement" by some. Johnson's "Avocado Cream Soup," from *The American Table,* fulfills both Strunk's and Fisher's edicts. He lists the necessary ingredients, including "1 large ripe avocado," "1 tablespoon light rum" and "Pinch of curry powder" at the top of the recipe, then writes his directions, which are the soul of simplicity:

> Whirl avocado, cream, stock, lime juice, and rum in a blender until smooth—going from a slow speed to a high one. Place in a bowl and add curry powder, salt to taste, and Tabasco (please, only a drop or two).
>
> Cover and refrigerate several hours. To serve, put in cold cups or soup plates and sprinkle with chives.
>
> Serves 4.

Johnson's own comment on the recipe begins, "*What could be simpler?*" (7) In typical recipe fashion, Johnson begins with a list of ingredients, which is remarkable for its *lack* of sentence structure; "Pinch of curry powder" may resemble a line of poetry, but it is not a sentence. The sentences come during the instruction part of the recipe, are emphatic, imperative, beginning with verbs like "whirl" and "cover" and "serve." This is not to say that the recipe is uninviting to the reader; Johnson's easy aside about "please" not adding too much Tabasco makes the recipe sound more intimate than it might otherwise. The genre itself requires barked orders that are muted by the form of the list that organizes them. The form assumes community; it relates specific, but not original, information. Originality may come in the act of cooking, but not in the "scoring" involved in the recipe itself.

ARK is "a community epic, cyclical / hung in the balance / stream sweet Time," as Johnson writes in ARK 93, *Arches XXVII.* Open *ARK* to BEAM 6, *The Musics,* or to ARK 52, *Fountain III,* or to ARK 86, *Arches XX, The Wreath* (among many possible examples). What you find is poetry written as imperative. For example, BEAM 6 consists of a list of sentences beginning with the paradoxical word "Let" (paradoxical because the word itself suggests volition, but the imperative does not):

> Let flick his tail, the darkling Lion, down to the primal huddle
>   fiddling DNA.

Let the Elephant ruffle the elements in The Great Looped
   Nebula with his uplift trunk.
Let the Binary, orange, emerald, and blue, in the foot of
   Andromeda run awhisker with Mouse.

The wording reminds us that science, too, requires recipes to fulfill its experimental imperatives, and that myths are also necessary, involved with science and with poetry both. ARK 52 begins with the word "Ask," and scrolls down the page in one-word lines. ARK 86 contains the imperatives "wreathe," "weld," "weave," "twist up," "spin," "ply," and "construct." These are verbs of the dance, or one of Johnson's mother's occupations, and of building, his father's (a carpenter), or what he is doing in this poem (composed as it is out of "beams" and "arches") out of quotation and into literary monument. Johnson's "Note," placed at the end of his book, can be read as a list of ingredients: he has mixed his poetry from portions of Pound, W. C. W., Zukofsky, and Olson, and William Blake, among others. According to Davenport's introduction to *Valley of the Many-Colored Grasses,* "All these voices quoted in RJ's poems are other modes of vision which he is allowing to play over the subject along with his own" (13). As we have seen, however, pastiche is not simply a modernist and postmodernist literary activity; it is also profoundly related to recipe-making and to cooking. Hence the metaphors hidden behind all of Johnson's work: cooking is building is writing poems.

Emily Dickinson is quoted by Ronald Johnson in *The American Table* before a section on "Quick Breads" (314). Her rhetoric in this poem about bread, based as it is on questions, is stereotypically feminine and community-oriented: "Shall I / Send it back? Will you have a / Loaf of mine—which is spread?" she asks. To share a loaf has associations at once Biblical and communal; this metaphysical poet offers physical sustenance, the "spread" loaf indicating not simply the act of buttering the bread, but also of sharing it. [I am reminded of a tour I took of Dickinson's house in 1997, when the tour guide rather defensively pointed out that Dickinson didn't just stay in her room writing all the time; she also did the family's baking.] Yet, as I've pointed out, recipe rhetoric doesn't question: it ordains. And what other poet, aside from Johnson perhaps, is so imperative in tone as Dickinson? Look at the "Index of First Lines" in her *Complete Poems*, edited by Thomas H. Johnson and you will find the following, selected nearly at random:

Alter! When the hills do, 729
Awake ye muses nine, sing me a strain divine, 1
Don't put up my thread and needle, 617
Make me a picture of the sun, 188
Put up my lute, 261
Take all away from me, 1640
Tie the strings to my life, my Lord, 279

ARK 72 is an elegy to many of Johnson's influences and, while it quotes Olson's "'man model of world'" it also invokes Dickinson:

stitch soul Emily but banner Walt
    —hound of the Lord
     snifffootfall belowground . . .

If the imperative mode is as visionary as is the apostrophe—obliging objects, materials to come into life because the poet says so—than it is also the mode of the recipe writer, whether that writer is Dickinson or Johnson. Where Johnson's imperatives have been read almost without counterexample as exemplars of visionary calls-into-being, I think they should also be read as models of a more feminine mode, that of calling a meal into being based on words found in a cookbook or on a scrap of paper handed down by a grandmother. If we read Johnson convention-ally, either as a poet or as a cookbook writer, we run the risk of perpetu-ating the tired dialectic: men write poetry and women cook; men argue about ideas and women about ingredients. That is, we do so unless we synthesize these two positions, namely that men and women write po-etry and men and women argue about ideas and ingredients. It troubles me that I am making this argument so late in literary history, but if these ideas need to be rehashed, then so be it. (I do not find a recipe for hash in Johnson's books, though I find one for haschish in Toklas's!)

I have perhaps belabored my quotations of Guy Davenport, but will cite him again, as a critic who *almost* catches what I take to be Johnson's central metaphor, but turns it in a masculine direction always. In an introduction to Johnson's 1969 volume, *Valley of the Many-Colored Grasses,* Guy Davenport writes: "If the finely textured geometry of words RJ builds on his pages is not what we ordinarily call a poem, it is indisputably poetry . . . It incorporates in generous measure the words of other men" (10). He goes on to comment on Johnson's "erudite" cookbooks as a sign of his "objectivity." Later in the introduction, Davenport comments on the way "all these voices quoted in RJ's poems are other modes of vision which he is allowing to play over the subject along with his own" (13). I have just argued that quotation may have come to Johnson as much from his work as a recipe writer as from the "objectivity" of his "vision." His skill at combining voices and ideas is apparent in a poem like ARK 37, *Spire called Prospero's Songs to Ariel (constructed in the form of a quilt from Roger Tory Peterson's A Field Guide to Western Birds).* In this section of his epic poem, Johnson reimagines Shakespearian songs from a play—*The Tempest*—about discovering the new world, through citations from a prominent book on birds (so long associated with poets). That Johnson describes this layering of voices first as a "spire" and then as a "construct[ion]" and finally a "quilt" usefully complicates the field, combining the male "spire" with the female "quilt" (one of the birds is described as following a "*sewing-machine motion*"). Yet the act of quotation is also one of leaving out, unless one rewrites *Don Quixote* as Borges's character once did. To quote another writer is also to silence him or her; the act is one of foraging and hunting, then presenting the other's text inside your own, having digested it. Johnson's poetry, which began in late Romantic country walks, reported in full sentences, developed over the three decades in which he published his work into a poetry more of leaving out. If Johnson is to be seen as part of a Miltonic tradition, it is because he "reduced" and "sifted" Milton, not because he was inspired to add on to Milton's language. Thus,

Of man's first disobedience, and the fruit
Of that forbidden tree, whose mortal taste
Brought death into the world, and all our woe,
With loss of Eden, till one greater man
Restore us, and regain the blissful seat,
Sing Heav'nly Muse, that on the secret top
Of Oreb, or of Sinai, didst inspire
That shepherd, who first taught the chosen seed,

In the beginning how the heav'ns and earth
Rose out of Chaos

becomes in BEAMS 21, 22, 23, *The Song of Orpheus:* adapted from *RADI OS 01:*

O

Tree

into the World,

Man

the chosen

Rose out of Chaos:

This is, of course, to alter the theology quite profoundly! Where Milton's emphasis was on an explanation of the ways of God to man, Johnson takes Man as his "chosen" text, and it is he who has the power to rise from chaos. No mention is made of disobedience or mortality in Johnson's reevocation of the muse-as-tree. What matters here is as much what is not quoted, as what is. Johnson creates by way of *reduction* as if he were boiling down a stock. One can suggest that Johnson's is a recipe for recreating or reconstructing Milton or paradise, but most important to me in this instance is the way in which the poem's form resembles that of a recipe in the way it's written and in its concentration on essences rather than on the all of it.[5] Reduction, in writing if not in cooking, comes of the generation of poetry out of one's conscious blocking of another—prior—writer's work. When Johnson erases Milton's connectives he arrives at a text consisting of what is not missing; it is as if Johnson installed the block from which Milton did not suffer. Call this the block of modernity or, more aptly for my purposes, an interruption of tradition rather than the continuation of it. Johnson brings the tradition he otherwise claims to participate in to a skidding halt, while using elements of that tradition to new (secular, postmodern) purpose. His operation (installing silence where there was language) reverses that of Susan Howe (whose silences, as we shall see, suggest voices already erased), but they both intervene in a canon that has excluded some voices to the benefit of others. If Johnson locates "Man" at the expense of "God," Howe gives us "Woman" (and "God"). But they arrive there through silences that they either highlight or create.

westward into darkness
in realms of whippoorwill
yet glinting off leaves
in the Forest of Arden (*To Do As* 147)

is a section of *The Shrubberies,* included in Peter O'Leary's edition of
Johnson's *To Do As Adam Did: Selected Poems* (2000). Characteristic of
Johnson's late work, this short lyric section has no real subject, except
perhaps the movement in darkness; certainly, it has no *lyric* subject.[6]
There is not an *imperative* movement in this poem, like the one I described in some sections of *ARK,* but there is a backwards one. "A Line
of Poetry, A Row of Trees" (1964) included the following passage, another invocation of Arden:

Where
the smokes curl up, the moss hangs down:
let us call it Arden

& live in it! (*To Do As* 3)

Thoughts of life in Arden (where gender identity was hidden in the
Shakespearian mists) are replaced by musings on death in Arden, yet it
is as if the self were not Johnson's primary focus here, but something
larger (if it has been the fate of the lyric to seem smaller and smaller in
its references over time). What I notice here, in addition, is the way Johnson has subtracted, reduced, condensed, his own work in something of
the same manner as his operation on Milton in *RADI OS.* Page 32 reads:
"the always revisiting / mind all-revising / yet another vision," combining "visit" and "vision" in a way that Dickinson would appreciate. No
inessential word takes its place on the thin staves of *The Shrubberies.* He
pays attention to his own silences, now, by taking out more than he puts
in. The Williams-like directive of the first poem becomes another kind
of directive in the second, more communal perhaps, because less personal. Where Williams and the Romantics (odd mix, indeed) informed
his early poems, here Johnson sounds like Susan Howe, operating from
sound more than the sense syntax offers automatically. (What direction
that influence ran is unclear to me, if it was indeed direct influence at

all, yet the idea that "vision" comes out of "re-vision"—a textual as well as a visionary practice—is central to the work of both poets.) It is only appropriate to hear so much Howe in *The Shrubberies,* since her *My Emily Dickinson* makes explicit that poet's link to her in ways that Johnson never did, but might have.[7]

At the end of *The Alice B. Toklas Cook Book,* Toklas comments on the genesis of the book the reader has just finished. She reports that she has only given a confidence twice; the first person to whom she gave it responded, "How very amusing." The second person asked with a start if Alice had ever "tried to write." The final words in this book that Toklas *did* write, answer that question, "As if a cook-book had anything to do with writing" (280). This seemingly off-handed remark gets at any number of American assumptions about authorship, that perhaps "writing" is not what one does for money and/or for an audience of women, that "writing" is what poets do, without hope of remuneration, for an audience stripped of its "ladies," to paraphrase James Joyce on the effect of *The Waste Land* on modern poetry. It is clear to me that what Johnson did, however differently in his cookbooks and his poems, was all *writing* in the sense Toklas gestures at, even if Johnson himself insisted on the differences between these genres, and tried on occasion to suppress knowledge of his cookbook writing. Of course we can read Milton, Blake, Pound, Olson, and other epic poets *in* and *through* Johnson's *ARK* and other poems, but I strongly suggest that we cannot read Johnson's poems without also considering his cookbooks, which raise issues of gender and form so crucial to Johnson's work from beginning to end.

But the stakes are, indeed, higher than this: Johnson is not the only "visionary" poet who has been read as if he belonged to an all-male, or nearly all-male, fraternity of poets. The narratives we create about poets are powerful, so powerful, in fact, that Johnson himself wrote about the poems this way in his brief commentaries on them, when he surely knew better. What we need are new narratives—ones with pauses for recipes, perhaps, like those of Fisher and Toklas—to point us in other directions, toward what comes to these poets' work from a female tradition, and toward those women poets whose work demands entry into the lists created by Johnson's first readers. Johnson's use of quotation resembles no other poet so much as Marianne Moore, it seems to me. Not only is her name typically left off the lists of Johnson's influences, but it has not appeared until now in this essay. Let me say that there is work left to do on gender and poetry, and that, although this may *still* seem an odd thing to say, there may be no better place to start than with Ronald Johnson's cookbooks.

6
The Stutter in the Text

Editing and Historical Authority in
the Work of Susan Howe

The complexities of history deserve our respect.
—Mark DeWolfe Howe

It does not matter whether the world is conceived to be real or only imagined; the manner of making sense of it is the same.
—Hayden White

Somewhere Thoreau says that exaggerated history is poetry.
—Susan Howe

If history is a record of survivors, Poetry shelters other voices.
—Susan Howe

I

For Susan Howe, history is at once impasse and possibility. Insofar as history has excluded and silenced women, it is in impasse; once these exclusions are noted, history becomes possibility. History represents a kind of authority that fascinates Howe, an authority she claims as a poet who does historical work. Howe's use of the archives fills in some of the gaps, but her work less involves the writing of a new history than the foregrounding of what is missing from original texts. She is less historian than editor and reviser (as she puts it at the end of *Singularities*), but her fascination with history is deep and her revisions of it worth exploring in the context of the historiography, much of it from the 1970s and 1980s, that has influenced her work. The particular story she tells, over and again, involves what Paul Naylor describes as "a resolute investigation of the 'dark side' of colonialism and imperialism" (43). Where Naylor is fascinated by the contradiction between Howe's storytelling and her paratactic style, my concern lies more with the ways in which Howe "earns" the authority to speak for characters lost to history. Authority breaks silence, for Howe, and finds voice in historical impasses.

Howe's poetry, while every bit as idiosyncratic in style as that of the Language poets, revises tradition through her self-proclaimed role as editor/interpreter of a series of prior texts. Where Bernstein's "dysraphism" describes a poetry constructed of mis-seaming, or the radical and ironic unraveling of tradition, Howe begins from a place of mis-seaming and reconstructs (or sews together) traditional texts.[1] She doesn't attempt to step outside tradition, but to redescribe and reframe an existing one in such a way that it admits women. While Howe is a formal innovator, her work rests always on *content* more than form, and should not then be associated as closely as it sometimes is with the Language school. As Hank Lazer writes, "A strength of Howe's writing . . . is that it is *not* an avant-gardism or aestheticism severed from history. Precisely the opposite" (*Opposing Poetries:* 2:66). And yet, as I hope to show, the *content* of her work depends to a great extent on the *styles* that lend authority to the historian. In that sense, her interests are very much in line with those of Charles Bernstein; where Howe uses a *style* of history as a model for her poetry, we will see Bernstein using writing *styles* as a way around the impasse of professionalized writing, both in poetry and in the profession of English.

The truest of Howe's originary metaphors for her "place"—or lack of one—in poetic tradition is that of the Harvard Library where she was forbidden access as a young woman. In *The Birth-mark* (*TBM*), Howe writes her own captivity and conversion narrative about her experience of that library as wilderness. "What is forbidden is wild," she writes. "The stacks of Widener Library [at Harvard, where her father taught law] and of all great libraries in the world are still the wild to me. Thoreau went to the woods because he wished to live deliberately in order to give a true account in his next excursion. I go to libraries because they are the ocean" (18). When she went to the (ironically named) Widener Library with her father, she was forced to remain outside the second-floor entrance to the stacks because, as her father told her, to go beyond there would be to "trespass." She waited outside the entrance while he "entered the guarded territory to hunt for books" (*TBM* 18), a phrase in which "hunting" loses metaphorical softening and reacquires a violent connotation. Howe's status at the frontier of learning made her a captive within the wilderness and so linked her to Mary Rowlandson, whom she calls "the mother of us all" (*TBM* 167), and to Native Americans who are the *other* of Rowlandson's captivity narrative. Howe writes that "a lot of my work is about breaking free: starting free and being captured and breaking free again and being captured again" (*TBM* 166). She is lost in the wilderness and denied entry into it. An escape *into* the wilderness or library will link her with the Native Americans whose lost voices so interest her in *Singularities*. But it also allies her with Mary Rowlandson's ambivalence about her captivity. Howe's authority stems, therefore, both from a sense of being a member of an oppressed group whose power can only come from solidarity, and, paradoxically, from her status as a representative of the dominant culture: white, historical rather than mythical, and editorial. In both cases, Howe is a "captive," but the nature of her captivity oscillates between that of someone forbidden language and of someone, like Rowlandson, who lays claim to a language and set of beliefs that are not hers, but those of male intermediaries—editors, publishers, authors of source texts like the Bible. Authority is still figured as male and white, marginality as female and "other." Howe's task as a poet who calls these roles into question is that of a cross-thinker who fashions her role by blending and blurring of traditional hierarchies. To the extent that she succeeds at this, her poetry offers a radical new interpretation of American history and literature. To the extent that she fails, merely turning the master narratives inside out, rather than dispensing with them or writing new ones, her work provides us with a problematic instance in the larger tradition of American works like William Carlos Williams's *In the American Grain* and earlier Puritan narratives of mythologized history. Problematic because these renovated myths cannot quite escape the originary stories they attempt to overthrow: witness Williams's replacement of the Founding Fathers with other powerful white men like Sam Houston and Aaron Burr.

Howe does not disdain the library, as she might; instead she infiltrates it like the scout in her poem, "Thorow," who inhabits the wilderness secretly and alters it by seeing, rather than by attempting to "civilize" it.[2] What is most radical in her work is her sense that the tradition is wild and that entry into the wilderness makes the poet into a scout or a captive, not an empire builder. If the scout is also an editor, or a reviser, however, then her territory is imperial rather than egalitarian; the burden of history, for Howe, is that it repeats itself, even as it is being edited.

How to avoid a historicity that is merely Steinian repetition (even insistence), provides Howe with one of her most formidable obstacles, tasks.

Howe's authority is paradoxical; while she uses elements of the historical record in her poems, she does not use them as would a conventional historian. For example, in "Articulation of Sound Forms in Time," a poem I will read in more detail later, Howe introduces a wanderer out of the historical record, namely Hope Atherton, only to assert that, since "hope" is a word used to represent the feminine in our culture, "he" can be used to retell the tale in transvestite fashion. Rachel Tzvia Back pursues the clothing metaphor in her discussion of Howe and Hope Atherton: "Paralleling Hope's 'movement . . . toward the Other' is Howe's movement toward Hope, effected by her 'assumin[g] Hope Atherton's excursion': putting it upon herself, as one would a piece of clothing— performing his transformative journey through her transformations of language" (40). "Sound forms in time," then, exist at the intersection of history and language; if history is told through language, and in some sense created by it, then history can be changed by altering and articulating sound forms in new ways.

History in Howe's work is dependent on the procedures of language; her authority as historian is based on her authority as a poet, not vice versa. Such authority, while based on the record, often depends on rhetorical moves rather than the introduction of new "data"—the language, not the history, takes her from one place to another. For Howe, language is an instrument for re-creating truth where none—or little— exists. That her work's authority is often based on a sleight of hand does not, of necessity, diminish its power, which is at once reconstitutive (the feminist project of returning women to the text that they'd been left out of) and "emotive" rather than "rational."[3] Yet such authority springs from the poet herself, rather than from an "objective" record; Howe is, in fact, a strong critic of objectivity. Where Howe's work is most problematic, perhaps, is in her assumption that the poet, or the poet-reviser, can carry this authority on her own back, that she can create out of herself a form of objectivity that is a new history by manipulating her (and our) language.

It is through the "wild" that Howe most directly links herself to the earlier "trespasser," Emily Dickinson, and stakes her claim to participate in the antinomian impulse behind Dickinson's brand of American literature. "Emily Dickinson's writing is my strength and my shelter. I have trespassed into the disciplines of American Studies and Textual Criticism through my need to fathom what wildness and absolute freedom is the nature of expression" (*TBM* 2). Howe's freedom is made, paradoxically, of a melding of voices and genres and forms, and the creation of a system out of texts that attempt to destroy systems governing them, including Puritan texts that conflate history with prophecy, American with religious history. As she explains it: "By choosing to install certain narratives somewhere between history, mystic speech, and poetry, I have enclosed them in an organization, although I know there are places no classificatory procedure can reach, where connections between words and things we thought existed break off" (*TBM* 45). This amazing sentence gestures both toward a system of organization and classification and toward a mode of writing that is able to capture or explore in less violent terms what lives beyond the frontier of a territory we might label "intelligibility." What she means to accomplish is a hybridization of writing practices in which her authority as a poet enables her to revise history, while her authority as a revisionary editor allows her to turn historical documents into poetry. Thus, the poet whose collection, *Singularities,* ends with the putative name of the author, "THE REVISER," finally takes liberties not unlike those of the male editors she so despises. "It was my postmodern editorial decision," she writes in "Submarginalia," "to turn some sections of the conversion narratives and Mary Dyer's letter into poems" (*TBM* 39).

Howe's authority, like that of the editors she attacks, is often arbitrary. It exposes the fundamental ambivalence in Howe's work, namely her conflict with preestablished authority, which is played out in Trojan horse fashion, as Howe adopts the myths of her elders and then shows the ways in which they collapse under the weight of alternative readings of history. Howe's work is in many ways, then, a search for a new kind of authority, one grounded in the history of places rather than of ideas, yet frankly indebted to histories of ideas imposed upon places. But for her, as for the Romantics, place is often another word for *language;* Howe reads the landscape with the same freedom, and often the same self-referentiality, as a Romantic poet. The Romantic poet's primary interest is not so much in reproducing place as in transcending it, a motivation that complicates Howe's work, rooted as it is both in the Romantic tradition and that of William Carlos Williams, Charles Olson, and other American anti-Romantic poets.

Howe's project, the stripping away of accretions of meaning from the historical and literary record, requires an asceticism similar to that found in the work of Laura Riding and Gertrude Stein. Their most significant intellectual precursors may be the Puritan minister and thinker, Jonathan Edwards and, less surprisingly, Emily Dickinson. Susan Howe, the descendent of them all, would lead us to that connection. In her blurred genre book of poetic criticism, *My Emily Dickinson* (*MED*), published in 1985, Howe paraphrases Edwards's argument for "each person's active participation . . . in the battle against sin. To be in the world but avoid serving Mammon, I must renounce attachment to friends and worldly accomplishment" (48). For a poet whose religion was poetry, as Howe claims was true for Dickinson, the renunciation of publication is "far from being the misguided modesty of an oppressed female ego," rather "it is a consummate Calvinist gesture of self-assertion by a poet with faith to fling election loose across the incandescent shadows of futurity" (*MED* 49). Where Dickinson refuses to participate in tradition, however, Howe constructs a tradition largely through her work on Dickinson. For Howe, that tradition is not only made up of poetry, but also of editorship. While Howe doesn't, to my knowledge, ever discuss the work of Laura Riding, her efforts to "avoid serving Mammon" resonate with Riding's condemnation of poetry as "profession"—not religious but secular profession. As we've seen, Gertrude Stein also attacked "Mammon" in her work, though her relationship with it was rather more complicated than was Riding's.

For the Puritans, who distrusted language, words are material, allied more to Mammon than to spirit. Howe describes the necessary Puritan renunciation of mammon in language that echoes some of William Carlos Williams's most earnest tirades in *In the American Grain,* and his review of Marianne Moore as a writer whose words are "clean" and free of an "aroma."[4] Howe writes: "If language imposes on the understanding names which familiarity has deadened, how does a minister preach a sermon when words and images have become predictable?" (*MED* 50). The answer comes through a process of denuding language, purifying it, stripping off its metaphorical clothing: "Ideas must be stripped to their essence, rhetorical embroidery torn off" (50). Howe makes the connection to Dickinson, whom she sees as a poet of positive negation: "The recipient of a letter, or combination of letter and poem from Emily Dickinson, was forced much like Edwards' listening congregation, through shock and through subtraction of the ordinary, to a new way of perceiving" (51).

In an America where, as Kenneth Dauber argues, "authority is . . . defined as rhetorical from the very start" (52), Dickinson's authority comes of a rhetoric of subtraction. Stephen Greenblatt might be describing her (and Howe) in *Renaissance Self-Fashioning: From More to Shakespeare* (1980), when he writes about the Protestant ethos of Tynedale that "the Protestant discourse of self [emerges] out of conflicting impulses: rage against authority and identification with authority" (85). For Howe, the original instance of this conflict was the antinomian controversy of the late 1630s, at whose center was a woman, Anne Hutchinson. Hutchinson, according to David D. Hall, represented a Puritan belief system that put an emphasis on inner spiritual experience. Like Dickinson, Hutchinson "devalued the outward material world" (xi) and claimed the authority of her own inspiration. In so doing, she "was openly defying the hierarchical authority that men derived from their gender, and from gender-restricted learning" (xi). As a result of her "enthusiasm" and her claim to possess authority in her own right, Hutchinson was banished, denied even the knowledge of where she was being exiled. In an interesting, but in many ways typical, conflation of nature and history, Howe writes that Hutchinson was then "murdered in the natural wilderness by history" (*TBM* 4).

Howe claims for Dickinson a similar fate—Dickinson who is as wild as her name's etymology: "Emily: Feminine of the Teutonic Emil, 'the industrious,' stems from Amalia of the ancient Goths; and Amalia, or Amelia, goes back to the wild forest people known as the Ameler" (*MED* 65). Although Howe does not see Dickinson's non-publication as banishment but as an instance of self-assertion, she regards the male editors of Dickinson's work as literary policemen bent on taming the poet's natural wildness. In this they are in some ways like the male editors of conversion and captivity narratives in New England: as Patricia Caldwell writes, "A woman, afraid of not speaking well, tells her story to a man who writes it down . . . All testimonies are bereft, brief, hungry, pious, authorized" (50). Using a concept crucial to Howe's sense of her own work, namely the "stammer," Caldwell adds: "many of these voices were not so much crying in the wilderness as they were stammering to themselves in the dark. But they did talk, because they had to" (114–15). The verb construction "had to" is provocatively ambiguous here; not only did Puritans have to speak of their experiences in the New World due to their severity and strangeness, but these women were obligated to speak through the medium of male editors. Their conversions were double, for not only did their spiritual worlds change, but so did their actual words.

Because women's words were, from the beginning, transcribed and edited by men, Howe begins *The Birth-mark: Unsettling the Wilderness in American Literary History* by connecting the rejection of antinomianism to editorial practice: "The issue of editorial control is directly connected to the attempted erasure of antinomianism in our culture. Lawlessness seen as negligence is at first feminized and then restricted or banished" (*TBM* 1). Such lawlessness disturbs the very commerce of a society that places commercial value—however little—on words: "The trace of her unapprehended passage through letters disturbs the order of a world where commerce is reality and authoritative editions freeze poems into artifacts" (*TBM* 19). Like Hutchinson, Dickinson is "tamed," disciplined, frozen, and then frozen out.

Dickinson lived, according to Howe, "really alone at a real frontier, dwelling in Possibility" (*MED* 76). It can be no mistake, then, that Howe devotes so much space and energy in her book about Dickinson to that poet's frontier poem written in the midst of the Civil War, "My Life had stood—a Loaded Gun," which Howe describes further as having as its subject "the lust for power" (85). Power, as Dickinson and Howe know, "will always demand sacrifice and subjugation of one group by another" (93) and also demands the creation of authority through a demonization of the Other. As Stephen Greenblatt writes in *Renaissance Self-Fashioning,* a book whose influence Howe acknowledges, "Self-fashioning is achieved in relation to something perceived as alien, strange, or hostile. This threatening Other . . . must be discovered or invented in order to be attacked and destroyed" (9). Historiographer Hayden White, in his collection, *Tropics of Discourse: Essays in Cultural Criticism,* also writes about the notion of "wildness" as part of "a set of culturally self-authenticating devices" and asserts that, "like the Puritans who came after him, Augustine found that one way of establishing the 'meaning' of his own life was to deny meaning to anything radically different from it, except as anti-type or negative instance" (151). In terms historically, if not psychologically, closer to Howe's own, Richard Slotkin writes that, "in opposing the Indian culture, the Puritan symbolically affirmed his Englishness" (22). Eric Cheyfitz goes even further when he writes: "As

Cronon's seventeenth-century Puritans were meeting his seventeenth-century Algonquians, the Puritan's God, we might say, was becoming truly American (as opposed to Native American): the ultimate individual, the infinite proprietor" (55).

Michel de Certeau helps link the notion of a wildness considered "other" to Howe's assertion that this move often depends on a "feminization" of the concepts. De Certeau is interested in "the possessed woman, the victim" (245) and writes that "there must always be a gap between what the possessed woman utters and what the demonological or medical discourse makes of it" (247). To that, Howe would add "editorial discourse," or that which tames the possessed woman's wildness (an especially evocative phrase when applied to a poet) by invisibly closing the gap between the woman's words and the way in which those words are printed. She also notes that, "If you are a woman, archives hold perpetual ironies. Because the gaps and silences are where you find yourself" (*TBM* 158). While print traditionally and historically is identified with power, de Certeau makes a fine distinction between the power of possession, which "is only a voice" (254) and writing, which possesses: "a person cannot be possessed while writing," he asserts (254). Women, whose power is here figured as "voice," lose power when their words are translated, edited, into print, which is a mechanism to control "possession." In Trinh T. Minh-ha's terms, the dominant culture imposes a mode of writing on minorities (and, one imagines Howe would insist, on women): "The Well Written. The master-servant's creed carries on: *you must learn* through patience and discipline" (16–17). Thus self-possession becomes the opposite of "possession," and the poet must govern her tongue even as she rescues it from an internalized editorial (magisterial) conscience.

II

In most of her work, Howe mixes genres, moving between prose and poetry, explication and enactment, performing her dual authority as historian and poet. If we are to look at her work within the context of its time, we see that Howe is not alone in her blending of genres; she is, in fact, very much a thinker of her own time. In a profound sense, the only contemporary or postmodern genre is a mixed one. I will explore the ways in which her poetic practice enacts a theoretical stance adopted in the 1970s by two historiographers, Hayden White and Michel de Certeau, whose work I have briefly cited already. I do this so that I can better discuss Howe's own conflation of history with poetry, her claim to authority as a chronicler of histories that happened but were not written down. White and de Certeau argue in remarkably similar terms that historical narratives cannot be distinguished from other kinds of narratives, that history and fiction have more affinities than differences. Furthermore, they claim that the writing of history is based on linguistic practices usually associated with poetry or poetic thinking. White and de Certeau respond to what they see as a lack of engagement by other writers with their subject; White claims that a good deal of twentieth-century literature is hostile toward historical thinking (31).[5] Their response to the deauthorization of history is to reclaim its authority by redescribing it, enlarging its field, opening its borders to the alien, the Other, poeticizing it.

In her essay "Incloser," Howe writes that "knowledge, no matter how I get it, involves exclusion and repression" (*TBM* 45). Perhaps the most significant exclusion involves a process that often relies on fictions, supreme or no. Hayden White argues that history is created out of the act of telling it, that "all discourse constitutes the objects which it pretends only to describe realistically and to analyze objectively" (2). Historians work from a preexisting set of explanatory paradigms, rather like a reservoir of plotlines for dramatic productions; they take material generated by their research and plug it into the paradigm that seems to them most reasonable. For this reason, history is not so much an objective chronicle of unique events, but something that happens over and again because the number of plot structures are limited. "There has been a reluctance to consider historical narratives as what they most manifestly are," he writes: "verbal fictions, the contents of which are as much *invented* as found and the forms of which have more in common with the counterparts in literature than they have with those in the sciences" (82). Thus histories are, like literary texts, symbolic organisms, not one-of-a-kinds. They are "fashions" that can be reproduced over and again, fashions that change over time. White's most radical statement to this effect is that "it does not matter whether the world is conceived to be real or only imagined; the manner of making sense of it is the same" (98). History, then, is a rhetorical activity, not a scientific one, and the historian, like the American authors discussed by Kenneth Dauber, creates authority through style rather than through documentation. The effect of questioning history's authority in this way is extreme, for it calls into question the discipline itself, much as Howe's poetry interrogates the notion of what makes a poet separate from a historian, an editor, or a prophet. In the end, what gives the poet power (her status as historian) may diminish the historian's power (as poet).

Because White believes that history and literature are like-minded in this way, he declares history's authority to be poetic instead of scientific. For him (as for Hart Crane, who describes metaphor as a kind of logic), metaphorical consciousness is "every bit as authoritative as logic itself" (10). He refuses to separate categories like "myth" and "poetry" and "history" from each other, or to assign to the first two the label of "primitive" and to the latter that of "civilized" (104). De Certeau develops this line of thinking further, arguing that "history becomes the myth of language," and, more radically, that the very documents used to create histories are invented. In describing his notion of what becomes historical documentation, he uses the word "scatter," crucial to Howe's definitions of history and poetry "[History's] work consists in creating the absent, in making signs scattered over the surface of current times become the traces of 'historical' realities, missing indeed because they are other" (46). Thus the historian is the "poet of meticulous detail" (80), historical "facts" are "figures" (85), and "historical figures" are "dummies" (9). Whether it is considered myth or history, however, chronicles of the Puritans' sojourn in the New World create authority for their tellers and for the community those tellers represent. There is, as Richard Slotkin puts it, "a constellation of compelling metaphors" (6) that transforms knowledge into power (7). And so, as Howe writes, Mary Rowlandson creates a narrative that is at once personal and communal history and mythology: "Each time an errant perception skids loose, she controls her lapse by vehemently invoking biblical authority" (*TBM* 100). As Sacvan Bercovitch has written, the Puritans attempted to create history out of their belief in religious symbology; history, for John Cotton, was backdated prophecy. History is controlled by the interpretation of it. Bercovitch writes, "The American jeremiad was born in an effort to impose metaphor upon reality" (62) or, as Howe might put it, to make scattered reality fit the traces of metaphor.

Of course the creation of history through metaphor was assigned only to certain members of the community; metaphor, which can be more wild than regulatory, was intended by Puritan fathers to help create an official story, not competing narratives. As Eric Cheyfitz has argued, "from its theoretical beginnings, then, metaphor comes under suspicion as the foreign, that which is opposed to the 'proper,' defined inescapably . . . as the *national,* the *domestic,* the *familiar,* the *authoritative,* the *legitimate*" (90). Metaphor, which exists at the "frontier between the national and the foreign" (94), is used by the powerful to patrol that boundary, not pull it down. "The master struggles to deny the slave access to the full potency of language, that is, eloquence, by asserting the frontier of decorum as an absolute, or natural, frontier" (172). By now it should be clear that Susan Howe is most interested in "figures" that crossed that frontier and were "tamed" by editors who have policed the frontier since the beginnings of American thought and literature. Hence her interest in the "Scapegoat Dialectic" (*TBM* 53), enforced against women who refuse to acknowledge preexisting boundaries of the Puritans' decorous metaphorical self-definition. The danger consists in creating new metaphors; where the metaphor of enforcement insists on Mary Rowlandson's comparison of herself to a biblical character foisted into the wilderness, only later to be saved, Rowlandson's own occasional comparison of her Indian captors to her own people is dangerous to the definition of the white community. Thus she ends up writing a narrative that undoes itself, one whose metaphors work to unravel rather than adjudicate the boundaries between worldviews. Howe writes: "Mary Rowlandson's thoroughly reactionary figuralism requires that she obsessively confirm her orthodoxy to readers at the same time she excavates and subverts her own rhetoric" (100). Howe blurs the boundaries of genre to redefine history and poetry in such a way as to give power to the voice of Rowlandson's subversions, to undo some metaphors so that others can be installed in their stead. While Howe joins White and de Certeau as fellow-thinkers of this re-placing of genres, she does it with an explicitly feminist agenda in mind; the "possessed" women about whom they write become her historians; they come to repossess the very histories that have excluded them. So Howe takes their manifestos of history's affinities to literature and enacts them through the figures of Puritan histories.

III

My reading of "Articulation of Sound Forms in Time"[6] makes two main arguments. The first argument is that Howe writes an American epic in reverse, in which she endeavors to undo the story told to us by the Puritans, that this poem is more like Williams's *In the American Grain* than it is like a Puritan jeremiad or even Crane's *The Bridge*. By performing and taking apart the central ideologies that separate Puritan theology from the Native American context in which they found themselves, Howe aims to get back to a point where the story can begin again, where it can be more inclusive. She also wants to tell the story that the historians did not: on the first page of "Articulation," she writes of a white attack on an Indian camp, "What the historian doesn't say is that most of the dead were women and children." The function of the poet-historian, then, is to reimagine the past so as to tell it again more completely, a role that makes the poet into a self-conscious creator of fictions. Yet, because *new* stories, according to a thinker like Hayden White, do not exist, Howe's "Articulation" does not so much tell a new story as attempt to deconstruct the old. What is new about her story is the way in which it dismantles the old narrative, not the way she invents a new one; in that sense, she is faithful to the historical record, which holds her to the gaps rather than liberating her out of them. The second argument is that Howe's epic is a feminine one, but that her rewriting of the narrative is at times undermined by the structure of her story. To use de Certeau for a moment: Howe reaches for the paradigm that best fits her historical details, but the best paradigm proves to be the old one with significant details transfigured. The way in which she tells the story in reverse, however, subverts the very authority of that paradigm. What she aims for, then, is a kind of revelatory impasse, one that returns us to an origin so that what accrues are fragments of what she calls, in "Thorow," "narrative in non-narrative," or a poetic history that acknowledges gaps and questions its own authority.

The first of Howe's transfigurations is the name change operation that she makes in her proem, "The Falls Fight," where the American wanderer, Reverend Hope Atherton, is by fiat re-"figured" as a woman. "In our culture," she writes, "Hope is a name we give women. Signifying desire, trust, promise, does her name prophetically engender pacification of the feminine?" (4) The answer to this question is complicated, since in some ways it does; the wanderer, Hope Atherton, is a white American (man or woman or word) lost in the wilderness of native America. Howe's attitude toward Hope resembles her attitude toward Mary Rowlandson; Howe at once admires Rowlandson's resilience, her ability to survive and to write about her experiences, and disdains her constant use of biblical authority to render the Indians as savages. Hope is, like Rowlandson, an ambivalent character. The extent to which the narrative is predetermined is made clear in Howe's notion of the origin of the poem itself. "Hope's epicene name draws its predetermined poem in" (4) she writes, asserting that her poem, too, comes of the kind of "Postdated Prophesie" alluded to in her quotation from John Cotton. The only way for the poet to liberate herself from the preconceived narrative is through the work of demythologization, work that she accomplishes by ending this poem with only the "Rubble couple on pedestal" remaining (38). "I assume Hope Atherton's excursion for an emblem foreshadowing a Poet's abolished limitations in our demythologized fantasy of Manifest Destiny" (4). The poet, then, has imperial designs of her own; only when she undoes the myth of Manifest Destiny can her poetry break the bounds imposed on it by the very force of that myth on American letters.

How does one untell a myth, demythologize a fantasy? Howe does so, in part, by setting up dichotomous terms to represent Puritan thinking and that of the Native Americans they displace. The most basic of these dichotomies is that of "system" or "logic," which is Puritan, and "intuition" or "lack of western system" (which is the Other). The world the Puritans enter is soon reduced to the grids that they place upon it, grids that Howe imitates on some of her pages, which are covered with fields of words arranged in rows. Thus, in "Taking the Forest," she writes of "Universal separation /—Distant coherent rational system" and of "Consciousness [that] grasps its subject / Stumbling phenomenology // infinite miscalculation of history" (17). That this system is created somehow counter to historical process becomes clear later on: "total systemic circular knowledge / System impossible in time," which is promptly called into question by "truant freedom of dream" (28). Systems are necessary to the act of "possession"; late in the poem, when Howe invokes Columbus's voyage she connects western system-making ("World as rigorously related System") to the destruction of "pagan worlds" (38).

The first of Howe's mirror pages presents the reader with a grid of words on the left-hand side of the opened book, and a similar grid on the right—one that is a mirror image of the first, with spaces between words erased so as to create one long, rather Germanic looking, word. The function of these grids is to present the conflict between worldviews and, perhaps, to gesture toward a way beyond the conflict. On the one hand, Howe presents us with "system" words: "border"; "possess"; "empirical"; "Kantian" and "force"; on the other, mixed in with these words, she provides: "*is*"; "open"; "Halo"; "Maoris"; and "Immanence" (14). The fact that these words are separated on the first page imitates separations caused by the systematizing imagination. On the second page, these words run together in reverse; taking from the middle of the grid: "UpConcatenationLessonLittleAkantianEmpiricalMaoris HumTemporal-spatioLostAreLifeAbstractSoRemotePossess ReddenBorder" and so on (15). But the most important word on both sides of this double page is the one that inaugurates the grid on the left and which concludes it on the right, namely "is," a word that suggests process, history, becoming, and a lack of system. So the second grid becomes an answer to the first. As the poem moves forward it becomes clear that Howe believes the myth must incorporate both these ways of thinking, that neither should possess the other, even if (or especially because) the end result is an undoing of both; thus she posits "Untraceable wandering" against the next line, "the meaning of knowing" (25) and "Kneel to intellect in our work" against "Chaos cast cold intellect back" (34).

And yet these binaries are, of course, too simple to be trusted entirely to do their own work. So we begin from the rather more complicated Hope Atherton, the Puritan Every-man/woman, wanderer in a wilderness that is at once the land and his/her own mind. Howe effectively collapses her symbology inward when she creates this "figure" (he/she is not really a character), because Hope serves at once to organize her text, by giving it a fulcrum, and to unravel that text by valuing "wandering" (like the later term, "scattering") over stasis. Though a kind of hero in Howe's book, as he/she might have been in Williams's *In the American Grain,* where the only American successes are seen to be its failures, Hope's historical fate was more absurd and more unhappy. According to a letter by Stephen Williams in 1781, which is quoted in Howe's text, Hope offered to surrender to the enemy, but they wouldn't have him (5). In her introduction, Howe relates that, "No one believed the Minister's letter. He became a stranger to his community and died soon after the traumatic exposure that has earned him poor mention in a seldom opened book" (4). Thus, like the text itself, Hope begins as a paradigmatic figure and dissolves into language like the systems he at first represents (religious and historical). His function is also linguistic; not only is Hope reborn as a word ("hope for the artist in America") and as a woman because of the "nature" of his name, but also because he speaks the language not of this place but of England. Thus, in "Hope Atherton's Wanderings," note the English accent on "matah" and "chirah":

And deep so deep as my narrative
Our homely manner and Myself
Said "matah" and "chirah"
Pease of all sorts and best
Courtesy in every place
Whereat laughing they went away (9)

Howe's critique here resembles Williams's; Williams points out that early immigrants from England, lacking words for animals they had never seen, still assigned the names of animals they knew well, calling the new bird a "robin" because they knew that "robin" was the name for a bird.

Part of the unraveling effect of Howe's own text occurs, not surprisingly, in and through language. She is especially effective when she puns between the world and its words, when she makes the landscape into language by echoing it (the verbal equivalent of her textual mirror). So, in a section that begins, "Bound Cupid sea washed," showing a western mythological figure bound and suffering in the wilderness, she writes: "Cries open to the words inside them / Cries hurled through the Woods" (23), where the inner (words) become one with the outer (Woods) and both scream out their pain at what must be seen as a bad "translation" of one mythology onto a new place. Then, in a section that begins again with a search, "Left home to seek Lost // Pitchfork origin," two things are made (nearly) synonymous through this sound play:

tribunal of eternal revolution
tribunal of rigorous revaluation (25).

Similar moments of transfiguration occur in her phrases, "Collision or collusion with history," where in fact both words are true; "Milestones bewitched millstones" (35); and at the end of the poem where her history begins, "Lif sails off longing for life" (38).

What Howe has done, then, is to take a historical system, that of the

Puritans, and desystematize it, in part by telling the story backwards, so that we end with Lif [Erickson] rather than beginning with him, as William Carlos Williams does. To desystematize history is to render it as myth, fiction, story, rather than assume its scienticity or truth-as-fact. This beginning has itself been altered; it is not a real origin, but one that is achieved through destruction, that re-arrives at a destructive moment created by "Stern norse terse ethical pathos" (38). Rather than recovering the Garden of Eden for its notorious couple, Howe recovers ruin—scattering—albeit in a state of nature:

> Rubble couple on pedestal
> Rubble couple Rhythm and Pedestal
>
> Room of dim portraits here there
> Wade waist deep maidsworn men
>
> Crumbled masonry windswept hickory (38)

What Howe does with the repeated word play, which here at the end involves the comical sound of "rubble couple," is to show how the deformations of language, its accidents, collide and collude with history. A rubble couple is not gendered, either, but forms the remnant of a cultural structure that takes gender as its primary sign. More importantly to Howe, what this shows is that history can be revised through language itself. This is where Howe comes closest, I suspect, to being among the visionary company of Language poets, although her puns are much more considered than are, say, those of Charles Bernstein. Through an oxymoronic principle of scatter, Howe shows how history can, in some sense, become prophecy—in countermovement to John Cotton's assertion that history is postdated prophecy. It can prophesy its own end, at the beginning. The end of "Articulation of Sound Forms in Time" is, therefore, not quite an end or a beginning, rather a beginning in the end of American myth, which is also history.

Susan Howe's work emerges from a paradoxical crossroads in thinking through the relationship between history and imaginative writing. On the one hand, in their work of the 1970s, Hayden White and Michel de Certeau presented history as writing that comes out of the same process as fiction or poetry; history is little more than the historian's imaginative reconstruction of it. The historian's authority is located not in the *truths* he or she discovers in the archive, but in his or her way of writing. Style *is* substance. On the other hand, and at the same time, literary theorists like Stephen Greenblatt and other New Historicists were searching for a way out of text-only systems of literary criticism that had installed themselves in the academy since midcentury; I'm thinking here of New Criticism and deconstruction. They found this new way in history and the authority it provided literary critics in examining texts as symptoms of larger cultural and historical issues rather than as "well-wrought urns," either intact or shattered. The authority they reached for was old-fashioned in the terms set forth by White and de Certeau, but their mode of writing criticism and history relied in great measure on the generic blurring of poetry, narrative, and history that interested these historiographers. Susan Howe's blurring of genres and authorities, her paradoxical and sometimes simultaneous deconstructions and reconstructions of history, participate in this intellectual intersection.

7

Local Vocals

Hawaiʻiʻs Pidgin Literature, Performance, and Postcoloniality

AT THE 1993 READING for Lois-Ann Yamanaka's book, *Saturday Night at the Pahala Theatre,* written almost exclusively in Hawaiian Creole English (usually called Pidgin), I sat quietly while an audience of upwards of 500 people actively and warmly participated in her reading. I had moved to Hawaiʻi from the mainland only three years before. When Yamanaka referred to details such as the "Japan pencil cases" used in school, the crowd roared. I felt puzzled. Every one of her details sparked astonishment and pleasure in her listeners; there was joy in simply naming these objects that had never found their way into poems before. The audience was participating to an extent that approaches performance theorist Richard Schechner's description of "social" drama, where spectators are performers. He opposes social drama to "aesthetic" dramas that separate audience from performer (171). In this case, I was attending an aesthetic drama and almost everyone else was participating in a social one. Never had I felt such a sense of other people's community at a poetry reading; rarely had I felt so foreign in an American place.

To write in Pidgin is to write in a language that has no standardized orthography; reading Pidgin can be difficult even for native speakers who are unaccustomed to seeing Pidgin words on the page and who sometimes remark with surprise on the spelling of words like "so-wa" (for "sore"). Linguist Suzanne Romaine writes: "Alterations to standard orthography of whatever kind are visual signals to the reader that something is significant. However, it isn't always obvious that each nonstandard spelling represents some significant phonetic feature" (541). Much of what may look like standard English in a book sounds like Pidgin only when it's read aloud by a native speaker. This is, I think, a crucial point; while the standard English reader is able easily to assimilate written Pidgin in the silence and privacy of her own reading, she cannot so easily do so when she hears Pidgin spoken by a native speaker. What we have is a "listener's block," which, as I shall show, was preceded, historically, by a "writer's block" imposed on the Pidgin writer from the outside—the dominant national culture, local schools, and the English department at the University of Hawai'i, where many of today's writers in Pidgin studied.

In their 1987 essay, "What is a Minor Literature?" Gilles Deleuze and Felix Guattari argue that in minor literatures, which they define as those created by minorities within major languages, "Language stops being representative in order to now move toward its extremities or limits." Minor writers are those who "hate all languages of masters," and who assert that "what can be said in one language cannot be said in another." Minor writers produce work that is inevitably political and which takes on collective value. Pidgin is such a nonrepresentative language, loud, extreme, and in this ironic manner, minor. For the Pidgin writer language does not stop being representative so much as it stops being "universal," a dangerous word that is too often used by thinkers like William Bennett to denote "dominant" rather than truly multicultural. The moment of strongest resistance by the Pidgin writer to the dominant language and its "major" literature comes, to my mind, when that writer performs his or her text, either in public or on tape. It is the *sound* of Pidgin, the resonance of its shared cultural references rather than its presence on the page, which is most different from standard English. It is also the sound of Pidgin that breaks a silence long enforced on Pidgin speakers. The audience's reaction to Yamanaka was not due to the fact that they were finally hearing her speak *her own* words, the operative dynamic at almost every poetry reading I've ever attended, but because they were hearing *their own* words in a language more often spoken than written: "This is the authority," writes Deleuze, "the autonomy of the stammerer, of him who has conquered the right to stammer, in opposition to the 'well-spoken' major" ("One Manifesto Less" 220). This phrase, "the autonomy of the stammerer," puts me in mind of Susan Howe's eloquent description of the "stutter" in literature, which she in turn takes from Charles Olson. Yet Yamanaka's stutter is different from Howe's, not because they aren't both steeped in culture and history, which they are, but because Yamanaka's language is, at base, a spoken, shared language, nonstandard because it has a separate syntax and vocabulary. Where Susan Howe's voice (for example) rises from the written page, Yamanaka's seems transcribed on the page, as if the page were an edited transcript of an already composed text, or the score for a musical performance. Unlike David Antin, Yamanaka does not compose in concert, yet her language emerges out of the oral tradition that his work imitates, even as he speaks a written discourse.[1] Deleuze is most interested in the ways in which minor languages transform major ones; he sees "the minoritarian as a potential, creative and created, becoming" ("One Manifesto Less" 150). While Yamanaka and other Pidgin writers will likely have that effect—her appearance on the United States of Poetry indicates the power of her words for an audience of non-Pidgin speakers—I am most interested in the ways in which the performance of Pidgin poetry, in public and on tape, has transformed Hawai'i's literature and, to some extent, its culture more generally.

There is only one poem in Yamanaka's book, *Saturday Night at the Pahala Theatre* (1993) that contains more than a short phrase of standard English, namely "Tita: On Boyfriends." What the brash Pidgin speaker, Tita, does is to shift into what might be called standard American California Valley Girl English at a strategic point in her conversation with her friend (the much berated listener in/to this series of Tita poems). The rest of the book, made up of a series of dramatic monologues by young female speakers talking about their lives, is in flat-out Pidgin. On the page, the poem is readily accessible to readers who are not native speakers of Hawaiian Creole English; Yamanaka's spelling of Pidgin words often overlaps with standard English spelling. The drama of the language switch is far clearer when Yamanaka reads the poem out loud, shifting from Pidgin to standard English and back again. The question I will pose is: why does Tita change languages? And, more importantly, what does this shift tell us about the relationship of Pidgin speakers to the dominant language and culture that so briefly makes its appearance in this poem? Finally, why is it that Yamanaka's performance of the poem is so crucial to our understanding of it—and to the very different understanding of native Pidgin speakers in Hawai'i?

The word "Tita" refers to a large woman with a loud voice, who is brash and often funny; she is a stock character in routines by such comedians as the late Rap Replinger and by Frank da Lima.[2] Titas gain their authority through their voices; Yamanaka's Tita, who is a preteen, is all voice, though she is insecure about her Japanese-American identity in a culture saturated with the signs of continental American dominance. She takes on the assumptions of the majority culture even as she cloaks them in local talk, constructing a highly ambivalent identity for herself. Tita is, above all, a performer, and her sense of herself is highly performative. As Judith Butler argues, in her discussion of performativity in *Bodies That Matter; On the Discursive Limits of "Sex"*, "the 'I' only comes into being through being called, named, interpellated, to use the Althusserian term, and this discursive constitution takes place prior to the 'I'; it is the transitive invocation of the 'I'" (225). In this poem Tita instructs her quiet (silenced) audience in the wiles needed to ensnare a boyfriend. As I hope to show soon, she thus mimics the dominant culture's silencing of Pidgin speakers. The following passage is crucial:

> Richard wen' call me around 9:05 last night.
> Nah, I talk *real* nice to him.
> Tink I talk to him the way I talk to you?
> You cannot let boys know your true self.
> Here, this how I talk.
> *Hello, Richard. How are you?*
> *Oh, I'm just fine. How's school?*
> *My classes are just greeaat.*
> *Oh, really. Uh-huh, uh-huh.*
> *Oh, you're so funny.*
> *Yes, me too, I love C and K.*
> *Kalapana? Uh-huh, uh-huh.* (41)

Tita's switch of languages is significant for many more reasons than that of explaining to her friend the way to get a date. Rather, it opens up a problem with historical, cultural, and economic ramifications to Pidgin and standard English speakers since at least the end of the last century, through Hawaiʻi's admission to statehood in 1959 (the last state admitted to the union), and on to the present moment. As a scholar and teacher of American poetry in Hawaiʻi, these are issues that I face every semester. Tita's conscious change of language as she asks her friend about school reveals her to be a savvy sociologist; the shift from Pidgin to standard is equally a shift from a "lower class" to a "higher class" language, and from what my students tell me is considered a less to a more feminine way of speaking. She is also switching from the local language to that of the "haole," or outsider. It is thus a "speech *act,*" rather than an act of unconscious speech, like that, say, of a native standard speaker who knows no Pidgin. The speaker is acting *up,* as it were. At the moment that Tita makes this move, she causes standard English—even for the standard English speaker/listener—to become "nonabsorptive," just as Pidgin is the "absorptive" speech of all the characters in Yamanaka's book, and in the milieu that she describes. Or, as the Martinican writer Edouard Glissant argues in a related context, she causes the dominant and Creole languages to seem *opaque* to each other (133). That this reversal of positions, Pidgin becoming the dominant language, standard becoming downright unstandard, is painful (if liberating) for the Pidgin writer is shown most clearly in the last poem of the book, "Name Me Is," where a girl and her older friend WillyJoe tattoo their names on each other: his on his back, hers on hers, as they literally bleed language. Here is Yamanaka's speaker's pidgin misprision of Rimbaud: "I IS. / Ain't *nobody* / tell me / otherwise" (140)—the last words of the poem and the book. "I is" is for these speakers every bit as revolutionary as Rimbaud's bit of proleptic postmodernism, "I is another." And every bit as self-estranging, in the way of so much self-knowledge.

Yamanaka's discussion of dating in "Tita: Boyfriends" is hardly egregious or unique. In a 1960 article, "Communication: A Problem of Island Youth," published in *Social Process in Hawaii,* Andrew W. Lind writes (remember that this was a year after statehood): "The widely recognized reticence of Island youth, particularly of Oriental ancestry, in speaking their minds in the presence of Haoles is in large part, so they themselves confess, a consequence of an unfounded fear that their expression may reflect a flavor of pidgin and hence of lower-class status" (48). He then quotes an unidentified "Japanese male" as saying that "Youths have hesitated to date because of the lack of social confidence. I have been asked many times as to how to act, how to ask for a date, and even as to what to do or where they should go on a date, by my friends" (48).

This young Japanese male also tells Lind that, "Oriental youths are afraid to speak up. These youths lack social ease, in that they feel that they will be laughed at every time they open their mouths. They feel that people will not accept them, and that a mistake will show their intelligence." Later, he adds that he has "seen youths actually perspire, while speaking" (48). (And which of us has not?) Stephen Sumida, whose *And the View from the Shore: Literary Traditions of Hawai'i* (1991) was the first important study of Hawai'i literature, writes: "Hawaii's local people have been stereotyped as being silent or quiet, not merely reticent but deficient in verbal skills and therefore incapable of creating literature of any merit, much less a literary tradition" (227). In 1994 Suzanne Romaine quotes a writer who reports that her university writing teacher told her to write in her Pidgin voice (an unusual event, mind you). Her response: "I cannot do it because I will be showing my ignorance to the whole class. I don't want them to think of me as stupid because of the way we talk everyone thought we were stupid . . . And then what happened is I found this kind of artistic freedom because I saw the history" (544).

Some historical background, of necessity streamlined and simplified. Pidgin developed as a "language of command" (Lind 44) that allowed lunas, or foremen, on the sugar and pineapple plantations of Hawai'i around the turn of the last century, to give orders to their workers. Plantations, which were developed in the middle of the nineteenth century and owned by "mainland haoles," brought foreign labor to work the fields, much of it from Asian countries: Japan, China, Korea, and the Philippines. The language that developed was a mix of Hawaiian, English, and the workers' native languages; these days, the vocabulary is recognizable as English, but the sentence structure more resembles that of the Hawaiian language. This morning a woman said to me: "cold the weather, ya?" The multiculturalism of Hawai'i's society, as well as its language, thus originated as part of a strategy of "divide and conquer" on the part of plantation owners. According to historian Ronald Takaki, "Though they imported workers as supplies, planters were conscious of the nationalities of their laborers. The employers were systematically developing an ethnically diverse labor force in order to create division among their workers and reinforce management control" (*A Different Mirror* 252). The extent to which the plantation system was stratified according to race and power structures is made sadly but comically clear by Milton Murayama in his novel, *All I Asking for Is My Body,* which was written in the late 1950s and published in the 1970s (a telling gap). The manager's house in the novel was located at the top of the hill, the Portuguese and Japanese lunas lived slightly below the managers, and below them were the run-down houses of Filipinos. "Shit too was organized according to the plantation pyramid," the narrator comments, as those at the bottom of the pyramid lived closer to the sewage ditches than those at the top.

Shit may not be so well organized in schools as it was on the plantations, but the late linguist, Charlene Sato, writes that with the demise of the plantation system in Hawai'i, "the locus of language contact and change . . . has moved from the plantation to the schoolyard" ("Linguistic Inequality in Hawaii" [LIH] 27). In 1924 an English standard school system was installed; children attended either a standard school or a nonstandard one. "Paradoxically," Sato writes, "the English Standard schools played a crucial role in the development of Hawaiian Creole English, simply because they helped maintain the distance between HCE speakers and English speakers for another twenty years" (LIH 18). The child, Lei, in Marie Hara's short story, "Fourth Grade Ukus," fails to get into Lincoln English Standard School (ironic name, that, since Abraham Lincoln is an American emblem of equity), because she pronounces "the volcano" "Da BO-LO-CA-NO" (48). Ukus, or lice, which stigmatize the student who has them, are also metaphorically words, Pidgin words.

A scene of instruction from Yamanaka's novel, *Wild Meat and the Bully Burgers* (1996): Mr. Harvey, the English teacher, "says for the fiftieth time [is this number 50 significant, I wonder, since Hawai'i was the 50th state?] this year: "*No one will want to give you a job. You sound uneducated. You will be looked down upon. You're speaking a low-class form of good Standard English. Continue, and you'll go nowhere in life . . .* Speak Standard English. DO NOT speak pidgin. You will only be hurting yourselves'" (9).

Public expressions mirror private ones; the father in Yamanaka's novel tells his daughter, shifting registers as he does: "'And you, you wanna be this, you wanna be that, you better learn how for talk like one haole like me.' 'Yes, sir, I would really appreciate this job. What a spell of nice weather we're having here. Oh yes, sir, I am a hardworking individual . . . Yes, sir, uh-huh, I am quite capable of speaking the haole vernacular'" (148). These are fictionalized examples of what might be termed a Pidgin speaker's primal scene, that of being silenced by a standard English speaker and his ideology, invariably based on economics (as was, ironically enough, the very creation of Pidgin). Many not so fictional characters have spouted the same line, however; in 1960, for example, Elizabeth Carr wrote, in *Social Process in Hawaii*: "This group [of Pidgin speakers] rightly deserves our concern, pedagogically, for, with the changing face of the landscape under statehood [in 1959] . . . these dialect-speaking citizens will find jobs to their liking increasingly hard to obtain and hold" (57). Seventeen years later, during one of the periodic and predictable language battles in Hawai'i, one woman wrote to the editor of the *Honolulu Advertiser:* "Pidgin English is as useless as weeds in the flower garden. Speaking English well is an essential part of finding a good job for any kids and making it in the future." Hawai'i is hardly the only place where this ideology is spelled out so neatly. Edouard Glissant, writing about another kind of plantation system in the Caribbean, which engendered another Creole, argues that, "According to traditional textbooks [and note that these are *books*] creole is a patois that is incapable of abstract thought and therefore unable to convey 'knowledge'" (182). But Glissant quarrels with the kind of knowledge represented by this argument: "We should state that, taken in this sense . . . abstraction is a presumption of Western thought, a presumption based on technological expertise and the means of dominating nature" (182).

Diane Kahanu has a short poem in Chock and Lum's *Best of Bamboo Ridge* that is quicker to the point, called "Ho. Just Cause I Speak Pidgin No Mean I Dumb" (43).

Along with the repressive scene of instruction, there is also a revenge narrative in Pidgin literature. In the 1981 Hawai'i issue of *Mana,* a journal published by the South Pacific Creative Arts Society, Leialoha Apo Perkins's "Manifesto for Pidgin English" tells the story of an English composition class taught by a Mr. Holmes, who "treat[s] a paper with a fury that looked like a literary orgasm" (5) and who insists on "correct usage" (8) of English. We all know what that means. He meets his match, however, in a Pidgin-speaking student from the Big Island town of Miloli'i, which is contrasted to the "important" cities where Mr. Holmes has taught previously. When Holmes (whose name is an ironic pun on "home," I suspect) challenges this student's essay, the student—for once—talks back. What the student asserts is that he knows *more* than Mr. Holmes, by virtue of his having been forced to learn about a history that has nothing to do with him. "Dass w'at I mean. Dass yo' history, *man,* not mine. So I know moah, an' you less; but all da time, you tellin' me I know not'in' when w'at you mean iss I no can never know w'at you know because yo' stuff is all yo' own an' you no can learn mine—mine no count for you, but yo's have to count fo' me. Dass bull, Mistah Holmes. Dass real bull" (11). Among themselves, once the smoke has cleared, the local students agree that this was their best composition class ever (12).

When Lois-Ann Yamanaka came to my class on island poets from the Caribbean and Hawai'i a few years ago, she spoke at length about instructors she'd had at the University of Hawai'i from the continent who told her not to write in Pidgin. One Distinguished Visiting Writer, for example, had told her that his English was better than hers. She was angry at these outsiders who told her how to write "well"; she was also angry when she told an interviewer on National Public Radio that James Michener's novel, *Hawaii*, portrayed Asians as "Asiatic beasts." The week after Yamanaka visited my class I noticed that the atmosphere was more highly charged than usual, and it had been charged almost from day one. After a moment of confusion, I realized that *I* was "the haole instructor." Because I perceived then—and at other times—that my voice was suspect, I discovered that the best way to run the class was to set up discussions that would run largely without my direct input. Silencing myself became my mechanism of defense against the strong emotions that circulated that semester. From that point forward, I better understood the dynamics of a sometimes angry silence.

But thirty years ago, the *lack* of a literature in Pidgin seemed a valid argument against the language. In his 1960 article in *Social Process in Hawaii*, Andrew Lind asserts that Pidgin's "limited vocabulary and modes of expression, as well as the virtual lack of any literature, give to this language a restricted sphere of usefulness" (45). A couple of sentences further on he ascribes the following characteristics to Pidgin speakers: "Servility, illiteracy, and slovenliness are of its essence and Hawaii's claims to maturity appear to be controverted by its widespread use." Going back a few decades, Lind's language of maturity finds its echo in John Reinecke's important study of Pidgin, written in the 1930s and republished by the University of Hawaii Press in 1969: "In some places the local dialect, under the influence of past or present nationalist or regionalist traditions, has come to be a cherished semi-literary form of speech to be used beside the standard speech." Its use in literature is unlikely, however, writes Reinecke, because "the local dialect wholly lacks prestige. Its only appearance has been in farce such as 'Confessions of Joe Manuel of the Raddio Patrol,' which appeared in the Saturday editions of the *Honolulu Star-Bulletin* between 1932 and 1933 . . . there will be no reason to use the dialect in writing, except for local color in fiction, in advertising . . . in foolery" (188–89).

"If there is no such thing as a Hawaii writer," asks the poet Eric Chock, "how can you teach a Hawaii kid to write?" (*Best* 8).

More recently Chock has said: "We in Hawaii are expected to believe that we are subordinate to the mainland. At best we are expected to believe that we are really no different here and can even be *like* the mainland if we try hard enough. We are asked to reject the feeling that Hawaii is special. And when we become numbed and lose the feeling, it then becomes possible to accept mainland history and mainland culture as our own" (quoted in Romaine 534). His poem, "Tutu on da Curb," is an elegy for island culture, disappearing like a traditional Hawaiian woman behind a cloud of smoke from a passing bus: "She squint and wiggle her nose / at da heat / and da thick stink fumes / da bus driver just futted all over her. / You can see her shrivel up / and shrink little bit more. / Bum bye, she going disappear / from da curb / foreva" (*Last Days Here* 63). In "War of Words: Oral Poetry, Writing, and Tape Cassettes in Somalia," Alexander Stille writes of the Somali poet Hadrawi that "it would be easy to dismiss Hadrawi's stance as romantic, Luddite nostalgia, [except that] he is registering an epochal change in Somali life: the disappearance of the world in which he grew up" (204). While Somalia, as Stille describes it, in many ways does not resemble Hawai'i, both Somali poets and poets like Eric Chock use contemporary technology, the tape recorder in particular, to get the news out about the quick rate of change in their societies. This is not to say that Pidgin is political in the sense Loretta Collins describes it in Jamaica during the Manley years, when she writes: "In a decolonized situation, and especially in the Caribbean, where the official languages of the colonizing nation have been creatively 'versioned' by creole speakers, natural sounds, the sounds of cultural resistance, and the disruption of normative sounds through sound *mediats* (technological manipulations) articulate a desire for self-determination" (*Sound States* 170). For one thing, Hawai'i is not a "decolonized situation"; Pidgin remains a subculture, rather than a true alternative to the dominant culture. The renaissance of the Hawaiian language and culture in Hawai'i poses more of a threat to the dominant culture, when it is linked—as it often is—with claims to sovereignty over native Hawaiian lands.[3]

In 1993 Darrell Lum, one of Hawai'i's most popular fiction writers in

Pidgin, told an interviewer: "We continue to deny the value of our language. Local literature is about validating a people. When you acknowledge a language, you acknowledge a people" (Romaine 533). Marie Hara, Arnold Hiura, and Stephen Sumida organized the Talk Story conference in 1978; it, along with the founding of Bamboo Ridge Press, launched a renaissance in local Asian-American writing. According to Chock and Marie Hara, the talk story tradition began when plantation workers gathered in the fields for meals and talked about political, social, and cultural issues. People talking story squatted on their haunches, low to the ground, and spoke softly, without moving, so that the authorities couldn't see them. The founding of unions early in the century, which brought together workers from different nationalities and ethnic backgrounds, came out of such moments of talking story—in Pidgin. Chock thinks that Hawai'i's local literature is in "the high period of the talk story form," a form that is necessarily oral in its origins. He himself didn't think of writing poems in Pidgin until he began talking (and I think it important that it's *talking*) about writing not with professors at the University of Hawai'i, where he was a masters student in the late 1970s, but with friends in the Talk Story group and the Bamboo Ridge Study Group, which was founded in the early 1980s.

The young writer R. Zamora Linmark organized the reading for his novel, *Rolling the R's,* as a performance—complete with drag queens and other costumed characters—because he wanted to "pay homage" to the voices he grew up with. As my colleague Craig Howes noted at a Local Literature Conference in 1994, most people first encounter local literature through performances, whether of Darrell Lum's plays or dramatized short stories, the popular rendering of fairy tales into Pidgin by Lisa Matsumoto (including *Once Upon One Nodda Time,* a translation of Shakespeare's *Twelfth Night* and the recent *Compleat Works of Wllm Shkspr.*) The creation of Hawai'i's literature in Pidgin is, above all, a collective effort.

"We say that a national literature emerges when a community whose collective existence is called into question tries to put together the reasons for its existence" (104) writes Glissant, who also (unfortunately) comments that "Martinique is not a Polynesian island. This is, however, the belief of so many people who, given its reputation, would love to go there for pleasure" (1). He claims that the movement from orality to literature is coming full circle, that Creoles will develop an *oraliture,* as

Haitian writers call it. Where better to represent this than in performance or on tape, in a "secondary orality" (Walter J. Ong's phrase) that is truer to the oral discourse of Pidgin than are words on a page?

Edward Kamau Brathwaite famously advocates a "nation language," or one that leaves behind the pentameter for a rhythm closer to that actually used by Caribbean people. It is also a public language: "Reading is an isolated, individualistic expression. The oral tradition on the other hand demands not only the griot but the audience to complete the community: the noise and sounds that the maker makes are responded to by the audience and are returned to him" (312).

But, when asked if he composes differently in Pidgin than he does in standard English, Darrell Lum said that no, when he is composing a story, he thinks of Pidgin as a written language.

Lois-Ann Yamanaka insisted on recording her tape twice. The first time, according to Rodney Morales, who was technical director for the recording, she said it didn't go well because she didn't move her hands. "The oral . . . is inseparable from the movement of the body . . . Utterance depends on posture, and perhaps is limited by it," writes Glissant (122).

The oral poet, according to Paul Zumthor, "unifies" his or her community. This is easy to see in work by Darrell Lum or Eric Chock, work that evokes a community united by values like family and Asian traditions carried on in the new world. Strange then that Yamanaka's construction of unity comes out of poems so occupied with violence; it is as if community is being formed around the sounds of community falling apart. Yamanaka's (and Linmark's) characters are people under siege, threatened by domestic violence, by self-hatred, by mainstream American pop culture.

"Late in the summer of 1987," writes Charlene Sato in her article "Sociolinguistic Variation and Language Attitudes in Hawaii" in 1991, "Hawaii's Board of Education (BOE) formulated a policy on 'Standard English and Oral Communication,' a preliminary version of which mandated that 'Standard English [would] be the mode of oral communication for students and staff in the classroom setting and all other school related settings except when the objectives cover[ed] native Hawaiian or foreign language instruction and practice'" (653). Opposition to the policy was, for once, loud, and the policy was not passed. But Pidgin is still censored, in practice if not by law. Yamanaka has been asked to give schools lists of the poems she wants to read to students; sometimes she's asked not to perform certain poems. I would argue that such censorship has at least as much to do with the poems' being in Pidgin as it does with their containing four-letter words. The poems are profane, but Yamanaka has taken this language from the world the students know, not from outside of it; after all, she used to be an intermediate school teacher. The poems' speakers are often racist, but the author distances herself from them in her poems, or so I would argue. Yamanaka's characters use violent language to talk about violence: in her poem "Parts," which begins with a flourish of language so intense and seemingly innocuous that members of the audience start laughing (I've witnessed this at two public readings and in the classroom, when I've played the tape), a mother yells at her child:

What I told you
about digging your nose?
Who taught you that?
You going get
two slaps
I ever see you
doing that
in public again.
Good for you
your nose bleed
and I hope you get
so-wa stomach too
for eating that shit. (68)

The laughing always stops suddenly in the middle of the poem, as audience members realize that they are laughing at child abuse. The effect, again, is much greater when Yamanaka reads to a large audience than when her work is read off of the page. Walter Ong asserts that "violence in oral art forms is also connected with the structure of orality itself. When all verbal communication must be by direct word of mouth, involved in the give-and-take dynamics of sound, interpersonal relations are kept high—both attractions and, even more, antagonisms" (45). Glissant certainly helps us again in this instance: "the traditional Creole text, folktale or song is striking in the graphic nature of its images" (125).

More specifically, according to Rob Wilson, "Yamanaka's local Japanese identity is hardly one of purity or ethnic wholeness, but one of self-division, self-hatred even, which includes a longing to be othered into haole (white) pop cultural styles" ("Bloody Mary" 146). To say this out loud, however, brings shame upon the community at large. And it must be said out loud in Pidgin. As Darrell Lum, who has a doctorate in education, remarks, educators still intensely resist Pidgin.

Many of Yamanaka's poems are *about* acts of censorship within a Pidgin-speaking community against its own language practices, including the potent use of profanity. In "Lickens" we hear:

Ho boy, one time my small sista wen' say *fut*
which we no could say 'cause the word
us had for use was *poot*
and she got lickens with the green brush
which was mo so-wa than the fly swatter
but both was less so-wa than the iron hanger. (87)

In the next poem in the book, "Dead Dogs RIP," the family's dog, Wiki, participates in the censorship:

Wiki wen' bite my friend Claude
on his ass 'cause he said fuck
in our house. My sista told him
no say f-word around Wiki
but Claude start screaming *fuckfuckfuck*
in my sista's face for fun
and Wiki wen' rush his ass, for real.
But now Wiki dead. (88)

Glissant comments on standard French bumper stickers in Martinique that are creolized by adding or subtracting letters. In Hawai'i you see bumper stickers that read: "no blame me: I voted for Bu." Bu (full moniker, Bula'ia), who sports a chaotic yarn wig and blacked out front tooth, ran for governor in the 1994 election as a protest candidate, although he didn't appear on the ballot. (My former and then-78 year old landlord voted for him.) He was in later years seen on TV advertising for Pacific Nissan, which shows that there can be a fine line indeed between language as protest and language as advertising tool. The connection between Pidgin and humor (often of the antiestablishmentarian kind, but also in Bu's case of the advertising kind) is doubtless older than Bu or even Rap Replinger, who became a local hero in the 1970s, but few are as acute at social commentary as was Replinger. In his "Room Service" skit, Replinger does the voices of a tourist asking for his meal and of the Tita who rather purposefully misunderstands, speaking in Pidgin and substituting local food for the hamburger that he wants. As Schechner argues, "Western thinkers have too often split ritual from entertainment[,]privileging ritual over entertainment" (155). If Hawai'i's readings and tapes represent a kind of communal ritual of self-affirmation, they do so often through sheer laughter, even when that laughter turns quickly to pain.

Glissant writes, in his "Cross-Cultural Poetics": "One could imagine— this is, moreover, a movement that is emerging almost everywhere—a kind of revenge by oral languages over written ones, in the context of a global civilization of the nonwritten. Writing seems linked to the transcendental notion of the individual, which today is threatened by and giving way to a cross-cultural process" (126). Is Hawai'i's literature on tape an "oraliture," as Glissant terms the return of the oral to literature? Are Hawai'i's literary artists more like griots than like writers? Yes and no. Certainly the act of writing in Pidgin is an assertion of a kind of "nation language," albeit in a place where most people speak the standard national language, American English. Reading that writing onto a tape recovers the sense of Pidgin as a spoken language, though at quite some remove. This is oral language that has been written and then reread to an audience that is either actual (at a reading) or abstract (if the listener is alone) or a bit of both (as in classroom use of the tapes). To record a speaking voice is to fix it as firmly in time as it is to transcribe that voice in writing. Yet this paradox, this image of voice (like the performance poet David Antin's "image of thinking"), is strikingly appropriate. For Pidgin is, among many other things, a language of resistance, of anger (in Yamanaka's case), of active nostalgia (in Chock's case), a language that resists the absorptive talons of a dominant language and culture. As Glissant writes: "the role of Creole in the world of the [Caribbean] plantations was that of defiance" (127). It is at once a language of colonialism and postcoloniality, a language by which plantation workers were branded by plantation owners and lunas, and at the same time the language through which these workers resisted the world outside of their "talk story" culture. At a time when American culture is only getting stronger in Hawai'i as it enters through radio and television waves, cable, and the new outlet malls that are springing up all over the island of Oahu, these taped voices alert their listeners to the dangers—and the curious pleasures—of assimilation.

If Chock's and Yamanaka's poems are written in something like a "nation language" (though they lack any vision of a political "nation" separate from the United States), the poems themselves are hardly pure instances of talk story unmediated by literary notions disseminated by members of the dominant culture. For these are carefully crafted workshop poems; for example, Chock bases his poems on images, his use of images on T. S. Eliot's notion of the "objective correlative," and he keys his use of Pidgin to the particular image at hand. Yamanaka creates ironic written distances between herself and her narrators, playing Mark Twain to Tita's Huck, foreshadows images and ideas, brings the poems' elements to neat (en)closures. They are not just the poets of Talk Story; they are also poets who've studied with mainland writers teaching at the University of Hawai'i-Mānoa. These twin influences are responsible for hybrid works, at once radical and conservative in the context of the Talk Story culture and in that of the university culture.

Work in Pidgin, therefore, is almost inevitably in dialogue with the language and ideology of the dominant culture. In "Tita: User," Tita argues that she hasn't stolen her friend's tapes:

Eh—no act. I no mo your Donny Osmond 8-track.
I hate Down by the Lazy Riva.
And I no mo your Captain and Tenille tape either,
so get off it. I so piss off right now
I like buss all the tapes
I *did* borrow from you. (35)

She then distinguishes, with the wit and wisdom of Huckleberry Finn, between "stealing" and "borrowing":

No get *wise*. No ac-cuse.
'Cause when you ac-cuse,
you *act* like I *use*,
and I no use, I borrow. (35)

In any meeting of dominant and nondominant cultures the question of "using" and "borrowing" is crucial; the characters in Yamanaka's world "borrow" American pop culture and standard American English even as they are "used" by it. Their modes of resistance are often seen as self-destructive; as we have heard, the very act of speaking Pidgin is still considered by many to be self-destructive in the face of a national job market and a school system that reflects—and enacts—mainland values. And yet there are now countertapes: contemporary Titas have not only the current avatars of Captain and Tenille and Percy Faith to borrow or use, but also the tapes of Lois-Ann Yamanaka, Eric Chock, and others. Now that there are Hawai'i writers and performers, to return to Chock's point, Hawai'i's children are becoming writers.

With the publication in 1996 of Lois-Ann Yamanaka's first novel, *Wild Meat and the Bully Burgers,* on the continental United States by Farrar, Straus & Giroux, a major New York publishing house, Hawai'i's local literature entered the mainstream, something that seemed impossible merely a decade ago. According to the poet Eric Chock, another major New York house told Darrell Lum about a decade before that his work was "too provincial." Signs of a mainland audience do predate the 1996 novel, however. Yamanaka's *Saturday Night at the Pahala Theatre* was the first book published by Honolulu's Bamboo Ridge Press (which was founded in 1978) that had blurbs on the back cover; none of these blurbs is by a local writer. They assert, by turns, that the poems are "universal" and that they "transcend place" (Faye Kicknosway); that Yamanaka "refuels the English language" (Jessica Hagedorn); that her writing is "raw and elegant" (Kimiko Hahn). Howard Junker, editor of the California based journal *ZYZZYVA,* goes so far as to say that "Lois-Ann Yamanaka speaks a language we all know in our heart of hearts, but never see on the page." *Do* we all know this language? (Have we read the new *Pidgin Grammar* by Kent Sakoda and Jeff Siegel, published in 2003?) If we do, have we then denuded language of its immediate value as a carrier of culture (as Ngugi wa Thiong'o would insist) and supplanted it with a metaphorical meaning that erases that function? How many of us can speak Pidgin? How many of us understand references like "Japan pencil cases" and "li hing mui"? The tapes that Bamboo Ridge Press has made of its authors since 1990 embody this paradox, that local literature is at once resistant to the dominant culture and is being rapidly assimilated into the multicultural lit biz. According to Darrell Lum, one of the founding editors of Bamboo Ridge, the audience for the tapes originally was thought to consist of mainland teachers who wanted to teach the texts in their classrooms but couldn't read the literature out loud. But the reception by local listeners is, as you may imagine, quite different. Now, according to Eric Chock, another of Bamboo Ridge's founding editors, the tapes sell mainly in Hawai'i, and the best-selling tapes are those by Lum and Yamanaka, namely those with the most Pidgin on them. For Hawai'i listeners the tapes reinforce a sense of community centered around the person of the writer/reader. They assert the importance of community (a central tenet of Lum's and Chock's definitions of "local") over that of individualism (or the eminently written American tradition of Ralph Waldo Emerson and Henry David Thoreau). But the fact that the tapes carry voices that are reading texts—even if those texts are written in a language that is almost always spoken—suggests that Hawai'i's literature is created out of a strategic reconstruction of the oral out of the written. Speakers of standard English, and most members of the University of Hawai'i English department, including myself, do not speak Yamanaka's language; I think that is precisely one of her points in writing Pidgin. That I have been speaking about—if not for—her, is ironic, and in some manner troubling to me. And yet, if I do not speak Yamanaka's language, I certainly recognize its importance. It is out of a double sense of that recognition and that lack of it that I have talked out this essay.

POSTTALK

What follows is added later, and in response to arguments that arose about Yamanaka's work in the late 1990s, after my essay was first written. The central argument, over whether or not Yamanaka's work is racist toward Filipinos, in some ways replicates an old argument over the role and power of literature between thinkers like Plato and Laura Riding and ironists like Richard Rorty and T. S. Eliot. If literature is to be taken as a vehicle for social practice, Yamanaka's work can, indeed, be troubling. If literature is considered a site for the *contestation* of ideas about social conditions, then Yamanaka's work can be used productively to talk about issues in contemporary Hawai'i. I begin with a quotation from a Filipina-American writer in Hawai'i, Darlene Rodrigues, who argues that Yamanaka's work is racist. Substitute "poetry" for "fiction" and the meaning still holds: "There's fiction, and then there's meaning. We cannot say that fiction holds no meaning in the world. There's meaning behind what we write, and there's meaning in the way people read what we write" (201).

Rodrigues is responding to Yamanaka's novel, *Blu's Hanging,* which caused a firestorm in the literary community here for its representation of a Filipino man as a sexual predator (a representation that many argue fits all too neatly into ethnic stereotypes that originated on the plantation in the nineteenth century). For Rodrigues (as indeed for Yamanaka when she performs her work out loud), reading is an activity that involves the body; the body grows out of history: "But the body remembers historical oppression. It's my mother's and father's pain passed down to me, but even beyond that, it is four hundred years of Spanish colonization and one hundred years of continuing American imperialism in the Philippines" (201).[4]

Thus, Yamanaka's writing, which I have claimed is postcolonial in its breaking of silences, is seen by Rodrigues and other writers as participating fully in the colonial regime that has silenced minority voices for so long. Those who defend Yamanaka often argue against censorship in literature; while there are compelling arguments in Yamanaka's favor, this is not one of them, as no one has the power to censor her work. They can only refuse to read it, or mount public campaigns to point out its weaknesses.

As Candace Fujikane notes in her essay "Sweeping Racism under the Rug of 'Censorship,'" the 1998 controversy over *Blu's Hanging,* which led to Yamanaka's having an award taken back by the AAAS, was not new to this novel. Fujikane argues that the first poem in Yamanaka's *Saturday Night at the Pahala,* namely "Kala Gave Me Anykine Advice Especially About Filipinos When I Moved to Pahala," contains the same stereotyping of Filipino men. Much of what is at stake in this poem rests on the reader's strategy, his or her interpretation of the poem. A New Critical reading of the poem, informed by knowledge of local culture, sees it as an ironic dramatic monologue; we are not meant to trust Kala's advice, in other words. Kala is simply too superstitious, too self-contradictory, too much a young girl, to be believed.

Yet Fujikane does not recognize poetry as the sole provenance of the academy; she is also concerned with readers who do not have access to readings that rely on irony, or readers for whom irony may be considered a cop-out. (Irony is much more a New York than a Honolulu trope, as well.) One of the subtitles to her essay condenses her argument effectively: "*Saturday Night at the Pahala Theatre* and the Use of Literary Criticism against Communities beyond the Academy." In this section of her essay, she argues that "Literary criticism has proven to be an effective means by which minority groups critique and challenge operations of power, but in its most established and familiar forms, it has been historically deployed against oppressed groups to sustain bourgeois, patriarchal, racist or colonial systems by privileging dominant world views" (165–66). Thus *readers* are not synonymous with *critics,* nor are they necessarily in tune with the *poet,* whose work has been considered so important to the development of Hawai'i's literature. Later in her essay, she notes that readers with power in the community (notably local white, Chinese, and Japanese readers), argue that Filipino readers simply "do not understand" the work. "The point is precisely that while these stereotypes are 'nonsensical' to privileged readers who assume that these images have no power, local Filipinos were testifying to the ways that these stereotypes continue to exert a material force on their lives" (168).

Admittedly, I am one of those readers for whom the poem performs an act of irony, acts within the very movement against racism that Fujikane claims "Anykine Advice" participates in. Within the framework of the book I am composing, however, I appreciate the dangerous dynamic of silencing she points to, even as I hearken to difficulty, both within the text and for the reader. The danger in Fujikane's argument, it seems to me, is that it posits the necessity of a literature that dispenses with rhetoric—in its own way, it resembles Riding's notion that poetry should be stripped of its "clothing." As a moral rather than a literary argument, it resembles the Puritan assertion that Truth must be opposed to Profession. Among Fujikane's arguments is one that takes on professionalism as a site where racism is perpetuated. It's perhaps no accident, then, that the issue came to a crisis over the awarding of a prize, certainly one way in which the academy professionalizes writing, where writers "get a name" in whatever communities in which they hope to sell their work. What I find most persuasive about Fujikane's argument is that it gives responsibility to the professional critic to pay heed to silences, both inside the text and inside their own classrooms, as well as to essays about work like Yamanaka's. Where Susan Howe calls the editor to account for his rendering of women's voices in Puritan texts, Fujikane calls the non-Filipino critic to account for his or her failure to read through the text and back out into the world where symbolism is all too real for many groups of people. She takes us out of the text, in a way that strikes me as a valuable counter to Riding's insistence on plunging us into it. At the same time, my hope is that such strong criticism, which in some ways treats fictional texts as if they more resembled sociological ones (lacking unreliable narrators and other outs fiction lets in), does not stifle—as indeed it has not seemed to—voices of new writers who need to risk the disapproval of their critics, as we've seen in the case of John Ashbery and Harold Bloom.

Of Time and Charles Bernstein's Lines

A Poetics of Fashion Statements

The first purpose of Clothes, as our Professor imagines, was not warmth or decency, but ornament.
　　　　　　　　—Thomas Carlyle, *Sartor Resartus*

Fashion is the supreme expression of that contemporary spirit. It changes constantly and remains necessarily incomplete; it is transitory, mobile, and fragmentary.
　　　　　　　　—Ulrich Lehmann, *Tigersprung: Fashion in Modernity*

See
the idea of form
is to fit tight
(Frank O'Hara said that)
& a sonnet seems like one
of those turtlenecks that if it's
a good color
& the shape hugs
then it becomes
one.
—Bernstein, "Sonnet" (*Islets/Irritations*)

The clothier makes the person (there's
a change in the sweater, a change
in the smock, from now on
they'll be a change in *you*).
　　—Bernstein, "Surface Reflectance"

My father pushed a
line of ladies' dresses—not down the street
in a pushcart but upstairs in a fact'ry

office. My mother was more concerned
with her hemline.
   —Bernstein, "Of Time and the Line"

[W]ord processor ideology reinforces the idealization of "clean
copy"—a defleshed, bureaucratic and interchangeable writing.
        —Bernstein, "Blood on the Cutting Room Floor"

To UNDERSTAND THE WORK of Charles Bernstein, one needs to think
hard about fashion, in clothing and in print(s). For Bernstein, unlike his
self-proclaimed precursor, Laura (Riding) Jackson, even nakedness is
disguise, and power is at once naked and hidden by the audience's desire,
if not under actual or metaphorical cloth.[1] The poet, quite simply and
comically, can never take off his clothes:

> Should I choose to take my tie off, the one with the embossed seals
> that is so carefully knotted over my Adam's apple, I do not fall into
> a state of undress. I remain clothed, in some fashion or other, until
> I am without clothes and indeed then my skin still encloses me,
> until I disappear. (The real moral of "The Emperor's New Clothes"
> is that power is always naked and by force of that concealed by the
> modesty of a people who cannot bear to look at the spectacle with-
> out mediation: the Emperor is clothed, that is, by the self-protective
> squeamishness of the collective subconscious.[)] (*Content's Dream*
> [CD] 306–7)

What the poet can do, and what Bernstein has done throughout his
nearly thirty-year career, is to critique fashions of writing that attempt
to conceal their status *as* fashion. His strongest critiques have been offered against what he calls "official verse culture" (represented by the
kind of work published in *The New Yorker* and *American Poetry Review*)
and the "frame lock" (we might rephrase that "frame block") that distinguishes (or fails to distinguish) writing in the profession of literary
criticism. The "official" in "official verse culture" comes about because
"it denies the ideological nature of its practice while maintaining hegemony in terms of major media exposure and cultural legitimation and

funding" (personal communication). And in his long essay-poem, a kind of poetics of what I've termed "reader's block," "Artifice of Absorption," he writes:

> Moreover, official verse culture
> of the last 25 years has engaged in militant . . .
> campaigns to "restrict the subversive,
> independent-of-things nature of the language"
> in the name of the common voice, clarity, sincerity,
> or directness of the poem, & specifically
> in the highly problematic equating, as in
> the passage from Wesling, of the "irrational"
> and the "artificial". (*A Poetics* [*AP*] 46)

Elsewhere he defines "frame lock" (in a poem by that title) "as an insistence on a univocal surface, minimal shifts of mood either within paragraphs or between paragraphs, exclusion of extraneous or contradictory material, and tone restricted to the narrow affective envelope of sobriety, neutrality, objectivity, authoritativeness, or deanimated abstraction" (*My Way* [*MW*] 92). The problem with both forms of writers' "lock," as we shall see, is that for Bernstein there can be no separation between form, style, and content; to write in a conventional style or form is to be conventional in one's thinking. In "Artifice of Absorption," he asserts that "Content never equals meaning" (*AP* 10); meaning cannot be located outside the purview of the language of the poem; "meaning" is not conveyed through language. Language is, in and of itself, highly artificial for Bernstein—not natural, as the post-Romantic confessional school claims it is; he asserts that their "comfortably furnished landscapes and confessed selves [are] often found in such venues as *The New Yorker*" (*CD* 157). Or, as Jed Rasula puts it: "Meanwhile poets, patiently laboring under a vast cultural misconception, imagine that authenticity is conflatable with subjectivity, not realizing that subjectivity is simply the most acutely engineered of all our technologies—voice-activated, setting in motion a replay of cultural 'memories' which are generic and thus belong to nobody" (49–50). Bernstein seeks "an alternative to the drab conformist fashion-minded thinking that blights our mental landscape full as much as the nineteenth-century mills poxed the English countryside" (*AP* 118).

In an essay that he might have titled "Tradition and the Individual Lack of Talent," Bernstein argues against the tradition of "plain speech" as one that limits the writer: "Rather it seems to me that, as a mode, contemporary expository writing edges close to being merely a style of decorous thinking, rigidified and formalized to a point severed from its historical relation to method in Descartes and Bacon" ("Writing and Method," *CD* 221). In much the same way that industrialization brought the standardization of goods, including clothing, writing has been standardized. Where writing becomes standard, Bernstein's argument goes, thinking itself atrophies. More recently, Bernstein has compared the obligatory styles of "dress and decorum" sported by job candidates at the MLA to the dissertation style that "[is] the bogeyman of frame lock" ("Frame" 92). As Bernstein argues punningly in "Writing and Method," "The contemporary expository mode was adopted because it effectively did the business of the society's vested interests" (224). Style, then, is a façade that becomes content—a content intended to sell. The product to be bought, if not consumed, is either the candidate at her MLA job interview (how well I remember my "power suit"), or the successful candidate marketing her dissertation as a book. In both cases, as anyone who has served on a hiring committee can attest, the style of writing and the writer's methodology are as important as content and often, in fact, dictate the content. Richard Ohmann made very similar judgments of the teaching of Freshman Composition in the early 1970s, when he wrote, "But of course freshman English does teach the style, broadly defined, of the managerial and professional classes. Style of thinking, style of work, style of planning and organizing, style of language" (167). Writing thus loses any revolutionary force it might potentially have and becomes the instrument of the discipline (in its various senses) that perpetuates, and is perpetuated by, a status quo.

In "Surface Reflectance," a long quasi-meditative poem in *The Sophist* [*TS*], Bernstein reflects on his father's business, without specifying which Mr. Bernstein he's describing.[2] The elder Bernstein worked as a dress manufacturer for Smartcraft Corporation, which sold imitations of designer dresses in the fifties. His business went belly-up in the early sixties, but rebounded later. Bernstein's father lived according to proverbial phrases, which reflected American wisdoms; in "Charles Bernstein: A Dossier," the son reports: "my father's concerns were centered foursquarely on success, and too often, and very painfully for him, failure in business. As he put it, 'One can achieve success and happiness if the right priorities are valued'" (Bové 24). Charles Bernstein, whose relationship with his father was apparently (so to speak) ambivalent, finds himself performing the same kind of work as his father, though within a different frame, and he hopes without the lock. He presents himself as a salesman for poetry: "I always say I am a professor of poetry, I profess poetry; think of me as a snake-oil salesman, a confidence man: I don't want to test your accumulated knowledge; I want to convince you of the value of poetry as a method, as a way of writing, as a form of vision" (Bové 63). Earlier in the interview he had emphasized the conjunctions of poetry and business:

> One day I woke up and found myself metamorphosed into a tiny businessman. All that I have done since, political and poetic, has changed this not at all. For poetry, after all, is the ultimate small business, requiring a careful keeping of accounts to stay afloat. . . . That is to say, I have wanted to bring poetry into the "petty, commercial," indeed material and social world of everyday life rather than make it a space in which I could remain "free" of these things, or, better to say, chained to an illusion of such freedom. (Bové 28)

If, as Langdon Hammer writes, "The work of the adman was, in a sense, a parody of the work [Hart] Crane wished to do in poetry" (*Land* xiii), then Bernstein takes on the role of the parodic poet, adman and artist combined. For Bernstein there is no paradox, or the paradox is itself a grounds for poetry and the business of advertising it.

Marjorie Perloff notes in another context that "Surface Reflectance" is not so much a Language poem as an exploration of "the relationship of the individual to those elusive but ever-present structures of big business within which one negotiates one's daily life" (*Radical Artifice* 174). The language of the poem (including the words "material," "style," and "'classics'") applies almost as well to poetry as to clothing (I assume that this Bernstein is Charles Bernstein's father):

> "Despite the disparaging
> things that less fashion-alert males have said
> about the chemise, Mr. Bernstein plans

to back it. He will risk
several thousand yards of material
which is what he has
set aside for this style. . . . Mr. Bernstein
has been known to sell as many as 12,000
copies of one style in the same week. . . . Of
course there are certain 'classics' that will continue
to sell and probably keep Mr. Bernstein
from closing up shop even
if he guesses wrong and cuts
thousands of dresses that buyers will never buy.
These classics include shirtwaist
dresses and full-skirted cotton with scooped
necklines." (*TS* 165)

Few poets have so well described the postmodern conundrum that "classics" are mass produced; that the language of poetry cannot often be distinguished from the language of advertising; and that style is absolutely crucial to clothes and to poems—more crucial, it would often seem, than content. It's no mistake that one of the most hilarious interludes in this long poem is the metaredundant, "And then we'll go axeroxing! / Axeroxing! Axeroxing" (164)! Here we find the amoralized landscape of "image consultants" like Dorothy Sarnoff, who writes that "surveys have revealed that only 8 percent of the audience pays attention to the content of a speech, 42 percent to the speaker's appearance, and 50 percent to how the person speaks" (quoted in Stuart Ewen 260–61). And so 92% of the listeners are concerned more with style than with content.

Later in this poem, Bernstein quotes the fashion-conscious voice of someone who says, "I just bought it because it came out" (168), which he follows with a parody of Martin Luther King's "I Have a Dream" speech: "One day people will be judged / not only by the color of their skin but by / the color in their eyes" (168). Later yet comes the quotation I used in my headnote to this essay: "The clothier makes the person (there's / a change in the sweater, a change / in the smock, from now on / they'll be a change in *you*)" (168–69). Toward the end of the poem, Bernstein takes the anaesthetist as a paradoxical hero in the fight against style-as-self. The poet is simply a potentially less toxic anaesthetist:

> To suppress a twitch
> or tone, the anaesthetist
> may wish to abolish it
> at its origin. A less toxic approach
> is to block the signals
> or otherwise interfere with their transmission
> from source to destination. (*TS* 171)

This blockage of signals becomes the basis for Bernstein's advocacy of "non-absorptive" writing, or writing that blocks the accustomed signals between sender and receiver, writer and reader. To block these signals is to perform the kind of operation on the language accomplished by George Orwell in his essay "Politics and the English Language."[3] While Bernstein does not succumb to a writer's block caused by the mass-marketing of language itself, his method for doing so involves, at least in part, a mode of writing that blocks the reader, that is willfully (but not unreasonably) difficult. To block the reader is to free the writer to write around, or through, the obstacle of formulaic language, of tired fashion, just as dressing baroquely, self-consciously, blocks the observer's gaze, shifts her interest from preestablished pattern to fertile chaos.

So fashion emerges out of the worship of conventional forms, the easily recognizable styles of dress or speech, and anti-fashion blocks recognition by altering style, purifying the language of the tribe, paradoxically, by rendering it less "understandable." Anne Hollander writes in her study of clothing: "If anything, clothes are rather like conventional expressions in a literary form, of which the canonical examples have been assimilated by the reading public" (xv). While Hollander, despite her example, still warns against equating clothing with language use, Roland Barthes makes the equation plain: "Fashion behaves like language itself, for which the novelty of a turn of phrase or of a word always constitutes an emphasis destined to repair the wear in its system" (15). At the same time that fashion is reparative, writing about fashion is what makes fashion fashionable; the fashion editor is one who "invests nothing of himself in his speech . . . he simply conforms to a certain conventional and regulated tone" (228). What is meant to stand out and apart—the fashion item—then, does so because it's described in the most conventional of languages, that of the magazine. This vicious process ends, rather predictably, with the garment becoming "a signifier of something which is yet nothing other than this very constitution" (287).

Bernstein's arguments about writing take Barthes's position as their starting point; he claims that intellectual fashion precludes thought because of the socialized fact of a "regulated tone" that discourages discovery and encourages conventionality. The "sanctioned prose of the profession" ("Frame") serves to perpetuate the profession itself rather than to create new knowledge, new approaches. Within the scholarly or poetic marketplace, then, the writing garment signifies little more than its fact as a commodity to be bought or argued over. Its "intrinsic" value gets lost in the ironic consumer economy of the academy (where cultural capital has far more value than actual capital). As I mentioned earlier, Bernstein coined the label, "official verse culture," for those poetries that work within convention, rather than challenging it. He often uses the language of clothing to make this argument; in his interview with Loss Glazier, for example, he claims that, "Official Verse Culture operated then, as it does now, by denying its narrow stylistic orthodoxy under the cloak of universalized and unassailable poetic principles" (Bové 42). Again, basing his logic on paradox, Bernstein goes on to argue that the emphasis on individualism in mainstream poetry, an emphasis that is defeated by the utter conformity of its conventions, could better be achieved through collective action: "If mainstream poetic 'individuality' breeds unreflected conformism, collective formations might actually provide the space for conversation as well as for difference" (42). Here, by moving from individual to communal field/fashion, he avoids the impasse (Riding) Jackson met with poetic silence. While she abhorred Arrow shirts and opted for nakedness, Bernstein abhors the shirt but opts for layers instead of taking off the linguistic cloak.

Bernstein has long been interested in the way in which language participates in the larger economy of "value," in its two senses. In his 1980 volume, *Controlling Interests,* whose title is a play on business lingo, Bernstein includes the poem "Sentences My Father Used." The title of this poem suggests that his father did not create his sentences, but "used" them, that they were prefabricated and hence that the language he used already used him. The poem is full of allusions to his father's business; just as significantly, however, one of the poem's subjects is the impressions that people leave on one another through their appearances. These appearances are crucial to the moral values that his father holds. Thus:

"The impression I got / is everybody. Or I should say well groomed. But / in appearances" (23). Or, closely following a passage about conformity: "Patent leather shoes. In a gentle way, I / wasn't very. I didn't have a / very, my appearance wasn't one of, that / one could take, well I didn't make / the. Nothing stands out" (24). And so, the man who conforms both in his clothing and in his language, goes on, "Those were my values. To me they were good values. I didn't want to / struggle. & I could live frugally" (25). Bernstein's poem is fascinating in its presentation of the most ordinary language (plain, common speech) that obviously mirrors an ordinary life that is created, at least in part, out of that language. And yet the poem, by cutting and mis-seaming its way from sentence to sentence, critiques that language and the "form" of life that it at once creates and mirrors. Where "values" are presented as clichés, they tend to lose their value; and, where the businessman discusses his "values," the consumer's use of the word cannot lurk far beneath the moral one. The father's "style" may be simple, but his business is in creating another sense of style, that of women's fashion. Stuart and Elizabeth Ewen write that "the construct that assumes a simple and austere man and a highly sumptuous woman still stands to underwrite masculine morality, feminine guilt" (*Channels* 107). Later I will discuss the way in which Bernstein turns away from his father's "masculine morality" and toward the "feminine guilt" of sumptuous literary fashion.

Bernstein has other fathers than Mr. Bernstein, of course; there are also the difficult poetic ones, including Ezra Pound, whose anti-Semitism makes him especially problematic. "Surface Reflectance," from *The Sophist,* moves quickly, jaggedly, and in unseamly fashion from the poet's father to Mr. Pound:

These classics include shirtwaist
dresses and full-skirted cotton with scooped necklines."
And went down to the ship
very bored. What has not been
made, what has not been
seen, what has not been
spoken: always in the fold of the
audible, visible
projection of desire: to launch
a care, munching a pear. (165–66)

The younger Bernstein's misprision of Pound connects the world of actual fashion to that of poetic style; were poetic traditions composed of a series of ready-mades, like the "classic" dresses his father manufactured, then literary tradition (beginning from the *Iliad*) would be terribly boring. Ulrich Lehmann presents Walter Benjamin's idea of fashion and quotation in terms that match Bernstein's take on Pound: "*Fashion is irreverent in its quotations. Its superficial appearance creates a strange independence from recognizable contents—and from this, its potential for hermeneutics ensues*" (xvii). That much of contemporary literature is dull is one of Bernstein's primary problems with it. So the poet emphasizes the ready-madeness of tradition by alluding to this ready-made allusion by Pound while, through his own method, attempting to break out of the prison house of allusiveness through a process of mis-seaming, or of rapid cuts from one thought-sentence to another. He offers only half an allusion, which then carries him somewhere else entirely, notably away from the literary world and into one that more resembles soap opera or advertising language. In this sense, and maybe in this sense only, he is the heir of Marianne Moore, who deflected the grandiose literary ambitions of the high Modernists by using quotations from Forest Service manuals and business texts. And yet there is something troubling, to this reader at least, in the way Bernstein moves from what seems an advocacy of "making it new" to the flip "to launch a care / munching a pear." Newness, at least here, comes at the price of wisdom, though perhaps, as Charles Altieri suggests, Bernstein's moments of wisdom are accidental, and not constructed. For Bernstein, however, the accident is already contained, as potential, in the garments that we wear. Some of these garments are, quite literally, nonsensical, like the sound of an advertising jingle at the end of a statement of poetics. Of course, poetics are also a form of advertising, and of that, Bernstein, as we have already seen, is terribly aware.

The process of radical disconnection between parts that forms the core of Bernstein's poetics is one that he refers to as "dysraphism," the title of another poem in *The Sophist*. He defines the term in a long footnote: "'Dysraphism' is a word used by specialists in congenital disease to mean a dysfunctional fusion of embryonic parts—a birth defect . . . *Raph* literally means 'seam', so dysraphism is mis-seaming—a prosodic device!" Bernstein links the method to the purveyor of that method, the poet: "But it has the punch of being the same root as rhapsody (*raph*)—

or in Skeat's 'one who strings (lit. stitches) songs together, a reciter of epic poetry.'" He finds the word adjacent to another, "'dysprosody'" [sic]: "disturbance of stress, pitch, and rhythm of speech'" (44). The poet, then, lets be the finale of seams—he stitches his epic out of speech's defects, not its seemlinesses or even its seaminess. His "allusion" to Pound alluding to the *Iliad* is, above all, not neat; rather, it is a parody intended to expose the Modernist habit of revering the tradition and trying to extend it by placing it within a different context.

Rather than argue against "fashion" per se, Bernstein claims time and again that, while fashion and style are inevitable, writers should define them in the plural, write unofficial verses. Where a "universal" style is problematic, Bernstein suggests that a plurality of styles is less so. As he told Tom Beckett, reversing the usual assumptions about style as a reflection of content, or a conduit of meaning: "It is not the valorization of style, and certainly not a style, that is fundamental, but the recognition that meaning is possible only through styles" (*CD* 388). New styles will inaugurate new modes of thinking. Official verse culture's greatest problem is that its perpetrators produce ready-mades, or poems that cannot be distinguished from other similar poems written in the same tradition. These ready-mades are bland, uniform, standardized, and (hence) empty. In response, Bernstein proposes a poetics of the nonstandard— an especially relevant term for a poet who often writes in his own nonstandard forms (or idiolects) of English. "Poetics," he writes, "is all about changing the current poetic course. Putting on a dress, not strapping yourself into a uniform" (*AP* 157). Here he taps into Barthes's vocabulary where that writer, borrowing a binary from Saussure, suggests that, "we might agree to call the structural, institutional form of what is worn *clothing* (that which corresponds to language), and this same form when actualized, individualized, worn *dress* (that which corresponds to speech)" (18). Dress, then, is what is individually tailored, just as uniforms (or uniformity) are what is mass-produced. That this is already a dead metaphor (we know that the dress is also mass-produced) matters less than that Barthes and Bernstein define their terms to distinguish between the multiply similar and the multiply different or eccentric and that they make clothing serve as a metaphor for language use. In arguing against ready-mades, of course, Bernstein is also setting himself against the model of his father and of Pound, for whom the allusion was a kind of ready-made to be slipped into the piggy bank of poetry. It is no accident that what often seems, in a Bernstein poem, to be (or to have been) a literary allusion, is a mis-copy, a flagrant mangling of the actual lines from a prior poem into something new, and very strange.

There is something else at stake here, and that is Bernstein's implicit critique of gender politics by way of his use of fashion statements in prose and poetry. For, in his assertion that one should wear a "dress" and not a "uniform," Bernstein subverts the traditional, "conventional" notion that fashion is feminine (Ulrich Lehmann notes that the word for fashion, or "mode" in French, is given a feminine article [18]), not masculine; he suggests instead that fashion is both. Lehmann develops his argument from the fact of the feminine article, in language as well as cloth: "The emphasis is on equating *la mode* with the ephemeral and the futile, which may be strong but is ultimately unimportant—as the woman does not really dominate anything but the consumption of an artificial reality of luxuries and vagaries" (19). As Fred Davis notes, "To the person on the street, and only slightly less so to the student of dress, the word *fashion* is more likely still to evoke images of women rather than men" (205). And as Jennifer Craik comments, "Women are fashionable but men are not. This lament is common in western cultures" (176). Likewise, Stuart Ewen quotes the maven of etiquette, Emily Post, who wrote in 1930 that modern spare design was "well suited to men. . . . Empty spaces, the absence of ruffles and curtains, and beautifully polished surfaces of wood and metal were masculine" (130). Femininity became associated with kitsch, which was associated with popular, rather than high, culture. Dorothy E. Smith's discussion of texts and femininity includes the following meditation, which could as easily and profitably be associated with poetry: "The relation between the standardized ideality of the discursive images of femininity and the imperfect body generates that perpetual renewal of desire into which the texts tying desire to commodity are inserted. Women are returned again and again as consumers to the retail outlets that will remedy their ever-renewed textually reflected imperfections" (208). Women, then, are the true commodities, filled with imperfections, but capable of being "upgraded" and "improved." To be a desirable woman is to take part in a constant process of improvement; there is nothing static about a woman's desire to be more desirable. Thus a woman cannot achieve the status of a "well-wrought urn"; she can only work toward that status through a series of strategies. The fashion industry creates and stokes that desire through an equal number of marketing strategies aimed at pointing out defects and proposing solutions through the use of their products. The kind of desire inspired in the woman, taking herself as an audience for herself, is above all surface oriented, visual. As Jane Grimes writes, "We are trained into clothes, and early become practiced in presentational postures, learning in the age of mechanical reproduction to carry the mirror's eye within the mind, as though one might at any moment be photographed" (quoted in Breward, 198). She can herself be rendered more perfect if her outward appearance improves. Women's fashion, since the watershed of the eighteenth century, has allowed for more superfluous touches than has men's fashion, which tends to be geared more toward the workplace than toward the work of being looked at.

The modernist masculine poetics of a writer like James Joyce was based on a spareness of style (if in manifesto only), a getting away from the "frilly" sentimentality of the Romantics. Bernstein, it seems to me, flaunts this distinction between male and female fashion in a poetry that elevates style into content, and foregoes all claims to participating in a "common speech," even when, as it often does, it imitates common speech quite uncommonly. The poet who wears a dress further admits to associating his identity as poet with his garb. He or she is a consumer of words, but not, according to Bernstein's notion of it, a consumer who seeks perfection, even if he or she does frequent malls in search of new vocabularies. He and she, as I should probably phrase it, also possess a larger potential market share than the poet whose uniform is more uniform and uni-gendered. And, as in the different cases of John Ashbery and Ronald Johnson, he finds a way around impasse by entering into a feminine, rather than a masculine, poetic tradition, whether consciously or no.

Yet Bernstein recognizes the subtle lacunae of his own argument, which situates him with and against the fashion industries of contemporary writing. While he distrusts fashion, he likes the idea of an anti-fashion that lurks within a larger system, an anti-fashion that can quickly become fashionable. As Stuart Ewen notes, "today's fashions offer the weapons of resistance and compliance in one, ready to wear" (187). Thus in an interview with Tom Beckett, Bernstein notes that, "'Fashion' might be a useful middle term between power and dominance, on the one side, and centrality as its legitimizing facticity on the other. Fashion seeks hegemony but produces *resistance*—not just to 'fashion itself' but also as the motor of fashion" (*AP* 188). In that sense, the fashion that Bernstein seeks to wear and write is an anti-fashion like the one described by Dick Hebdige in his important study, *Subculture: The Meaning of Style:* "However, the challenge to hegemony which subcultures represent is not issued directly by them. Rather it is expressed obliquely, in style" (17). Hebdige goes on to say that subcultures "represent 'noise' (as opposed to sound) and violate the taboos that protect "the sanctity of [a preexisting] language" (90–91).

This connection between anti-fashion in clothing and in writing is crucial, I think, in a discussion of Bernstein's work, either as poet or as critic, especially as Language writing generally has been so often critiqued as "noise" rather than as "music."[4] The comparison of fashion and writing, although it can be misleading, as Ann Hollander argues, is especially pointed in Bernstein's case since his father sold ready-made copies of designer dresses. This is an irony that is surely not lost on the poet, who has expended much energy in attacking the ready-mades, the easy copies, of literary fashion. And yet, to complicate the matter further (a characteristic of Bernstein's thinking), he has argued in "Living Tissue / Dead Ideas" that, "Language is the first technology, the extension of the body outward toward an articulation, *forging,* of the world, which is immediately transformed by this act, hence a *forgery*" (*CD* 364). In this sense art can only deal with the world by rendering it as a "forgery"; language, which is above all not "natural," is the artifice by which we describe—and hope to change—the world.

For Bernstein, then, forgeries and copies are at once the symptom of our failure to use language "well" (which often means "badly" in the conventional sense of the term) and the only hope to intervene in that world, now filled with disposable ready-mades. As he writes in the autobiographical, "Three or Four Things I Know About Him": "Ethics & aesthetics become increasingly 'out there'. Dress & syntax & right behaviour are copied from presented models, a process of emulation rather than interpretation. Clerks & secretaries spend their time typing neatly, removing idiosyncracies from the language & presiding over a tan neutrality" (*CD* 25). Bernstein, then, is interested in breaking certain taboos about language, taboos not often discussed openly but held very strongly by cultural conservatives and others. "Notions concerning the sanctity of language," writes Dick Hebdige, "are intimately bound up with ideas of social order. The limits of acceptable linguistic expression are prescribed by a number of apparently universal taboos. These taboos guarantee the continuing 'transparency' . . . of meaning" (91). Hence the turmoil caused by Bartleby's refusal to copy language, and thus the anger directed against an avant-garde writer such as Bernstein who writes but refuses to copy.

The metaphor that Bernstein employs to link conventional thinking to nineteenth-century industrialization is apt, as is his attempt to inoculate the language against conformity through his own, almost homeopathic, use of "styles." As early as 1859, Oliver Wendall Holmes was cautioning against the time when the "image would become more important than the object itself, and would in fact make the object disposable" (quoted in S. Ewen); transpose this discussion of image onto one about writing, and you get the thrust of Bernstein's critique of fashionable thinking, which is simply another manifestation of a consumer culture more interested in acquiring and dispensing thoughts than in actual thinking. According to Stuart Ewen, the nineteenth-century became the originary site of a paradox fundamental to "style"—that the mass production of clothing and other items made possible a greater democratization and, at the same time, undermined the democracy it helped to spread: "The new consumer democracy, which was propelled by the mass production and marketing of stylish goods, was founded on the idea that symbols and prerogatives of elites could now be made available on a mass scale. The values of elite culture were simultaneously upheld and undermined by this peculiar variant of democracy" (32). Whereas mass-produced clothing had originated for the working-class market (blue jeans come to mind), it soon became a marker of elite status, even if that status was only symbolic. Aesthetic values became less important for their own sakes and more so for the sake of promotion; as advertising man Ernest Elmo Calkins wrote, "Beauty is introduced into material objects to enhance them in the eyes of the purchaser" (46). Then, in much the way that Barthes describes the actual garment being transformed into the "written garment" (3), Egon Friedell in 1931 saw fit to declare: "Neither are there goods any more, *but only advertisements* . . . We call all this 'Americanism'" (S. Ewen 47). It was not so much that everyone became a true democrat by sporting an egalitarian fashion of clothing, but that every democrat became an elitist by donning the "uniforms" of the rich and of celebrities. In 1930, for example, one Bernard Waldman, garment executive, began making copies of a wedding gown from the film *King of Jazz,* which inaugurated the Modern Merchandising Bureau, which made copies of movie fashion (S. Ewen 99).

The most long-lasting result of the increasing supremacy of fashion over substance was not that the fashion of clothing changed, but in the link between surface appearances and identity that developed. Stuart Ewen refers to style as "a tool for constructing personhood" (79) and adds, "The utility of style in this regard is to find for oneself, and for others, the evidence of meaning in one's life" (79). Proliferations of style and emphasis on consumer goods led to the conflation, immediately after the fall of the Berlin Wall, of democracy with consumer goods; many of us remember images of stunned East Germans wandering through the shops of West Berlin and pointed remarks by television commentators that these East Germans were discovering the benefits of a "free [sic] society." Democratic values are measured by the production of goods that have a good style. These values are tied in with leisure time rather than with work. As Ewen explains it: "With the rise of mass fashion, the language of elegances and luxury entered the common vernacular of perception and expression. The garment industry, initially a supplier of clothes designed explicitly for workers, and *for work,* now began to dress its public in wares that suggested the common accessibility of prosperity and leisure" (130). But Bernstein himself recognizes the distinction between the makers of garments and the wearers of them, when he tells Glazier that, "'The right priorities' [his father's words] was not a particularly elastic concept for him and in this he represents, more than less, a new-immigrant generation that didn't have the leisure to question what their very hard work made possible for my generation" (Bové 24).

Poetry has traditionally been associated more with leisure than with work in American society, in large part because it doesn't easily fit into a consumer mind frame; poetry is that which cannot be bought and hence, the argument might go, also cannot so easily be disposed of. The contortions of Hart Crane's arguments to Otto Kahn, in September 1927, illuminate the problem he had in communicating the *value* of his work to a man who ran a successful business (in that sense a man very like his own father). As Langdon Hammer points out, Crane's first collected letter is to his businessman father, and in it he requests money (*Land* xiii). Later, Hammer adds that, "Together Crane's parents symbolized for him the legacy of 'materialism' and "Puritanism" against which, he felt, the modern American artist had to struggle" (*Land* 50). Ironically enough, Crane's only claim to work experience, which he mentions to Kahn, is as "a perfectly good advertising writer" (*Land* 349). He uses these skills to attempt to persuade Kahn of the "value" of his work. Part of what Crane knows might disturb this man of business is the fact that poets need free time to meditate about their work, time that looks to the outside eye as if it's being "wasted." So he writes: "It has taken a great deal of energy—which has not been so difficult to summon as the necessary patience to wait, simply wait much of the time"; his metaphors take a materialist turn as he continues the sentence, "until my instincts assured me that I had assembled my materials in proper order for a final welding into their natural form" (345). *The Bridge,* then, must be explained as if it were the actual Brooklyn Bridge and the poet its real engineer. Any less material metaphorical field would confirm the businessman's suspicion that poets live more in the clouds than among the steel girders of the bridge. Most telling, however, in this request for funds, is Crane's final (and in some ways heartbreaking) use of metaphor in the letter: "There is no monetary standard of evaluation for works of art, I know, but I cannot help feeling that a great poem may well be worth at least the expenditure necessary for merely the scenery and costumes of many a flashy and ephemeral play, or for a motor car" (349). He concludes his request for money with a sentence that puns between the worlds of art and business: "But that is a speculation which depends entirely on your interest" (350). Here we see the poet's metaphors used to convey "value" as a monetary quality, not an "inherent" one. The pathos of the letter is that these two forms of value are so removed from each other that Crane's attempts to link them through metaphor seem rather a false currency. That they resemble the words of Bernstein's father, in "Sentences My Father Used," is symptomatic of the continuing split in American culture between the worlds of poetry and of products. That they resonate in Bernstein's own conception of himself as a "confidence man" or "small businessman," points to the continued desire of American poets to place themselves within the actual economy of value, if only metaphorically.

While Crane, whose poetry is notoriously difficult to comprehend, paradoxically wished for a large audience and wondered why readers found his work inaccessible, Bernstein—arguing as he does against the poetry of plain speech—embraces difficulty, obscurity as a homeopathic cure of the obscurity of political and advertising language. His "Defence of Poetry," written exclusively in "typos," barely conceals a plea for comprehensible, honest talk by politicians (George Bush the Elder being the representative inarticulate man here). If the goal of much contemporary poetry is to convey meaning through as simple a vehicle as possible, then Bernstein's intent often seems to be that of the owner of a uniquely stylish vehicle who finds meaning in the vehicle itself. Another vehicle would make another meaning, an idea that is anathema to writers who aim at absolute "organicism" of form and vocabulary. As he writes in "Artifice of Absorption," "The obvious problem is that the poem said in any / other way is not the poem" (*AP* 12). The obvious solution is linked to this obvious problem; to make a poem that means something new, the poet must begin from a concern with style and form. And so, where the poet of plain speech aims to "absorb" the reader and hence to make it easy for the reader to "absorb" the poem's meanings, Bernstein proposes a theory of non-absorptiveness, of language as block rather than as conveyer belt. The poetics of non-absorptiveness is his long essay-poem, "Artifice of Absorption," whose deliberate obscurity of genre forces the very question he addresses. Non-absorptive poetry is, of necessity, a poetry that values style at least as much as substance; the merchants of substance want to sell the content of their work and aim to find as simple a vehicle as possible to convey that substance. Bernstein's work begins from the desire to make that transaction difficult; his poetry is not easily consumed on the open market. And yet this argument conflicts with Bernstein's desire to be a business man for the avant-garde; in that sense, he is very like the Gertrude Stein who writes plain-spoken advertisements for her most obscure work.

In "Artifice of Absorption," Bernstein sets up a binary distinction between "absorption" and "non-absorption," a distinction that will not last out the poem. It's interesting to note that, if nakedness be a natural state, then sartorial fashion is an artificial one; Bernstein's fascination with artifice allies itself "naturally" with his fashion concerns. His definitions of terms are as follows:

> By *absorption* I mean engrossing, engulfing
> completely, engaging, arresting attention, reverie,

attention intensification, rhapsodic, spellbinding,
mesmerizing, hypnotic, total, riveting,
enthralling: belief, conviction, silence. (*AP* 29)

By way of contrast:

Impermeability suggests artifice, boredom,
exaggeration, attention scattering, distraction,
digression, interruptive, transgressive,
undecorous, anticonventional, unintegrated, fractured,
etc. (*AP* 29)

Here he reverses Hart Crane's terms, at least those that Crane uses in his
letter to Kahn. No longer are "belief" and "conviction" and Romantic
"reverie" to be valued over "digression," lack of "integration," and refusal
of "convention." The very style in which Bernstein defines his terms signals the ascendancy of a willful obscurity:

The terms began to consume
my imagination, a pataphysical extravaganza
of accumulating works & fields absorbed
into this tropic zone without benefit
of underlying unity of perspective. There seemed no
limit to what
the absorption/antiabsorption nexus could
absorb. (*AP* 20)

Bernstein's fashion statement here bears some similarity to that of poems in *The New Yorker*, one of his favorite whipping-magazines. After
all, the line about limitlessness is ever so much longer than the line
that follows, a line whose subject is, after all, limitation. Bernstein knows
a thing or two about enjambment. And yet, precisely what is lacking
from his poem is any reference to image or landscape, what Charles Altieri calls the "scenic style" of much contemporary verse.[5] The extent
of Bernstein's discursiveness leaves a self-proclaimed discursivist like
Robert Pinsky in the prosaic dust.[6] Instead, "Artifice of Absorption"
sounds like an essay written in the professional mode of literary criticism. In that sense, Bernstein is using the vocabulary of one of the styles

he's been known to attack in order to decalibrate the vocabulary of the poetic style he means to dislodge from its "official" status. Bernstein knows that he cannot step outside the styles that are available to him; styles, like voice (in his important essay, "Stray Straws and Straw Men") are for him a possibility, but not an end.[7] While he cannot escape the possibility of voice, he can try to dislodge it from its status as the true reflection of a unique sensibility, unique precisely because it fits so well the form(ula) of the age. Or, as Jed Rasula puts it, "Driven by a taste of novelty, Americans seem intent on celebrating as sublimely original only those achievements that are servile imitations" (9).

Novelty turns transhistorical, if one believes Walter Benjamin (as parsed by Ulrich Lehmann): "*In quoting from past clothing styles, fashion is able to break the historical continuum and to become both transitory and transhistorical*" (Lehmann xvii). The adequate representation of sensibility comes, according to Bernstein and Benjamin, through ready-made vocabularies. In using these ready-mades, however, Bernstein risks his own authority, at least the kind of authority one arrives at through a tone of sincerity. He arrives at a sincerity that is oddly based either on a highly performative use of other people's vocabularies or one acquired through non-sense. So he aims to be the wise fool on the stage of his own creation, a status that is ever risky, because it can cut both ways.

Bernstein's antiestablishmentarian stance was made considerably more difficult to sustain in 1989, when he stopped writing freelance medical texts for a living and became the David Gray Professor of English at SUNY-Buffalo. It may be made more difficult still by his recent move from Buffalo to the Ivy League University of Pennsylvania, emblem of an establishment whose ambivalent avatars have included Ezra Pound, H.D., and William Carlos Williams. All at once Bernstein was "authorized" both as a critic, who used the jargon of the profession well before he entered it, and as an academic poet—or, at the least, a poet in the academy. I take his 1994 book, *Dark City,* to be an extended (and very zany) meditation on the paradoxes of achieving success within the academy. For Bernstein realizes that he has entered into another consumer economy, that poetry in (and out of) the academy is marketed like any commodity, and that there is, to follow Barthes, not just an *image* poem but also a *written* poem. The "written" poem is the advertising copy that accompanies the poem in its travel outward toward audience: it may include the blurbs on the back cover of a book of poems, and it may also include the polemical positions taken by poetic movements—those for which Laura Riding had such disdain. As a charter member of the group of L=A=N=G=U=A=G=E poets who achieved a certain distinction in the 1980s, Bernstein knows how to promote poetry. He was for a time the publisher of the Segue catalogue of experimental poetry books, and he "owns" the Poetics list at SUNY-Buffalo and moderated a radio show on poetry, Linebreak. An issue of *boundary 2* was devoted, in large measure, to his work.[8] He and Hank Lazer edit a series of books about poetics through the University of Alabama Press, in which series this book takes its place. And so on. Most of his work appears not in one, but in several venues. How to market poetry without becoming a pawn to consumer culture in the process is one of the central questions addressed in *Dark City*.

The first poem in the volume, "Lives of the Toll Takers," asks the question rather directly: what if one's insistence on rebellion is itself a problem? What if it has been reduced to a style emptied of content? Bernstein seems to operate from an assumption perhaps best expressed by Stuart Ewen in his *All Consuming Images,* who argues that, "In the contemporary world, where the mass media serve as increasingly powerful arbiters of *reality,* the primacy of style over substance has become the normative consciousness" (2). Ewen's is a learned manifesto against the all-pervasiveness of style in consumer society, one that reflects an emphasis on appearances rather than on convictions. Art is made less for its own sake than for the sake of control in the marketplace (50). For Ewen, the worst aspect of this ascendancy of style is that it has become "an intimate component of subjectivity, intertwined with people's aspirations and anxieties" (22). These aspirations, like the products marketed through a careful use of style, are themselves mass-produced and, ultimately, disposable. Finally, like Bernstein, Ewen asserts that "style—as a form of *information*—discourages thought" (263). Bernstein's method, in the poems from *Dark City,* is to play with advertising language in such a way as to show its emptiness in any discussion of poetry. He has long argued against poetry that reflects its author's subjectivity, claiming that he is not interested in himself but in language. This is certainly one way around—or out of—the problem of identity that Ewen addresses in his book. But, at the same time and unlike Ewen, Bernstein doesn't step outside the fashion system he critiques. Instead, he operates as someone whose identity *is* composed of advertising slogans. His critiques of poetry strangely become defenses of its importance, as he exposes the ironies of discussing art as if it were merchandise. In "Lives of Toll Takers" he even questions the relevance of continuing to rebel, since he knows that rebellion, too, is a style:

> What if
> success scares you so much that at the point of some
> modest acceptance, midway through
> > life's burning, you blast out
> onto the street, six-shooters smoking, still a rebel.
> > For what? (*DC* 21)

The response comes in the guise of a self-help transcript:

> Of course new ventures always require risk, but by carefully
> > analyzing the situation, we became smart risk
> > > takers. (21)

This leads the poem into a consideration of poetry as a business, the poet as a businessperson who takes risks only insofar as he expects to reap rewards, and one who considers himself part of the "service economy." "Our new / service orientation / mea / nt / not only changing the way we wrote poems but also diversifying / into new poetry services" (22). (This reminds me of a colleague whose application for full professorship included a listing of her poetry readings as "community service"—and why not?) Such consideration of poetry as a business leads the "speaker" (if I dare call him that) to talk about justifiable reimbursement for services delivered. "Besides, our current fees / barely cover our expenses; any deviation from these levels / would / mean working for nothing" (22–23). The poem is as hilarious as it is, in some real sense, serious. Why, the reader wonders, are poets NOT paid for their services? Poets do, as the poem tells us, "deserve compensation / for such services" (23), which include "alliteration, / internal rhymes, / exogamic structure, and / unusual vocabulary" (23). The poet then includes material from a poet's own career:

I had decided to go back
to school after fifteen years in
community poetry because I felt
I did not know enough to navigate
through the rocky waters that
lie ahead for all of us in this field.
How had Homer done it, what might Milton
teach? Business training turned
out to be just what I most needed.
Most importantly, I learned that
for a business to be successful, it
needs to be different, to stand out
from the competition. In poetry,
this differentiation is best
achieved through the kind of form
we present. (*DC* 24–25)

In a conversation I had with Bernstein in early 1993, he said that when he first started out to be a poet, he asked himself what he could do to distinguish himself, to write something genuinely new. So this discussion of poetry and business sense has beneath its hilarious veneer a terribly serious "content," having to do with the way in which poets construct careers for themselves in a "business" that has so little to offer of "value" in the pecuniary sense.

In another poem from this volume, "Emotions of Normal People," Bernstein again frames a discussion of poetry around its commercialization. He presents chunks of writing, much of it in advertising-speak, that concern everything from relationships to a book review (of the book by a different Bernstein), to a return notice, to a marketing questionnaire, to the promotional writing in a book about marketing poetry. The marketing questionnaire contains such questions as, "Which best describes your dress size? What brands of bar soap have been used in your household in the past 6 months?" and so on (93). The most telling of segments, however, is the one taken from *Poet's Market,* a book that lists journals and presses to which one can send poems, and also includes interviews with "successful" poets an aspiring poet might want to emulate. What we have in this section is the "stylization" of poetry, which presents the perfect paradox of much contemporary work that it must be both unique and yet formulaic enough to fit the "market." The poet herself must find her own way by imitating the "saint's lives" of poets like Richard Wilbur, 1987 Poet Laureate of the United States, and Rita Dove, winner of the 1987 Pulitzer Prize for poetry. The irony, of course, is that Wilbur and Dove are among the poets who harvest poems out of their own experiences, so that the notion of learning from them how to write and publish poetry is, in some sense, quite a stretch. If, in fact, subjectivity is the primary subject of poetry, which members of Bernstein's "official verse culture" believe, then one should not be able to share privileged knowledge about it. It's as if Emerson were to set up a writers' colony whose purpose would be to teach its participants how to have their very own moments of transcendence on Boston Common.

The poet most steeped in the contemporary language of advertising, Bernstein has been attacked on the grounds that his poetry accentuates style over substance, that it is itself lacking in convictions. In *After the Death of Poetry,* Vernon Shetley argues that Bernstein's poem, "The Kiwi Bird in the Kiwi Tree," markets only in surfaces. "There is nothing to penetrate because no meaning is hiding behind any other"; Shetley writes, "all are equally available, and the poem offers no ground for choice. But if this poem is ultimately too easy to read, it's also too easy to write" (151). Shetley has problems with poems written under the rubric of Language writing, that they are sometimes "all meaning or all randomness, but the interesting area, and the area of genuine difficulty, lies between" (153). Shetley's mistake, I think, is to focus exclusively on this one poem; one poem does not a context make. Nor does one poem, of necessity, set up the grounds for choices.

The central problem with Bernstein's critique of what might be called, by extension, "official writing cultures" is that his own language so often resembles that of the writers he is critiquing; as he himself writes in "Characterization": "Oddly, I have lately found myself writing things that would fit some of the prescriptions that the MLA, etc., puts forward. And I'm not quite sure why I've done that" (*CD* 450–51). Bernstein immediately posits his own unconsciousness in his claim not to know why he writes in MLA style; he becomes what Barthes calls a "looker" rather than a "reader," or someone who knows fashion without understanding it. Certainly, despite Bernstein's frequent claims that poetry and prose are not separate genres but *writing,* his essays do read differently from his poems. The dress and the uniform are distinct in his practice, if not in his theory.

I think it worth looking closely at a piece of writing that Bernstein presented at the Modern Language Association meeting in 1992, namely "Frame Lock," an essay that later appeared, rather surprisingly perhaps, in *College English,* and has since been reprinted in Bernstein's *My Way* (the publishing history of this piece itself makes a fascinating trajectory from research to pedagogy to poetics). I've already discussed the main thrust of Bernstein's argument in this essay—that the language of the "profession" has been so standardized that new thinking is discouraged, and that professional "fashions" (both in the interview suit and in the dissertation) are constricting. Bernstein advocates pulling the lock from the stable door here and changing professional style so that thinking can once again take place. In a conversation with Jonathan Monroe, Ann Lauterbach, and Bob Perelman, Bernstein discusses the relish he feels when he talks to MLA convention goers, a relish that is as much performative as anything: "I would always write something that was too long for the twenty-minute slot—and I don't like to go over the time—so what you can do is just collapse the time and read faster . . . They wake up, they're interested, and it's nice to be able to have almost a 'Captive Audience,' to borrow the title of one of Mr. Perelman's books, a trademarked item . . . " (Monroe 207).

So how does Bernstein present his argument against "frame lock," a phrase he adopted from Erving Goffman's *Frame Analysis*? In what style or styles does he present these ideas? How do his styles reflect his ideas, which are themselves part of an ongoing professional dialogue on the questions of the role of theory and the oft-times dreary presentation of theoretical ideas in the "major" journals? Bernstein does indeed mix (and match) his styles in this piece of writing, but instead of mixing styles together, he "frames" an essay in professional discourse with the kind of rhetoric usually reserved for his poems. The "frame," then, is revolutionary, but the meat of the piece is "locked" in place; it is the MLA style that he admits to using, though without knowing why.

Thus, in the third paragraph, Bernstein indulges in a verbal carnival once he has stated, quite soberly, that "Frame lock, and its cousin tone jam, are the prevailing stylistic constraints of the sanctioned prose of the profession." And goes on to say, "No matter that the content of an essay may interrogate the constructed unity of a literary work or a putative period; may dwell on linguistic fragmentation, demolition, totality, continuity, narrative progression, teleology, or truth and may insist that meaning is plural, polygamous, profligate, uncontainable, rhetorical, slippery or sliding or gliding or giddy and prurient" ("Frame" 90). Yet compare this verbal high-wire act to some of the prose that follows, which makes essentially the same point though in a different manner: "Professionalization is the criteria [sic] of professional standing but not necessary [sic] professional values; nor are our professional writing standards at or near the limits of coherence, perception, edification, scholarship, communication, or meaning" (91). This long sentence, I would argue, is more interested in making sense than in making style; it also participates in the rhetoric of the profession that Bernstein is criticizing. Again, later in the piece, he writes, in a style that imitates the very fault he points to: "In frame-locked prose, the order of sentences and paragraphs is hypotactic, based on a clear subordination of elements to an overriding argument that is made in a narrative or expository or linear fashion" (92). What Bernstein is doing here is not developing a new line of argument so much as running that argument through two or more machines of rhetoric, two or more languages. He is not evading style, he is just trying out more than one style in his critique of "frame lock." Like "official verse culture," "official professional speak," as he might call it, insists "on a univocal surface" and a minimum of shifts or mis-seams.

It is not entirely clear what the shifts in style in this piece actually do for the writer or his audience, except insofar as they render it more entertaining (a word hardly ever applicable to professional writing of any sort). The meaning here comes patently before the style; Bernstein has a central point and he manipulates his style to make that point at once more clear and more slippery. The humor of the piece comes at the expense of the profession, but does not open the way to a genuinely new idea about it. What are the new ways of thinking opened up for us by this manic whirl of language? In this piece, at any rate, Bernstein doesn't offer us a new field so much as new ways to play on the same field. This is perhaps appropriate, since Bernstein ultimately comes down on the side of style—if not over substance, then *as* substance. Like Adorno, Bernstein believes that "Fashion enthrones itself as something lasting and thus sacrifices the dignity of fashion, its transience" (quoted in Davis 121). Given a world in which fashion and style rule, Bernstein plays with them, granting them transience but also hoping that in the transient moments of his own writing a new thought emerges. Or, if not, that Bernstein himself becomes the "model," striding down the literary runway time after time, never repeating himself, as Stein cautioned, but always insisting on a new manner, a new cloak, a new divestiture of meaning.

But the most radical way in which Bernstein uses style may have less to do with the language he writes than with the way in which he challenges our assumptions about style itself. In "Of Time and the Line," his own brief presentation of his family's romance narrative: "My father pushed a / line of ladies' dresses—not down the street / in a pushcart but upstairs in a fact'ry / office. My mother has been more concerned / with her hemline" (*RT* 42), Bernstein posits his mother as the one who actually cares about style. His identifications with stylishness are identifications with what is generally interpreted as "feminine" practice; Bernstein refracts and deflects the reader's "gaze" through a blinding sequence of fashions, styles. A writer who argues against subjectivity as a worthy position in poetry, he takes on disguises as his subject and multiplies himself both in the poetic and scholarly marketplace and in the quick changes of the poems and essays themselves. As he writes in "Frame Lock," mimicking Whitman: "I've only just begun to contradict myself. But I contain no multitudes; I can't even contain myself" (*MW* 97). And, as Barthes states it, using the feminine as his subject: "we see the woman of Fashion dreaming of being at once herself and another": "the multiplication of persons in a single being is always considered by Fashion as an index of power; *you're demanding, and you're sweet, too; with the couturiers you discover you can be both, you can lead a double life:* herein lies the ancestral theme of disguise, the essential attribute of gods, police, and bandits" (256). So, while Bernstein does not put forward a feminist agenda in his work, the poems and essays can be seen within the frame of a challenge not just on "official verse culture's" claim on tone and style in poetry, but also the implicit masculinity of its claims. The simplicity and directness of "official verse" can be seen as part of the modernist project to make literature again the province of male writers intent on cleaning up the ruffles and lace of Romanticism. Yet Bernstein's feminism cannot but be partial; he attempts to rid contemporary poetry of its mass-produced fashions, which might be seen as analogous to the work of a male designer making women's clothes. By creating a fashion that is averse to conformity, he reinstitutes the individualism that feminist critics often oppose; fashion can at least sometimes be seen as an expression of community, though not in Bernstein's view of things. Like the Ronald Johnson of the cookbooks, about whom I wrote in Chapter Five, Bernstein's poetic practice suggests that one way around the impasse posed by a traditional canon—or its purveyors, in the case of Harold Bloom—is by way of recognizing a feminine tradition, either in a lineage that moves from Dickinson through Moore and Stein, or by putting fashion in a positive light.

As I mentioned at the beginning of this essay, Laura Riding made important arguments against professionalism, equating professional behavior with "fashion" and style of dress, and attempted to denude herself of these encumbrances and so to arrive at "truth." This sequence itself derives from the notion that spareness of voice equals authenticity, that fashion is suspect; it is, in some ways, an antifeminist argument, hardly surprising in view of the masculine will to power in modernist circles, including her own. It is interesting that Bernstein begins from a similar place, arguing against professional poets and critics for their attending more to fashion than to thinking, which is of necessity an unfashionable activity in a consumer society. And yet Bernstein has become the most consummate of professionals; he had a chair at SUNY-Buffalo and now a full-professorship at the University of Pennsylvania; he has edited numerous books on poetics; he has published three volumes in which his own criticism is reprinted; he has published a couple of dozen books of poems. He is, even more importantly, and as a result of these successes, the creator and propagator of a style. His work has, in recent years, become fashionable. Like many poets, he has arrived at the point where his is a recognizable style—albeit a pluralization of styles—associated not just with himself but with a "school."

Unlike Riding, however, and more like Gertrude Stein, from whom he takes more than any other writer, Bernstein relishes his position and destabilizes it at every turn. Like Stein, he uses his criticism (much more standard than hers) to advertise his poetry. It remains to be seen, however, to what extent Bernstein is able to maintain his anti-fashionable status at the moment when fashion is catching up with him, or if his strategy of disavowing fashion by indulging in it, succeeds in dismantling other, more ready-made styles. I will end this essay with a final paradox: Bernstein does not so much disavow authority in his work as reconceptualize it. Given a climate in which authority is a suspect term, Bernstein realizes that the only way to have it may be to disavow it. When Jonathan Monroe asks him about the issue of authority and writing, Bernstein responds by talking about graduate students who are advised how to make themselves attractive on the job market:

> But it is a naive idea of authority. People advise graduate students— and I read these manuals that try to do so—in a way that's not likely to get them authority. It's fine to say that if you do what everybody is doing and you don't stray and you use the references everybody else uses that people will think, "Aha, this person knows what he's doing," but also, if there are so many other people who are doing the same thing—just in the most crass, capitalist sense of market differentiation, this kind of manufacture of dullness doesn't nec- essarily create the authority that people think. (Monroe 208).

One could argue easily, I think, that Bernstein is misreading what we often call "the profession"; for better or for worse, the system does re- ward those who use the right references, and use them well. Bernstein's use of the metaphor of "manufacture," as in "the manufacture of dull- ness," is another gibe at the ready-made culture his father—and many others—made. But to argue against manufacture and for a kind of cot- tage industry of idiosyncracy is to ignore the very market system that Bernstein invokes. If Charles Bernstein is successful because he has cre- ated a cottage industry in an era of ready-mades, then he has done some- thing that most graduate students (if not all of them) cannot do. His invocation of Emerson in what directly follows the previous quotation, is appropriate, since Bernstein's criticism seems at times to echo that of his unlikely forerunner: "It's an Emersonian idea, but *not* being dull is perhaps not as risky as people tend to think. You don't fall off the earth. You're not as incomprehensible as you may fear. . . . It's a risk in some way, and people experience it as a risk, but what is actually on the other side of that risk?" (Monroe 208). It is that risk that has made Charles Bernstein's career unique, a one-of-a-kind, one of which the "old-fashioned" Emerson might even approve.

Coda
"Word Trade Center"

Writing after 9/11

ONE OF MY STRONGEST, strangest memories of September 11, 2001, was its silences: aside from the constant hum of the television, communications with friends in New York and Washington over e-mail (virtual sound only), public places in Hawai'i were quiet. There were no airplanes in the sky. People were walking around Longs Drugs in Kane'ohe as if enclosed in their own—and the world's—silences. "Did you know anyone?" was often as far as we got those first days, even in Hawai'i (where our neighbors did lose a friend) or, "the world has changed, but I don't know how," all tentative attempts at speech that lacked elaboration. I asked my students to write "I remember" poems so they could think about the day, while still performing some of the work of the class. Many did not want to, as all their teachers were asking them to talk. Recently, as the work of the 9/11 commission began to be aired publicly—and revelations of the Bush administration's attempts to silence the record emerged—I asked the fifty-odd members of a poetry e-mail list[1] to write "on the effects of recent world events on your work. Were you at any point 'silenced' by them? Have you incorporated those silences into your own in some way? How did you (or did you?) keep writing?"

But before I begin to parse the responses I got from poets on that list, let me step back to September 11 itself. The fact of impasse was vivid on that day, during the week that followed; we, whoever we were, had been silenced. Charles Bernstein, on whose poems I've ruminated in the last chapter, as in the first, was aware of the problem, and addressed it quickly. His strategies for continuing to write parallel those of the poets I asked; they are, for him, surprising strategies, at least if we consider him as the author of "dysraphism," whose poetics is based on mis-seaming, not sewing together, and on fashioning, not in going naked.

On September 11, 2001, Bernstein wrote an e-mail to the Buffalo poetics list to describe what he could not otherwise describe. He offered a series of vignettes—of a coffee shop; his memories of Simon and Garfunkel singing "Feeling Groovy"; of the skies of New York City; the hair salon run by his neighbor Andrew; the blanket television coverage of 9/11. He described the day's events as being like those in a movie, "One with an unbelievable plot at that." While recognizing that e-mail (whose poetics have yet to be written) is not poetry, or even perhaps prose as we've known it (certainly not critical prose), I want to consider how Bernstein reacted to 9/11 in this, immediate, form. It matters, I suspect, that the form is *not* poetic, that it is the most banal form of written communication available to most of us, that his message was addressed not simply to friends but to much of his poetry's readership. These were not intimate letters, but they were also not the kinds of poems he usually composes in which the "I" is simply an option. There is an "I" in these e-mails, it is the "I" of Charles Bernstein, and that matters, I would argue, for the continuation of writing in the aftermath of 9/11.[2]

For here, from a poet who has always expressed disinterest in himself as a poetic subject (there are autobiographical moments in the poems, but they are often cloaked) we have e-mails that say nothing more than what happened to Charles Bernstein on those few days. It's no stretch, I suspect, to say that much of what he writes is what we would, under other circumstances (even these?) term "banal." The only substantive hint that the author is the poet Bernstein comes in the third e-mail, which begins by describing the weather in Manhattan, then digresses to report that, "By mistake I first wrote 'Word Trade Center.'" But, where the language of "mistakes" can usually be found front and center in Bernstein's work, we find him telling stories with beginnings, middles, and ends, written in language none too far from the simple lyrics of a pop song, like one by Paul Simon. In his e-mail of September 12, for example, Bernstein tells of dropping his son, Felix, off at a friend's house across from a fire station. After expressing "relief" to see firefighters cleaning their trucks, Bernstein reports, "Then we hear that nine of the thirty men stationed there perished." As a life event, this is shattering, dramatic; as writing, it is conventional, following formulas that Bernstein has elsewhere attacked in his writing on writing.

The trauma of this event reduces the poet of dysraphism to simple reportage of what seems. And, while the form of his e-mails is disjunctive, small vignettes separated by spaces or by asterisks, there is an evident attempt, conscious or no, to link these blocks together. Andrew the hairdresser, for example, appears more than once as a neighborhood presence, staying outside his store because his customers might want to see him there. And there is the return to the sky, the weather. There are seams in the text, but they are not intended to separate, rather to patch together. What we see in these e-mails is a community, a family, trying to deal with 9/11, mainly by observing it. This is the case, despite Bernstein's admission that the "image" cannot represent the reality of the event. The last lines in the third e-mail hearken to Eliot's conclusion to *The Waste Land* in their disjunctive sewing together of elements:

the image is greater than the reality
the image can't approach the reality
the reality has no image
*

our eyes are burning

In an e-mail to me, Bernstein writes that 9/11 affirmed his commitment to poetry and to teaching:

Because my work originates, at least in part, out of a desire to both confront and acknowledge catastrophe (bad turns, impasses), in the wake of September 11, I felt a continued commitment to poetry, to poetics, and indeed to teaching. If anything, 9/11 made me feel an intensified sense of the relevance of the office of poetry. Not the demeaning sense of poetry as 'comforting' in a time of crisis, put forward by such places as *The New York Times*. Rather, by this 'office of poetry' I mean poetry and poetics as a way of thinking in, around, and through 'the real', and in particular, a way of going beyond the deafeningly deceptive representations of 'reality' provided by the massed media.

Bernstein has long written against the "massed media," as he calls it, but he has not often written as a diarist himself. The journal, with its "and then" clauses and its tentative record of "what happened," proved to be the first form Bernstein, and many others, turned to after the events of 9/11. My own "Report from Hawai'i," published in *Masthead,* an on-line journal out of Australia, rested very much in the everyday; writing was for me a way to re-create what seemed normal, including sentences, syntax, ordinary language, the very items experimental and avant-garde poetries so often attempt to break open. While the oft-quoted remark by Stockhausen about 9/11, to the effect that it was a "work of art," was rightly seen as despicable, there is a way in which the cracking of ordinary bounds of sense and logic demands their return via other means— in e-mail exchanges, in poetry.

It turns out that Bernstein was not alone in his strategy for writing about the catastrophe of 9/11. While there were a couple of responses to my questions to the effect that poets *had* stopped writing, or were writing less, because they were angry and felt powerless, most of my respondents from the e-mail list had recognized the possibility of impasse and had consciously attempted to deal with it. The typical trajectory of this perhaps atypical poet was to feel silenced; to keep writing by "taking notes," making journalistic records of what he or she was doing amid the world's explosions; and putting many of these notes together into collage pieces, or writing, in two cases, using the Google news search engine. In several cases, poets wrote of changing their methods radically after 9/11.

One of the first respondents was Allison Cobb, a New York poet who was in the subway beneath the Twin Towers when the attack occurred.[3] Despite that proximity to the attack, she writes that she "felt wary of focusing too much on my own subjectivity." What she describes as "her own subjectivity," is actually, by extension, a national trait: "I wanted to avoid a reaction that's been critiqued many times: As the United States collectively seemed to turn its rage outward it also turned inward, suddenly regarding the individual experiences of suffering by its citizens as more profound, more important for informing action, than the suffering of anyone else in the world." This passage sheds light on the way in which Bernstein's e-mails, for example, while they are personal, are not in any sense "testimonial." Bernstein is not speaking *for* or even really *about* the victims of 9/11; he is speaking about those who in some (astonishing) cases were still rollerblading in the park that evening. Thus Cobb, like Bernstein, writes that she "felt compelled to record what [she] was experiencing." She wrote "journalistically," "just recording." Even

then, she turned back from her experience, and tried to make a link between it and previous texts, "using language from the death rituals of
various cultures," which made her scope larger than self; later on, she
began work on Christine de Pizan's "Lament on the Evils of Civil War."
While she is not writing memoir, which is often a form of testimony,
her responses and those of others to the catastrophic events of 9/11 and
later, speak to Miriam Fuchs's description of what she calls "life writing
and catastrophe." Fuchs argues that "This duality [between catastrophe
and narrative] generates text while simultaneously thwarting it." As a
result, she continues, "catastrophe narratives are highly dynamic, with
the urgencies of their conception dispersed throughout their progressive,
yet irregular structures" (198). The irregularity of structure in post-9/11
poetry writing is reflected in records of the event and attempts to write
about it, stitched together roughly, as they must be. While poets like
Cobb and Anselm Berrigan[4] try to avoid "testimonial" writing, meaning
writing that's focused on their subjectivities, they are doing the important work of bringing together the event with the language that people
use to talk about it. Such writing reaches out to the subjectivities of the
reader, in any case, reminding them of the dynamic instabilities of their
own reactions to catastrophic events.

This unexplicated link between note-taking, collage, and the poet's
paragraph-style pages is one that ushers up the question of poetic fashioning, a question whose primacy to Bernstein's project I hope to have
shown in the last chapter. Collage is a form that italicizes interrelation-
ships between different source texts, even as it permits those sources to
remain separate in voice, in tone, in rhythm. Collage is not a form that
gestures toward scattering, although it incorporates it; rather, collage asserts that where there are seams, there are things to be joined. This is not
dysraphic, even as Bernstein's e-mails are not dysraphic, even in their
scattered presentation of material (poetry approaching the status of
information, perhaps). I confess still to being stunned when the very
word "seams" began to spring up in the e-mail conversation, invoked by
K. Silem Mohammad[5] in response to a post by Anselm Berrigan. First,
Berrigan, who moved from "flow" poems to carefully worked poems
based on "notes" taken as he walked around New York. (He writes: "I was
very determined not to have an impasse," even as he adds that, like Cobb,
he did not want to write testimonial work.)

Once Berrigan had pages of notes, he writes: "the practice of stitching together notes or snatches of writing has become more and more my regular process, with working on the seams being a major technical aspect of it . . . It's a completely torturous method of writing for me, but I've accepted it recently as what I'm doing in order to make a certain kind of personal advance in terms of content-focus, for lack of a better way of putting it." Mohammad makes the "stitching" metaphor into one with "seams": "Like him [Berrigan], I found myself shifting almost entirely into a constructivist (in my case, heavily assemblage-based) mode of composition, in which the bulk of my attention went into working on the seams rather than generating the germinal phrase or line that had often been the starting point in a lot of my earlier work." Mohammad does not link this "working on the seams" with a later remark in his post, that he, like Berrigan, finds himself "using less and less punctuation." But if punctuation is itself a kind of "seaming," then to work those seams, to construct a poem in which they can be brought into relationship with each other, means the building of poems that lack punctuation. The seams will speak to themselves, it seems.

Mohammad uses Google to construct many of his poems; another poet who Googles is Juliana Spahr, who writes that "after 9/11 it felt really important for me to be writing but it felt important not to be writing knowing the answers, so I felt I had to keep writing to try to understand what the range of answers were." In another e-mail, she writes that "I can only talk about the events and nothing else, so something [is] silenced I guess." For Mohammad, the Google-based method of writing poems meant that his poetry was saturated with immediacy, and he relates that "his self-justifying theory is that the poems ironically register their own complicitness in the same social systems they puke at." Spahr's piece, "Poem written from November 30 to March 27," performs this work lyrically; as the poem accumulates, using the language of erotic love and Google news items, the lyric joins the worlds of love and the military industrial complex until they cannot be divorced. The poem gets at the "intimacy" Spahr wants to consider, that between "things [she] would rather not be intimate with. . . . " Her poem's form is that of lines and paragraphs that are separated by white space—a patchwork held together, in other words, by its seams.

I have only gestured at a much larger body of poetic evidence responding to the events of 9/11, and to the wars in Afghanistan and Iraq. Suffice it to say that this is not a poetry of "ease," as Oren Izenberg calls it, noting how little of it there is these days. Izenberg, in a *Boston Comment: Avant-Garde Debate,* argues that contemporary poetry has lost "a range of feeling," and is dominated by a sense of humiliation, however wryly and comically expressed by poets.[6] Transpose "humiliation" to "anger" and you do have the tone, or the origin, of much contemporary experimental poetry; this is not an age of ease, and its poets cannot impose ease upon dis-ease. But the poetry of seams that poets describe enables them to "construct," literally and figuratively, a world out of the pieces.

Not all of the poetry that emerges post-9/11 will work; poetry only rarely, perhaps, actually works, even less performs "real" work in the larger society, as Hart Crane knew, writing his tortured letters to Otto Kahn. Not all of the poetry that comes out of 9/11 will appear to address the impasse or block such events force (if not create), or break out of the silences they impose. The questions of relevance, of audience, of efficacy, will always haunt us. And solutions to the problem of impasse that I have described throughout this book may no longer apply, in this new world (disorder). Where I described Bernstein's poetics in the chapter on Crane as taking all language as its form, creating a nearly imperial expansiveness, I do not see such expansiveness in his new work, or in that of many of the other poets whose work I read. Instead, there is a drawing back, a new skepticism about language that goes beyond that of the Language writers, who intended to cure language by using a lot of it. (Such a statement is, I realize, horribly reductive!) John Ashbery's liberating model reveals its age these days, even if his work still speaks to us out of its moments; while he is more of a political poet than many of us acknowledge with regularity, his use of language may seem unquestioning in the face of current world events. And, while he works his way out from under his archcritic, as I hope to have shown in my chapter on his "conversation" with Harold Bloom, that does not solve the problem of *world.* The question of "flow," raised by Anselm Berrigan and others, is equally a problem of form in the face of acts of formlessness and deformation. The poem no longer "takes off" from a phrase or from language as ongoing process, as K. Silem Mohammad comments, but from fact, and grim fact at that. This is not to say that the new poetry will be humorless, but that its ostensible reach may be reduced, and not for reasons of Bloomian belatedness. Within that reduction, however, are crucial fields for poetry; in political terms, poets have such language as that implicit in the "Patriot Act" to deal with (Adrienne Rich's "a patriot is not a missile" is instructive here); in social terms there is the language of intolerance to "correct" (my language slips knowingly into the moral realm). While I do not buy the argument that the language has been so infected by bad use (by Donald Rumsfeld as one example, George W. Bush an equal and opposite case, and so on), I would suggest that taking these uses of language as our text, which we must do, is a dangerous business. We will need all the tools given us by avant-garde and Language poets, as well as those more steeped in vocabularies of subjectivity.

And there are lessons to be drawn from the writers I've considered, as well. Ronald Johnson's reductions of text are illustrative here, though his poetic texts are literary, if not his recipes. To "reduce" a text, as Johnson does, is to recontextualize it, give it space in a new historical period, much as a poet like Allison Cobb claims to do with language from Christine de Pizan, say, or the Google poets with online wizardry. But these contemporary poets are recontextualizing texts with a view to speaking *through* source texts about political issues, to write "poems including history" (though hardly Poundian poems with Poundian politics). In using source texts and making them into stories, however full of seams, these poets are taking Susan Howe as one of their crucial models. And, in letting the voices of those who have not spoken (in a long time, or ever) ring through, they take Yamanaka's speakers as examples, whether they know it or not. Contemporary poetry, by which I mean the poetry being written *today,* is as political as any written in this nation's history. That it addresses the impasses and imperfections of our history goes without saying.

Notes

INTRODUCTION

1. Marjorie Perloff asks about the form of this "essay," which is so obviously indebted to Charles Bernstein's "Artifice of Absorption" (see note 2). I have used the poem/essay form for a couple of reasons. It allows me to combine critical and creative discourses in ways that propel both of them. And it pays homage to Bernstein's essay even where, at crucial moments, it takes that essay to task. A related, but different, use of the term "reader's block" can be found in David Markson's 1996 novel by that name.

2. See Charles Bernstein's "Artifice of Absorption," in *A Poetics,* where he argues against an "absorptive" model of writing and reading (what one gets in romance or sci-fi), in favor of an "anti-absorptive" model, or one more likely to be found in avant-garde poetry and fiction.

3. See Juliana Spahr's *Everybody's Autonomy* for a detailed model of reading based on Language writing, but worked out in readings of writers such as Theresa Hak Kyung Cha and Harryette Mullen, not usually included in the Language "canon."

4. See Ron Silliman's essay "The New Sentence" in his book by the same name, for his theory of prose poetry as disjunction, hence as vehicle for the reader's creation of meaning, especially: "The new sentence is a decidedly contextual object. Its effects occur as much between, as within, sentences" (92).

5. Quoting Emily Dickinson here, from a poem about the brain, where she points to a distinction between "syllable and sound" that is also a brain-breaker in the classroom. (#632)

6. Lyn Hejinian, 40–58.

7. Since the time that remark was made, circa 1989 or 1990, Yamanaka has published a book of poems in Hawai'i, namely, *Saturday Night at the Pahala Theatre* (Bamboo Ridge Press, 1993) and nearly half a dozen novels with New York publishing houses. Yamanaka told this story to a group of my students several years ago; the force of her anger was apparent years after the event.

8. The phrase "da kine" originated on the plantations, where speaking in code was an important strategy for avoiding notice by the "luna," or field boss. Hence, "da kine" is a phrase that refers to something both speaker and listener understand, but an outsider might not. As one of my students put it, "It's amazing that you always know what it means when you hear it." *Da Kine* is the name of a Hawai'i gay publication, and reveals another use for this language of secrecy. "He's, you know, da kine," can mean, "He's gay, you know."

9. For what it's worth, the Spring 2003 Small Press Distribution catalogue lists Kanae's book as "poetry," Tonouchi's as "cultural writing."

10. Sondheim's "Philosophical Text: Theology and Colonialism" was posted on May 30, 2003 to the Poetics List in Buffalo. The first word of the posting is "hanai." When I queried him about his use of Hawaiian, and brought attention to the word "hanai," Sondheim wrote, "Could you say more about hanai?" indicating that he did not know what it means. His post of June 1 relates that he's "been reading a Hawaiian grammar and another Hawaiian dictionary; I've also been reading some of the history, mythology, etc. of Hawaiian." While his recognition that theology and colonialism are, in Hawai'i, related issues is correct, his use of the language without having studied it makes his project problematic, to put it mildly, in the context of the very colonialism he seeks to fight.

11. See Rob Wilson's *Reimagining the American Pacific: From South Pacific to Bamboo Ridge and Beyond* for a sympathetic history of Bamboo Ridge from its origins in the late 1970s to the near-present.

12. For material on George Helm, see Rodney Morales's collaged text about the activist's life, *Ho'i Ho'i Ho: A Tribute to George Helm,* and his recent novel, *When the Shark Bites,* in which Helm's life and work is fictionalized.

13. See Steve Evans's Third Factory Web site for an essay on *Fence* magazine that is relevant here, for its inclusions and exclusions (*http://thirdfactory.net/resistible.html*). I do not mean to single Evans out, however; most practitioners of avant-garde criticism, including this one, perform similar acts of exclusion.

14. The more current term for "mainland" is "continent," which avoids the linguistic trap of marking Hawai'i as marginal, "off the map," where it so often finds itself (or can't, as the case may be).

15. See Claudia Keelan's book, *Utopic,* for a marvelous synthesis of what one might call "MFA writing" with more avant-garde moves and sentiments.

16. See Steve Evans's "The American Avant-Garde After 1989: Notes Toward a History."

17. See Bill Luoma's *Dear Dad* and his poem "My Trip to New York City" in *Works and Days.*

18. Eric Chock, *Last Days Here.*

19. In "Late Echo," John Ashbery writes, in Bloomian fashion: "Alone with our madness and favorite flower / We see that there really is nothing left to write about. / Or rather, it is necessary to write about the same old things / In the same way" (*Selected Poems* 267; originally printed in *As We Know* (1979).

20. In *Poetic Epistemologies,* Megan Simpson quotes Jerome McGann on the performative nature of Howe's poetics, an idea that is quite relevant to my own thinking about Howe's work, and experimental poetry more generally (166).

21. The MELUS conference was in 1997. Trask has several books of poetry and political criticism, including a recent book of poems, *Night is a Sharkskin Drum.*

22. Anne Brewster read and discussed her ideas about "whiteness" at the University of Hawai'i in May 2003.

23. Hank Lazer, Raintaxi.com review of my *Memory Cards & Adoption Papers.*

24. "Nature poetry" provides sloppy shorthand here for notions of "organic form," generally associated with nature poetry in the twentieth century.

25. See Marjorie Perloff's new introduction to *The Futurist Moment* for a discussion of plans for replacing the Twin Towers at ground zero.

CHAPTER 1

1. James Longenbach writes persuasively about the relationship between Crane and the New Critics. He argues that "one has only to place Crane's work within the literary and political context of the Twenties to realize that his friends' judgments have more to do with the debates over the New Humanism and the New Criticism than with the intrinsic merits of *The Bridge*" (82).

2. The best study of Crane's relationship to Allen Tate is Langdon Hammer's *Hart Crane & Allen Tate: Janus-Faced Modernism.* That Hammer's narrative ends with Lowell, and mine in this essay includes Allen Ginsberg and Charles Bernstein, indicates the pervasive (if often unacknowledged) force of Crane's influence on poets who followed him.

3. For an extended argument about Crane's "homosexual text," see Thomas Yingling.

4. In "General Aims and Theories" Crane writes: "It is as though a poem gave the reader as he left it a single, new *word,* never before spoken and impossible to actually enunciate, but self-evident as an active principle in the reader's consciousness henceforward" (*Complete Poems* 221).

5. See Miriam Fuchs's brief discussion of Crane's relationship (personal and professional) with Otto Kahn in "Poet and Patron."

6. Allergies plagued Crane throughout his life. He suffered from hay-fever, and wrote about it often to his family. In a May 7, 1927 letter, for example, to his father he wrote, linking his allergy to "bridges":

> I am refer[r]ing to such divers matters as hay fever and 'bridges'. I'm sure I've mentioned more than once that this particular valley out here—for God knows what reason—does, however, as a proven fact furnish me almost complete immunity from that nightmare affliction. It has so happened that for a number of years you haven't seen me under the benign influence of Ohioan pollens during the months of June, July, Sept. & October,—so you probably don't so sharply recollect what a miserable looking critter I become during

those twelve or so weeks every year . . . I used to be asked to remain away from the office—often for several days—during my hay-fever period with Corday & Gross. (T. S. W. Lewis 558)

CHAPTER 2

1. There are only two book-length studies of her work: Joyce Wexler's *Laura Riding's Pursuit of Truth,* and Barbara Adams's book, *The Enemy Self: Poetry and Criticism of Laura Riding,* as well as a biography by Deborah Baker, *In Extremis: The Life of Laura Riding.*

2. I agree with Lentricchia in *Ariel* insofar as he criticizes Gilbert and Gubar's work as essentialist and hence ahistorical: "The claim that Gilbert and Gubar make on behalf of the female writer rests on their inability to keep from assenting to what they do not want to assent to, a keystone premise of patriarchal thought that grants the male debilitation of reason known as emotion . . . " (182).

3. See Gilbert and Gubar's *The War of the Words,* especially the third chapter, "Tradition and the Female Talent: Modernism and Masculinism," 125–162, and *Sexchanges.*

4. Adams argues that Riding was "unable to unite the perfected poetic self with the real self" and that she divided herself into a "good self," associated with the poems, and the " 'bad' actual self who yields to the usual needs of the senses and the flesh" (1–2). I would associate the former with what Riding considered to be her "masculine" side, the latter with her "feminine" side.

5. As Diana Fuss argues, this opposition between essentialism and constructionism is inevitable, for constructionism is impossible "without a fundamental dependency upon essentialism" (*Essentially Speaking* 4). Yet Riding's brave attempt to deconstruct essences in much of her poetry was derailed by her simultaneous belief in them. Elsewhere Fuss states the problem at the center of my essay as follows: "Is it possible to be an essentialist deconstructionist, when deconstruction is commonly understood as the very displacement of essence? By the same token, is it legitimate to call oneself an anti-essentialist feminist . . . ?" ("Reading" 77). Fuss proposes a compromise, according to which essentialism would be saved for political purposes, if not for artistic ones. Such a position, which I find problematic for its Rorty-esque splitting of the public from the private realm, was not one that Riding discovered, or which she would have found useful.

6. The Fugitives explained their award of the 1924 prize to Riding as follows: "With a diverse play of imagination she combines in her poetry a sound intellectuality and a keen irony which give her work a substance not often found in current American poetry, . . . she has developed her own idiom of expression" (Wexler 10). Louise Cowan writes at some length about Riding's experiences as a Fugitive poet.

7. The ultimate problem with Imagism, according to Riding and Graves, is that it only repeats old saws in new ways: "They [the Imagists] *believed* in free verse; and to believe in one way of writing poetry as against another is to have the attitude of a quack rather than of a scientist toward one's art, to be in a position of selling one's

ideas rather than of constantly submitting them to new tests . . . they could only go so far as to say everything that had already been said before in a slightly different way" (117).

8. This and all other poems by Riding cited in this chapter are from *The Poems by Laura Riding: A New Edition of the 1938 Collection.*

9. Quoted in Gilbert and Gubar, *Shakespeare's Sisters,* 584.

10. For material on the gaze see Jacques Lacan's essay. For the feminist revision of the concept see the first chapter of Homans's *Bearing the Word* and E. Ann Kaplan's essay on the male gaze in film.

11. *Sulfur* published Riding's essay, "Engaging In the Impossible," in 1984. This does not go much farther than her essay that accompanied the collected poems in 1938 in explaining her ideas about poetry. The Language poets, like Riding, seek to write poems that are more about the language in which they are written than they are about the world outside the poem. Like Riding, they are formalists, if not the authors of New Critical poems. I am thinking now particularly of Michael Palmer's "Baudelaire Series," in which he describes himself as a poet who watches his poem—possessed of a life of its own—appear on the computer screen (31). Not everyone includes him among the Language group, I should add.

12. T. S. Matthews's recollections are not necessarily to be trusted as the "truth." Barbara Adams, for one, thinks it impossible at present to speculate on the reasons for Riding's renunciation of poetry (19). Whatever the truth-value of Matthews's story, it certainly reflects a larger, though perhaps ill-defined cultural myth, which has to do with a woman's self-silencing. Even if we take it as myth rather than history, this account is faithful to the situation of the modernist woman poet.

CHAPTER 3

1. As Perelman writes, "And the 'I' embodies the problematics of Stein's career: her seemingly endless output was not selfless meditation: she insisted on its value as masterpiece and her own value as genius" (130). Perelman's thesis, in short, is that Stein *is* a genius.

2. See Whitman's "When Lilacs Last in the Dooryard Bloom'd," where half of section 14 is in the voice of the bird (*Poetry and Prose* 464–65).

3. See Eliot's "Tradition and the Individual Talent" (in *Selected Essays,* 3–11).

4. This is not a view Wyndham Lewis would have shared. In *Time and Western Man,* he goes out of his way to attack Stein for her "child mind" (53–58).

CHAPTER 4

1. For information on the specifics of Ashbery's career and awards, see Lesniak (20–22).

2. See John Ernest's marvelous critique of "influence" as a theoretical term in "Fossilized Fish and the World of Unknowing: John Ashbery and William Bronk." Ernest discusses two poets who are in some ways similar, but who had no influence on each other. Ernest argues, "Fundamentally, narratives of influence are acts of

appropriation in the name of historical coherence, acts geared toward identifying the contours of a possible community of understanding" (169).

3. Bloom begins an essay from *Agon*, which became the introduction to the Chelsea House collection of essays *Modern Critical Views: Hart Crane*, by remembering the first time he read Crane: "I remember reading these lines [from *The Bridge*] when I was ten years old, crouched over Crane's book in a Bronx library. . . . I still have the volume of Crane that I persuaded my older sister to give me on my twelfth birthday, the first book I ever owned" (1). Such is the critic's version of Abe Lincoln's log-cabin-to-the-White House narrative.

4. Andrew Ross also argues for Ashbery's position as part of a larger tradition, though the tradition to which he assigns the poet is very different from Bloom's. Ross writes that "at least one of [Ashbery's] volumes [*The Tennis Court Oath*] directly aligns itself with the formal spirit and repertoire of techniques espoused by the historical avant-garde of Europe between the wars" (201).

5. Ammons dedicated "The Arc Inside and Out" to Harold Bloom and also wrote a poem entitled "For Harold Bloom" (*Selected Poems* 101, 105).

6. See especially the last lines of Bishop's "Poem": "Our visions coincided— 'visions' is / too serious a word—our looks, two looks: / art 'copying from life' and life itself" (38).

7. Fredric Jameson has famously argued that postmodernism can be characterized by the appearance of pastiche rather than parody: "Pastiche is, like parody, the imitation of a peculiar or unique, idiosyncratic style, the wearing of a linguistic mask, speech in a dead language. But it is a neutral practice of such mimicry, without any of parody's ulterior motives, amputated of the satiric impulse, devoid of laughter and of any conviction that alongside the abnormal tongue you have momentarily borrowed, some healthy linguistic normality still exists" (17). Ashbery, as I hope to show later in this essay, complicates this formulation; while he doesn't always seem to subscribe to the notion of a "healthy linguistic normality" (whatever that may be), his use of other poets' language is often parodic, and quite funny. His is a mimicry with motives, in other words.

8. Speculative studies on the growth of writers' careers and reputations include Lawrence Lipking's *The Life of the Poet*, John Rodden's *The Politics of Literary Reputation*, Michael Bérubé's *Marginal Forces/Cultural Centers*, and Libbie Rifkin's *Career Moves*.

9. For further discussion of *Three Poems*, see Mills-Courts, Murphy, and Schultz ("The Lyric Crash").

10. See Lentricchia on Stevens's change of titles (*Ariel* 163).

11. For Bloom's use of Orphism to read Crane, see his introduction to the Chelsea House collection on that poet.

12. Ashbery is playing with the mythical backgrounds to *The Waste Land*.

13. In "The Fire Sermon" section of *The Waste Land*, the speaker relates, "By the waters of Leman I sat down and wept" (36).

14. John Shoptaw writes of Ashbery's "crypt" words, tying Ashbery's practice to

that of Charles Bernstein, who also parodies the tradition through what one might call mis-mimicry. A crypt word, according to Shoptaw might be "borders," which would then be changed (utterly) into "boarders" (Schultz, *Tribe* 204).

15. See Stephen Paul Miller's analogous reading of "Self-Portrait in a Convex Mirror" as a poem about Watergate.

16. Miller reports that Ashbery said to him, "Oh, Nixon was a great president. I wish he was still president" (148).

17. John Shoptaw relates that in the fall of 1987, some few months after the death of Ashbery's mother, "Trevor Winkfield, whose own mother had died recently, suggested that Ashbery write a 'one-hundred page poem about his mother.' Ashbery recalled thinking to himself, 'Say, that's something I haven't done before!' yet hastened to add, 'of course, it's not about my mother' " (141).

18. See Bernstein's *A Poetics,* where he introduces his essays as follows: "if there's a temptation to read the long essay-in-verse ["Artifice of Absorption"] . . . as prose, I hope there will be an equally strong temptation to read the succeeding prose as if it were poetry" (3).

19. Mary Kinzie writes that "Ashbery is the passive bard of a period in which the insipid has turned into the heavily toxic" (17). Mark Jarman considers Ashbery's poetry to be "musical noise, like easy listening jazz."

CHAPTER 5

1. This phrase comes out of Johnson's *Company Fare: Effortless dishes for intimate gatherings* (1991).

2. In a November 19, 1995 interview, Johnson told Peter O'Leary that, "I've found some of the greatest lines I've ever written are in iambics. [laughing]" When pressed to come up with some, he responded by citing one of his cookbooks: "Do I have any [lines] on hand? Oh, I was thinking about the ending of one of my cookbooks; what was it?—You can analyze lines and you don't think about it beforehand, but when you look at it you realize it is "ta-tum, ta-tum, ta-tum, and that's why it has that ring, of an ultimate." [Page 12 of 14: http://www.trifectapress.com/johnson/interview.html.]

3. See especially M. F. K. Fisher's *The Art of Eating,* which collects five of her gastronomical works; Alice B. Toklas's cookbook, and Ruth Reichl's *Tender at the Bone.*

4. The *Joy of Cooking* is a model of erudition. The 1975 edition quotes Goethe (headnote), Thomas Jefferson (14), Horace (15), Mark Twain (123), and Dr. Johnson (850), among others. Need I add that these calls to authority are to the work of male writers?

5. In Milton's Eden, the author and the cook were not to be confused. *Paradise Lost* is not just a great book about the Fall of Adam and Eve (due to her desire to eat a new food), it is also a book about the consequences of *taste.* Book V concerns a meal, cooked by Eve, but ultimately authored by "our Nourisher." To eat is divine, but to taste is disobedient. From Book VIII:

This Paradise I give thee, count it thine
To till and keep, and of the fruit to eat:
Of every tree that in the garden grows
Eat freely with glad heart; fear here no dearth:
But of the tree whose operation brings
Knowledge of good and ill. . . . shun to taste (293).

6. See my omnibus review in *Talisman:* "'Called Null or Called Vocative'": A Fate of the Contemporary Lyric" (70–79), in which I develop an argument about the "voiceless lyric," or the lyric poem written without the intervention of an "I."

7. Many sections of *The Shrubberies* resound with Susan Howe's sounds, her plays on words, her word lists. I offer but a few short examples. On page 9: "zephyr sparkle drizzle / whistle up the wind / ask only sequence / & consequence . . . "; 13: "loft bare plain"; 113: "stroke unlimited amethyst." Any of these lines, and the following, could also be heard to echo Dickinson: "path—interfering patterns / moiré in depth & incidence / path—huge darknesses settle / all fireflies' nightingales" (102).

CHAPTER 6

1. In *The Sophist,* Bernstein defines the term "dysraphism" as follows: "'Dysraphism' is a word used by specialists in congenital disease to mean a dysfunctional fusion of embryonic parts—a birth defect . . . *Raph* literally means 'seam,' so dysraphism is mis-seaming—a prosodic device!" (44)

2. The "hero" of "Thorow," collected in *Singularities,* 1991, is a "scout" or "spy" in the wilderness. That this scout is also Susan Howe, scouting out the wilderness of texts, becomes clear in the prose preface, where she discusses the poem's origins in her visit to the Adirondacks in 1987.

3. Alasdair MacIntyre's *After Virtue* discusses the conflict between "emotive" and "rational" modes of thinking. See especially "The Nature of Moral Disagreement Today and the Claims of Emotivism," 6–22.

4. In "Marianne Moore," a review of Moore's work, Williams writes that "Miss Moore gets great pleasure from wiping soiled words or cutting them clean out, removing the aureoles that have been pasted about them or taking them bodily from greasy contexts. For the compositions which Miss Moore intends, each word should first stand crystal clear with no attachments; not even an aroma" (317–18).

5. Peter Middleton and Tim Woods introduce their book, *Literatures of Memory: History, Time and Space in Postwar Writing* (2000), by noting that their starting point "was the widespread conviction among literary and cultural critics and these historians, that the past has been killed, destroyed, lost or at best thinned out so much that it no longer seems relevant" (9). Their book offers important testimony that this is, in fact, not the case—that "even avant-garde poetry . . . still devotes much of its inventive energy to rethinking the relations between poetic form, individual memory, history and temporality" (188). Middleton and Woods are most in-

terested in the ways in which poets present personal memory, however. The poets they discuss are more mainstream, conventionally lyrical, than is Howe.

6. "Articulation of Sound Forms in Time" is the first section of *Singularities*. It was previously published by Awede press in 1987. For other close readings/explications of the poem, see Perloff (*Radical* 50–53), Back (37–57), Lazer (2:60–69).

CHAPTER 7

1. In "durations," David Antin talks/writes that he is interested in "that kind of performance in which the moment directs me which way to go." He speaks because spoken langauge is spontaneous, resembles the movement of thinking; Yamanaka speaks because her language belongs more to an oral culture than to a literate or literary one. The irony is that Antin speaks first and transcribes second, while Yamanaka writes her work first and then performs it. See Antin's "durations," page 65.

2. Rap Replinger's tape, *Poi Dog with Crabs* (1992) is only one of many comedy tapes available in Hawai'i. Local humor features the use of Pidgin and ethnic jokes that would make mainlanders blush.

3. There has been an explosion of publishing in and about Hawaiian language and culture. Most notable in the literary arena is the journal, '*oiwi*, founded by the late Mahealani Dudoit, and carried on by Ku'ualoha Ho'omanawanui. The journal features contemporary and archival writing by native Hawaiians; by presenting historical documentation, the journal aims to create a historical context for a larger struggle.

4. For an extension of such arguments, see *Whose Vision? Asian Settler Colonialism in Hawai'i*, a special issue of *Amerasia Journal* (2000), guest edited by Candace Fujikane and Jonathan Y. Okamura. Especially valuable are essays by Haunani-Kay Trask, Candace Fujikane, and Darlene Rodrigues.

CHAPTER 8

1. Laura (Riding) Jackson's dislike of fashion, in clothing and in poetry, can be found throughout her poetry and her polemics, from the beginning to the end of her bifurcated career. In "Poetry and the Literary Universe," collected in *Contemporaries and Snobs* (1928), she attacked "contemporary poetic gentlemanliness" in the following terms: "tortoise-shell spectacles natural history, toupee'd comparative religion and Arrow-collared Aristotelianism" (119). In the posthumous tome that she cowrote with her husband, Schuyler B. Jackson, which is introduced by Charles Bernstein, one finds this conflation: "The 'writers' lead the army of cultural intellectualism. They carry the language with them, or what seems to be the language. It is a version of the language adapted to the new compartmental principle of human understanding, the new wisdom-fashions'" (431).

2. In *Dark City,* Bernstein quotes (or invents) a review of another Bernstein's book: "Bernstein's argument is an important one and his discussion is consistently thoughtful, energetic, and smoothly handled. Any reader of the modern verse epic

will find *The Tale of the Tribe: Ezra Pound and the Modern Verse Epic* stimulating and provocative" (92). This is Michel André Bernstein.

3. Of course Orwell prefers a remedy by clarity, but his notion that "In our time, political speech and writing are largely the defence of the indefensible" (206) and that the fault lies in the (mis)use of language, resembles Bernstein's argument that, insofar as our politics are indefensible, the language did it to us.

4. Language writing has been variously attacked by its enemies (from the "scenic style" camp, among others) and, more recently, by its friends. One of the sharpest critiques of Bernstein's work is by Vernon Shetley, who prefers Ashbery's style of compromise to what he sees as Language writing's "radically dualistic schema" that sets traditional poetry and avant-garde poetry at extremes (142). More recent critiques include Susan Smith Nash's "Death, Decadence, & the Ironies of Language Poetics" and that of the four editors of *apex of the m* in 1994.

5. Charles Altieri writes of contemporary poetry much indebted to Romanticism that, "The central aim of the art is not to interpret experience but to extend language to its limits in order to establish poignant awareness of what lies beyond words. There is virtually never any sustained act of formal, dialectical thinking or any elaborate, artificial construction that cannot be imagined as taking place in, or at least extending from, settings in naturalistically conceived scenes. As shorthand I will call this the scenic style" (11).

6. Robert Pinsky, in *The Situation of Poetry*, writes that, "The poet's medium, then, is abstract, more or less discursive, and in some senses conventional" (5).

7. In "Stray Straws and Straw Men," Bernstein argues that "Voice is a possibility for poetry not an essence" (42).

8. The issue of *boundary 2* on Bernstein's work was edited by Paul Bové and includes a personal interview with Bernstein by Loss Pequeño Glazier; the interview is remarkable for the openness with which Bernstein talks about himself and his family.

CODA

1. The subpoetics list (by nomination only). This list is populated largely by poets in their thirties, centered in New York, Washington, and Boston.

2. Bernstein's e-mails were posted on September 11, 12, and 16, 2001, on the Buffalo-based poetics list. The archive is located at the Electronic Poetry Center site at UB: http://epc.buffalo.edu.

3. Allison Cobb is the author of *Born Two* from Chax Press, 2004.

4. Anselm Berrigan is author of *Strangers in the Nest* (Dolphin, 2002), *Zero Star Hotel* (Edge, 2002) and *Integrity & Dramatic Life* (Edge, 1998), among other books of poetry. He currently runs the reading series at the Poetry Project in New York City.

5. K. Silem Mohammad is author of *A Thousand Devils* (Combo Books, 2004), *Deer Head Nation* (Tougher Disguises, 2003) and *Hovercraft* (Kenning, 2000).

6. This was the *Boston Comment: Avant-Garde Debate*, printed online at

http://www.bostoncomment.com/debate.html. In it, Izenberg, writes, "When I read the poetry of my contemporaries who locate themselves in the tradition of radical innovation, I find there many shades of humor to enjoy . . . The negative emotions are also broadly represented—by many flavors of rage and indignation, passionate bewilderment, mourning and even flatness in response to loss. Both of these spectra of feeling belong, by and large, to the *humiliated* person, to the voice whose occasions for speaking are instances of the world's failure either to accommodate its existence or to provide a justification for its desire to exist" (page 30 of my printout).

Works Cited

Adams, Barbara. *The Enemy Self: Poetry and Criticism of Laura Riding*. Ann Arbor: UMI Research Press, 1990.

Allen, Graham. *Harold Bloom: A Poetics of Conflict*. New York: Harvester, 1994.

Altieri, Charles. *Self and Sensibility in Contemporary American Poetry*. New York: Cambridge UP, 1984.

Ammons, A. R. *The Selected Poems*. New York: Norton, 1986.

Andrews, Bruce, and Charles Bernstein, eds. *The L=A=N=G=U=A=G=E Book*. Carbondale: Southern Illinois UP, 1984.

Antin, David. "durations." *what it means to be avant-garde*. New York: New Directions, 1993. 65–92.

Ashbery, John. *As We Know*. New York: Viking, 1979.

———. *The Double Dream of Spring*. New York: Ecco, 1970.

———. *Flow Chart*. New York: Knopf, 1991.

———. Interview with Sue Gangel. *American Poetry Observed: Poets on Their Work*. Ed. Joe David Bellamy. Urbana: U of Illinois P, 1984. 9–20.

———. *Selected Poems*. New York: Viking, 1985.

———. *Self-Portrait in a Convex Mirror*. New York: Viking, 1975.

———. *The Tennis Court Oath*. Middletown, CT: Wesleyan UP, 1962.

———. *Three Poems*. New York: Viking, 1972.

———. *A Wave*. New York: Viking, 1984.

Back, Rachel Tzvia. *Led by Language: The Poetry and Poetics of Susan Howe*. Tuscaloosa: U of Alabama P, 2002.

Baker, Deborah. *In Extremis: The Life of Laura Riding*. New York: Grove Press, 1993.

Barthes, Roland. *The Fashion System*. Trans. Matthew Ward and Richard Howard. Berkeley: U of California P, 1990. Originally published in French, 1967.

Beard, James. *Delights and Prejudices*. New York: Barnes and Noble, 1964.

Begley, Adam. "Colossus Among Critics: Harold Bloom." *New York Times Magazine* (25 September 1994): 32–35.

Bercovitch, Sacvan. *The American Jeremiad*. Madison: The U of Wisconsin P, 1978.

Bernstein, Charles. *A Poetics*. Cambridge, MA: Harvard UP, 1992.

——. *Content's Dream: Essays 1975–1984*. Los Angeles: Sun & Moon, 1986.

——. *Controlling Interests*. New York: Roof, 1980.

——. *Dark City*. Los Angeles: Sun & Moon, 1994.

——. "Frame Lock." In *My Way*. 90–99.

"An Interview with Tom Beckett." In Bernstein, *Content's Dream*. 385–410.

——. *Islets / Irritations*. New York: Roof, 1983, 1992.

——. *My Way: Speeches and Poems*. Chicago: U of Chicago P, 1999.

——. "Narrating Narration: The Shapes of Ron Silliman's Work." In *Content's Dream*. 305–20.

——. Personal communication, e-mail of 12/5/2004.

——. *Rough Trades*. Los Angeles: Sun & Moon, 1991.

——. "Stray Straws and Straw Men," in *The L=A=N=G=U=A=G=E Book*. 39–45.

——. *The Sophist*. Los Angeles: Sun & Moon, 1987.

Bérubé, Michael. *Marginal Forces / Cultural Centers: Tolson, Pynchon, and the Politics of the Canon*. Ithaca: Cornell UP, 1992.

Bishop, Elizabeth. *Geography III*. New York: Farrar, 1976.

Bloom, Harold. *Agon: Towards a Theory of Revisionism*. New York: Oxford UP, 1982.

——. *The Anxiety of Influence: A Theory of Poetry*. New York: Oxford UP, 1973.

——. *Figures of Capable Imagination*. New York: Seabury, 1976.

——. "Harold Bloom on Poetry." *New Republic* (29 November 1975): 24–26.

——. Introduction. *Modern Critical Views: Hart Crane*. Ed. Harold Bloom. New York: Chelsea House, 1986: 1–15.

——. *A Map of Misreading*. New York: Oxford UP, 1975.

——. *The Western Canon: The Books and School of the Ages*. New York: Harcourt, 1994.

Blume, Peter. "A Recollection of Hart Crane." *Yale Review* 76:2 (March 1987): 152–156.

Bourdain, Anthony. *Kitchen Confidential: Adventures in the Culinary Underbelly*. New York: Bloomsbury, 2001.

Bové, Paul, ed. *boundary 2* 23:3 (Fall 1996): 1–72.

Brathwaite, Edward Kamau. "Nation Language." In Bill Ashcroft, Gareth Griffiths, and Helen Tiffin, eds. *The Post-Colonial Studies Reader*. London: Routledge, 1995. 309–313.

Breward, Christopher. *The Culture of Fashion: A New History of Fashionable Dress*. Manchester: Manchester UP, 1995.

Bridgman, Robert. *Gertrude Stein in Pieces*. New York, 1970.

Brooks, Cleanth. *Modern Poetry and the Tradition*. 1939; rpt. New York: Oxford UP, 1965.

——. *The Well-Wrought Urn: Studies in the Structure of Poetry*. Harvest Books, 1956.

Brooks, Cleanth, and Robert Penn Warren. *Understanding Poetry*. New York: Holt, Rinehart and Winston, 1938.

Brunner, Edward. "'The Farewell Day Unkind': The Fragmentary Poems Of Hart Crane's Last Five Years." In *The Green American Tradition: Essays and Poems for Sherman Paul.* Ed. H. Daniel Peck. Baton Rouge: LSU Press, 1989. 155–170.

Butler, Judith. *Bodies That Matter: On the Discursive Limits of "Sex."* New York: Routledge, 1993.

Caldwell, Patricia. *The Puritan Conversion Narrative: The Beginnings Of American Expression.* New York: Cambridge UP, 1983.

Campbell, Julie D. "M. F. K. Fisher and the Embodiment of Desire: A Study in Auto-biography and Food as Metaphor." *Biography* 20:2 (Spring 1997): 181–202.

Carr, Elizabeth. "A Recent Chapter in the Story of the English Language in Hawaii." In *Social Process in Hawaii* XXIV (1960): 54–62.

Cheyfitz, Eric. *The Poetics of Imperialism: Translation and Colonization from The Tempest to Tarzan.* New York: Oxford UP, 1991.

Chock, Eric. Interview with Susan Schultz in February, 1996.

———. *Last Days Here.* Honolulu: Bamboo Ridge Press, 1989–90. Also on tape.

Chock, Eric, and Darrell Lum, eds. *The Best of Bamboo Ridge: The Hawaii Writers' Quarterly.* Honolulu: Bamboo Ridge Press, 1986.

Cixous, Hélenè. "The Laugh of the Medusa." *The Signs Reader: Women, Gender, and Scholarship.* Ed. Elizabeth Abel and Emily K. Abel. Chicago: U of Chicago P, 1983. 279–97.

Cowan, Louise. *The Fugitive.* Baton Rouge: LSU P, 1959.

Collins, Loretta. "Rude Bwoys, Riddim, Rub-a-dub and Rastas: Caribbean Perfor-mative Sounds." In Adelaide Morris, ed. *Sound States: Innovative Poetics and Acoustical Technologies.* Durham: U of North Carolina P, 1998. 169–93.

Craik, Jennifer. *The Face of Fashion.* London: Routledge, 1994.

Crane, Hart. *The Complete Poems and Selected Letters and Prose of Hart Crane.* Ed. Brom Weber. New York: Anchor, 1966.

Dauber, Kenneth. *The Idea of Authorship in America: Democratic Poetics from Frank-lin to Melville.* Madison: U of Wisconsin P, 1990.

Davenport, Guy. *The Geography of the Imagination: Forty Essays.* San Francisco: North Point, 1981.

Davidson, Michael. *The San Francisco Renaissance: Poetics And Community at Mid-Century.* New York: Cambridge UP, 1991.

Davis, Fred. *Fashion, Culture, and Identity.* Chicago: The U of Chicago P, 1992.

De Certeau, Michel. *The Writing of History.* Trans. Tom Conley. New York: Colum-bia UP, 1988. Published in French in 1975.

DeKoven, Marianne. *A Different Language: Gertrude Stein's Experimental Writing.* Madison: U of Wisconsin P, 1983.

Deleuze, Gilles. "One Manifesto Less." Trans. Alan Orenstein. In *The Deleuze Reader.* Ed. Constantin V. Boundas. New York: Columbia UP, 1993. 204–22. Trans. from *Superpositions,* by Gilles Deleuze and Carmelo Bene. Paris: Les Editions de Minuit, 1979.

Deleuze, Gilles, and Felix Guattari. "What Is Minor Literature?" In Russell Ferguson, et al, eds. *Out There: Marginalization and Contemporary Cultures.* Cambridge: The MIT P, 1990. 59–70.

DeShazer, Mary K. *Inspiring Women: Reimagining the Muse* New York: Pergamon Press, 1986.

Dickinson, Emily. *The Complete Poems of Emily Dickinson.* Ed. Thomas H. Johnson. Boston: Little, Brown, 1960.

Douglas, Mary. "Deciphering a Meal." *Implicit Meanings: Essays in Anthropology.* London: Routledge, 1999. 249–75.

DuPlessis, Rachel Blau. "Echological Scales: On *ARK* of Ronald Johnson." In manuscript.

Dydo, Ulla E., ed. *A Stein Reader.* Evanston: Northwestern UP, 1993.

——. "Reading the Hand Writing: The Manuscripts of Gertrude Stein." In Bruce Kellner, ed. *A Gertrude Stein Companion: Content with the Example.* New York: Greenwood P, 1988. 84–95.

Eliot, T. S. *The Waste Land and Other Poems.* New York: Harcourt, 1962.

——. *Selected Essays.* New edition. New York: Harcourt, 1964.

Ernest, John. "Fossilized Fish and the World of Unknowing: John Ashbery and William Bronk." In Schultz, ed. *Tribe* 168–89.

Evans, Steve. "The American Avant-Garde after 1989: Notes Toward a History." In Edward Foster and Joseph Donahue, eds. *The World in Time and Space: Towards a History of Innovative American Poetry in Our Time.* Jersey City: Talisman House, 2002.

——. http://www.umit.maine.edu/%7Esteven.evans/3F-1

——. "*The Resistible Rise of Fence Enterprises.*" http://thirdfactory.net/resistible.html

Ewen, Stuart. *All Consuming Images: The Politics of Style in Contemporary Culture.* New York: Basic Books, 1988.

Ewen, Stuart, and Elizabeth Ewen. *Channels of Desire: Mass Images and the Shaping of American Consciousness.* Minneapolis: U of Minnesota P, 1982, 1992.

Fisher, M. F. K. *The Art of Eating.* 5th ed. Hoboken, NJ: Wiley, 2004.

Fuchs, Miriam. *The Text Is Myself: Women's Life Writing and Catastrophe.* Madison: U of Wisconsin P, 2003.

——. "Poet and Patron: Hart Crane and Otto Kahn." *Book Forum* (VI:1) 1982: 45–51.

Fujikane, Candace. "Sweeping Racism under the Rug of 'Censorship': The Controversy over Lois-Ann Yamanaka's Blu's Hanging." In Fujikane and Okamura. 158–94.

Fujikane, Candace, and Jonathan Okamura, eds. *Asian Settler Colonialism in Hawai'i.* Special issue of *Amerasia Journal* 26:2, 2000.

Fuss, Diana. *Essentially Speaking: Feminism, Nature, and Difference.* London: Routledge, 1989.

——. "Reading Like a Feminist." *Differences: A Journal of Feminist Cultural Studies* 1.2 (Summer, 1989): 77–92.

Gilbert, Sandra, and Susan Gubar. *The Madwoman in the Attic: The Woman Writer and the Nineteenth-Century Literary Imagination.* New Haven: Yale UP, 1979.

———, eds. *Shakespeare's Sisters: Feminist Essays on Women Poets.* Bloomington: Indiana UP, 1979.

———. *No Man's Land: The Place of the Woman Writer in the Twentieth Century.* Vol. 1: *The War of the Words.* New Haven: Yale UP, 1988.

———. *No Man's Land 2: Sexchanges.* New Haven: Yale UP, 1989.

Glissant, Edvouard. *Caribbean Discourse: Selected Essays.* Ed. and trans. J. Michael Dash. Charlottesville: U of Virginia P, 1989.

Goldberg, Natalie. *Writing Down the Bones: Freeing the Writer Within.* Boston: Shambhala Publications, 1986, 1998.

Graves, Robert. *The White Goddess: A Historical Grammar of Poetic Myth.* 1948; rpt. New York: Farrar, Straus & Giroux, 1988.

Gray, Paul. "American Poetry: School's Out." *Time* (26 April 1976): 95–98.

Greenblatt, Stephen. *Renaissance Self-Fashioning: From More to Shakespeare.* Chicago: U of Chicago P, 1980.

Grossman, Allen. "Hart Crane and Poetry: A Consideration of Crane's Intense Poetics." In *Modern Critical Views: Hart Crane.* Ed. Harold Bloom. New York: Chelsea House, 1986. 221–54.

Hall, David D. *The Antinomian Controversy, 1636–1638: A Documentary History.* 2nd ed. Durham: Duke UP, 1990.

Hammer, Langdon. *Hart Crane & Allen Tate: Janus-Faced Modernism.* Princeton: Princeton UP, 1993.

Hammer, Langdon, and Brom Weber, eds. *O My Land, My Friends: The Selected Letters of Hart Crane.* New York: Four Walls Eight Windows, 1997.

Hara, Marie. *Bananaheart & Other Stories.* Honolulu: Bamboo Ridge Press, 1995.

———. Interview with Susan Schultz in March, 1996.

Hebdige, Dick. *Subculture: The Meaning of Style.* London: Methuen, 1979.

Hejinian, Lyn. "The Rejection of Closure." In *The Language of Inquiry.* Berkeley: U of California P, 2000. 40–58.

Hollander, Anne. *Seeing Through Clothes.* New York: Viking, 1975.

Homans, Margaret. *Bearing the Word: Language and Female Experience in Nineteenth-Century Women's Writing.* Chicago: U of Chicago P, 1986.

———. *Women Writers and Poetic Identity: Dorothy Wordsworth, Emily Bronte, and Emily Dickinson.* Princeton: Princeton UP, 1980.

Hoover, Paul, ed. *Postmodern American Poetry: A Norton Anthology.* New York: Norton, 1994.

Howard, Richard. "A Formal Affair." *Poetry* 127 (1976): 349–51.

Howe, Mark DeWolfe. *The Garden and the Wilderness: Religion and Government in American Constitutional History.* Chicago: U of Chicago P, 1965.

Howe, Susan. *My Emily Dickinson.* Berkeley: North Atlantic Books, 1985.

———. *Singularities.* Hanover: UP of New England, 1990.

———. *The Birth-Mark: Unsettling the Wilderness in American Literary History.* Hanover, NH: UP of New England, 1993.

Howes, Craig. "Tradition, Literary History, and the Local Talent." In Lorna Hershinow, ed. *Hawai'i Literary Conference: Reader's Guide.* Honolulu: privately printed, 1994.

Huyssen, Andreas. *After the Great Divide: Modernism, Mass Culture, Postmodernism.* Bloomington: Indiana UP, 1986.

Inness, Sherrie A., ed. *Kitchen Culture in America: Popular Representations of Food, Gender, and Race.* Philadelphia: U of Pennsylvania P, 2001.

Jackson, Laura (Riding). *First Awakenings: The Early Poems of Laura Riding.* New York: Persea, 1992.

———. *Lives of Wives.* Los Angeles: Sun & Moon, 1995.

———. *The Poems of Laura Riding: A New Edition of the 1938 Collection.* New York: Persea, 1980.

———. *Progress of Stories.* New York: Dial, 1982.

———. *The Telling.* London: the Athlone Press, 1982.

———. *A Trojan Ending.* Rpt. Manchester, UK: Carcanet Press, 1985.

———. *The Word "Woman" and Other Related Writings.* New York, Persea, 1993.

Jackson, Laura (Riding), and Schuyler B. Jackson. *Rational Meaning: A New Foundation for the Definition of Words and Supplementary Essays.* Ed. William Harmon. Charlottesville: U of Virginia P, 1997.

Jameson, Fredric. *Postmodernism, or, The cultural logic of Late Capitalism.* Durham: Duke UP, 1991.

Jarman, Mark. "The Curse of Discursiveness." *Hudson Review* 45 (1992): 158–66.

Johnson, Ronald. *The American Table: More Than 400 Recipes That Make Accessible for the First Time the Full Richness of American Regional Cooking.* New York: Morrow, 1984.

———. *ARK.* Albuquerque: Living Batch Press, 1996.

———. *Company Fare: Effortless Dishes for Intimate Gatherings.* New York: Simon & Schuster, 1991.

———. *RADI OS OI-OIV.* Berkeley: Sand Dollar, 1977.

———. *To Do As Adam Did: Selected Poems.* Ed. Peter O'Leary. Jersey City, NJ: Talisman, 2000.

———. *Up to Now.* Unpublished typescript, 1997. 1–29.

———. *Valley of the Many-Colored Grasses.* New York: Norton, 1969.

Juhasz, Suzanne. *Naked and Fiery Forms: Modern American Poetry by Women, a New Tradition.* New York: Harper & Row, 1976.

Kalaidjian, Walter. *Languages of Liberation: The Social Text in Contemporary American Poetry.* New York: Columbia UP, 1989.

Kanae, Lisa Linn. *Sista Tongue.* Kane'ohe, HI: Tinfish Press, 2001.

Kaplan, Ann E. "Is the Gaze Male?" *Powers of Desire: The Politics of Sexuality.* Ed. Ann Snitow, Christine Stansell, and Sharon Thompson. New York: Monthly Review Press, 1983. 309–27.

Keelan, Claudia. *Utopic.* Farmington, ME: Alice James Books, 2000.

Kenner, Hugh. *The Pound Era.* Berkeley: U of California P, 1971.

Kinzie, Mary. *The Cure of Poetry in an Age of Prose: Moral Essays on the Poet's Calling.* Chicago: U of Chicago P, 1993.

Knight, Alan R. "Masterpieces, Manifestoes and the Business of Living: Gertrude Stein Lecturing." In Shirley Neuman and Ira B. Nadel, eds. *Gertrude Stein and the Making of Literature.* Boston: Northeastern UP, 1988.

Kostelanetz, Richard, ed. *The Yale Gertrude Stein.* New Haven: Yale UP, 1980.

Lacan, Jacques. *The Four Fundamental Concepts of Psychoanalysis.* Ed. Jacques-Alain Miller. Trans. Alan Sheridan. New York: Norton, 1978.

Lazer, Hank. *Opposing Poetries: Volume One: Issues and Institutions.* Evanston, IL: Northwestern UP, 1996.

———. *Opposing Poetries: Volume Two: Readings.* Evanston, IL: Northwestern UP, 1996.

———. Review of *Memory Cards & Adoption Papers,* by Susan M. Schultz. Raintaxi.com (Winter 2002/2003). http://www.raintaxi.com/online/2002winter/schultz.shtml

Lehman, David. "Yale's Insomniac Genius." *Newsweek* (18 August 1986): 56–57.

Lehmann, Ulrich. *Tigersprung: Fashion in Modernity.* Cambridge, MA: The MIT P, 2000.

Lentricchia, Frank. *Ariel and the Police: Michel Foucault, William James, Wallace Stevens.* Madison: U of Wisconsin P, 1988.

Lesniak, James G., ed. *Contemporary Authors: A Bio-Bibliographical Guide to Current Writers.* New Revisions Ser. Vol. 37. Detroit: Gale, 1992.

Levenstein, Harvey. *Paradox of Plenty: A Social History of Eating in Modern America.* New York: Oxford UP, 1993.

Lewis, Thomas S. W. *Letters of Hart Crane and His Family.* New York: Columbia UP, 1974.

Lewis, Wyndham. *Time and Western Man.* (1927.) Ed. Paul Edwards. Santa Rosa, CA: Black Sparrow, 1993.

Lind, Andrew W. "Communication: A Problem of Island Youth." In *Social Process in Hawaii* XXIV (1960): 44–53.

Linmark, R. Zamora. *Rolling the R's.* New York: Kaya, 1996.

Lipking, Lawrence. *The Life of the Poet: Beginning and Ending Poetic Careers.* Chicago: U of Chicago P, 1981.

Longenbach, James. "Hart Crane and T. S. Eliot: Poets in the Sacred Grove." *Denver Quarterly* 23:1 (Summer 1988): 82–103.

Lum, Darrell. Interview with Susan Schultz in February, 1996.

Luoma, Bill. *Dear Dad.* Kaneʻohe, HI: Tinfish Press, 2000.

———. *My Trip to New York City.* Hard Press Editions, 1991.

Lyotard, Jean-Francois. "Answering the Question: What is Postmodernism?" Trans. Regis Durand. In *The Postmodern Condition: A Report on Knowledge.* Trans. Geoff Bennington and Brian Massumi. Minneapolis: U of Minnesota P, 1984. 71–82.

MacIntyre, Alasdair. *After Virtue: A Study in Moral Theory.* Notre Dame: U of Notre Dame P, 1984.

Markson, David. *Reader's Block.* Normal, IL: Dalkey Archive, 1996.

Masuda, Barry. "Holoholo Style." *Tinfish* 1, Honolulu: Tinfish Press. October 1995. 28–29.

Matthews, T. S. *Under the Influence: Recollections of Robert Graves, Laura Riding and Friends.* London: Cassell, 1977.

McFeely, Mary Drake. *Can She Bake a Cherry Pie?: American Women and the Kitchen in the Twentieth Century.* Amherst: U of Massachusetts P, 2000.

Menand, Louis. *Discovering Modernism: T. S. Eliot and His Context.* New York: Oxford UP, 1987.

Meyerowitz, Patricia, ed. *Gertrude Stein: Writings and Lectures 1911–1956.* London: Peter Owen, 1967.

Middleton, Peter, and Tim Woods. *Literatures of Memory: History, Time and Space in Postwar Writing.* Manchester: Manchester UP, 2000.

Miller, Stephen Paul. "Periodizing Ashbery and His Influence." In Schultz, ed. *Tribe* 146–67.

Mills-Courts, Karen. *Poetry as Epitaph: Repesentation and Poetic Language.* Baton Rouge: LSU Press, 1990.

Milton, John. *The Complete Poems.* Ed. John Leonard. New York: Penguin, 1988.

Minh-ha, Trinh T. *Woman, Native, Other: Writing Postcoloniality and Feminism.* Bloomington: Indiana UP, 1989.

Moi, Toril. *Sexual/Textual Politics: Feminist Literary Theory.* New York: Methuen, 1985.

Monroe, Jonathan. Special Editor. *Diacritics* 26: 3–4 (Fall-Winter 1996).

Morales, Rodney, ed. *Hoʻi Hoʻi Ho: A Tribute to George Helm and Kimo Mitchell.* Honolulu: Bamboo Ridge Press, 1984.

———. Interview with Susan Schultz in January, 1996.

———. *When the Shark Bites.* Honolulu: U of Hawaiʻi P, 2002.

Morris, Adelaide, ed. *Sound States: Innovative Poetics and Acoustical Technologies.* Durham: U of North Carolina P, 1998.

Murayama, Milton. *All I Asking for Is My Body.* Honolulu: U of Hawaii P, 1988. Originally published 1977.

Murphy, Margueritte S. "John Ashbery's *Three Poems:* Heteroglossia in The American Prose Poem." *American Poetry* 7.2 (1990): 50–63.

Nash, Susan Smith. "Death, Decadence, & the Ironies of Language Poetics." *Talisman* 10 (Spring 1993): 201–5.

Neuman, Shirley, and Ira B. Nadel, eds. *Gertrude Stein and the Making of Literature.* Boston, Northeastern UP, 1988.

Naylor, Paul. *Poetic Investigations: Singing the Holes in History.* Evanston: Northwestern UP, 1999.

Ohmann, Richard. *English in America: A Radical View of the Profession.* New York: Oxford UP, 1976.

O'Leary, Peter. "An Interview with Ronald Johnson." *Chicago Review* 42:1 (1996): 32–53.

——. "Ronald Johnson Interview, November 19, 1995." http://www.trifectapress. com/johnson/interview.html 1–14.

——, ed. *To Do As Adam Did: Selected Poems of Ronald Johnson.* Jersey City: Talisman House, 2000.

Ong, Walter J. *Orality & Literacy: The Technologizing of the Word.* London: Routledge, 1982.

Orwell, George. "Politics and the English Language." In Paul Eschholz et al., eds. *Language Awareness: Essays for College Writers,* 7th edition. New York: Martin's Press, 1997. 199–210.

Ostriker, Alicia Suskin. *Stealing the Language: the Emergence of Women's Poetry in America.* Boston: Beacon, 1986.

Palmer, Michael. *Sun.* San Francisco: North Point, 1988.

Parkinson, Thomas. *Hart Crane and Yvor Winters: Their Literary Correspondence.* Berkeley: U of California P, 1978.

Perelman, Bob. *The Trouble with Genius: Reading Pound, Joyce, Stein and Zukofsky.* Berkeley: U of California P, 1994.

Perkins, Leialoha Apo. "Manifesto for Pidgin English." In *Mana: A South Pacific Journal of Language and Literature: Hawaii Edition.* Ed. Richard Hamasaki and Wayne Westlake. 6:1 (1981). 4–13.

Perloff, Marjorie. *Radical Artifice: Writing Poetry in the Age of Media.* Chicago: U of Chicago P, 1991.

——. "Modernist Studies." *Redrawing the Boundaries: The Transformation of English and American Literary Studies.* Ed. Stephen Greenblatt and Giles Gunn. New York: MLA, 1992. 154–72.

——. *The Futurist Moment.* Chicago: U of Chicago P, 2003.

Pinsky, Robert. *The Situation of Poetry: Contemporary Poetry and its Traditions.* Princeton: Princeton UP, 1978.

Pitzer, Sara. *How to Write a Cookbook and Get It Published.* Cincinnati: Writer's Digest Books, 1984.

Ransom, John Crowe. *The World's Body.* New York: Scribner's, 1938.

Rasula, Jed. *The American Poetry Wax Museum: Reality Effects,* Urbana: National Council of Teachers of English, 1996.

Reichl, Ruth. *Tender at the Bone: Growing Up at the Table.* New York: Broadway Books, 1999.

Reinecke, John. *Language and Dialect in Hawaii: A Sociolinguistic History to 1935.* Honolulu: U of Hawaii P, 1969 (originally written 1934).

Replinger, Rap. *Poi Dog With Crabs.* Tape. The Mountain Apple Company, 1992.

Retallack, Joan. ":RE:THINKING:LITERARY:FEMINISM:(three essays onto shaky grounds)." In Lynn Keller and Cristanne Miller, eds. *Feminist Measures: Soundings in Poetry and Theory.* Ann Arbor: U of Michigan P, 1994. 344–77.

Riding, Laura. *Anarchism Is Not Enough.* Ed. Lisa Samuels. [1928]. Berkeley: U of California P, 2001.

——. *Contemporaries and Snobs.* Garden City, NY: Doubleday, 1928.

———. *Four Unposted Letters to Catherine.* Rpt. New York: Persea, 1993.

Riding, Laura, and Robert Graves. *A Survey of Modernist Poetry.* 1928; rpt. New York: Haskell House, 1969.

Rifkin, Libbie. *Career Moves: Olson, Creeley, Zukofsky, Berrigan, and the American Avant-Garde.* Madison: U of Wisconsin P, 2000.

Rodrigues, Darlene. "Imagining Ourselves: Reflections on the Controversy over Lois-Ann Yamanaka's *Blu's Hanging.*" In Fujikane and Okamura, 196–207.

Rodden, John. *The Politics of Literary Reputation: The Making and Claiming of 'St. George' Orwell.* New York: Oxford UP, 1989.

Romaine, Suzanne. "Hawai'i Creole English as a literary language." In *Language and Society* 23 (1994): 527–54.

Ross, Andrew. "Taking the Tennis Court Oath." In Schultz, ed. *Tribe* 193–210.

Sakoda, Kent, and Jeff Siegel. Pidgin Grammar: An Introduction to the Creole English of Hawai'i. Honolulu: Bess Press, 2003.

Sato, Charlene. "Linguistic Inequality in Hawaii: The Post-Creole Dilemma." In N. Wolfson and J. Manes, eds. *Language of Inequality.* Berlin: Mouton, 1985. [Used manuscript copy with other pagination.]

———. "Sociolinguistic variation and language attitudes in Hawaii." In J. Cheshire, ed. *English Around the World: Sociolinguistic Perspectives.* Cambridge: Cambridge UP, 1991. 647–63.

Schechner, Richard. *Performance Theory.* Revised and expanded edition. New York: Routledge, 1988.

Schultz, Susan M. "'Called Null or Called Vocative': A Fate of the Contemporary Lyric." *Talisman* 14 (Fall 1995): 70–79.

———. "Hawaii Report." *Masthead.* http://au.geocities.com/masthead_2/us/schultz.html

———. "'The Lyric Crash': The Theater of Subjectivity in John Ashbery's *Three Poems.*" *Sagetrieb* 12:2 (1993): 137–48.

———, ed. *The Tribe of John: Ashbery and Contemporary Poetry.* Tuscaloosa: U of Alabama P, 1995.

Selinger, Eric. "Ronald Johnson." In *Dictionary of Literary Biography: American Poets Since World War II: Fifth Series.* Detroit: Gale Research, 1996. 146–56.

Shapiro, Laura. *Perfection Salad: Women and Cooking at the Turn of the Century.* New York: The Modern Library, 2001. Originally published 1986.

Shetley, Vernon. *After the Death of Poetry.* Durham: Duke UP, 1993.

Shoptaw, John. "*Flow Chart:* The Unauthorized Autobiography." *New American Writing* 10 (1992): 136–50.

Silliman, Ron. *The New Sentence.* NY: Roof, 1987.

Simon, Marc, ed. *The Poems of Hart Crane.* New York: Liveright, 1986.

Simpson, Megan. *Poetic Epistemologies.* NY: SUNY P, 2000.

Slotkin, Richard. *Regeneration Through Violence: The Mythology of the American Frontier, 1600–1860.* Norman: U of Oklahoma P, 1973.

Smith, Dorothy E. *Texts, Facts, and Femininity: Exploring the Relations of Ruling.* New York: Routledge, 1990.

Sondheim, Alan. "Philosophical Text: Theology and Colonialism" was posted on May 30, 2003 to the Poetics List in Buffalo (listserv@listserv.buffalo.edu).

Spahr, Juliana. *Dole Street.* Honolulu: Self-Publish or Perish, 2001.

——. *Everybody's Autonomy.* Tuscaloosa: U of Alabama P, 2001.

——"Poem Written from November 30, 2002 to March 27, 2003." *This Connection of Everyone with Lungs.* Berkeley: U of California P, 2005.

Stein, Gertrude. *Everybody's Autobiography.* New York: Cooper Square Publishers, Inc., 1971.

——. *The Autobiography of Alice B. Toklas.* In Carl Van Vechten, ed. *Selected Writings of Gertrude Stein.* New York: Vintage, 1972. 1–238.

——. *The Geographical History of America or The Relation of Human Nature to the Human Mind.* Baltimore: Johns Hopkins, 1995.

——. *How to Write.* Afternote by Douglas Messerli. Los Angeles: Sun & Moon, 1995.

——. *Lectures in America.* Boston: Beacon Press, 1985.

——. "Pictures." In *Lectures in America.* 59–92.

——. "Poetry and Grammar." In *Lectures in America.* 59–92.

——. "Stanzas in Meditation." In Richard Kostelanetz. 316–464.

Steiner, George. *On Difficulty and Other Essays.* New York: Oxford UP, 1980.

Stille, Alexander. *The Future of the Past.* New York: Picador, 2002.

Sumida, Stephen. *And the View from the Shore: Literary Traditions of Hawai'i.* Seattle: U of Washington P, 1991.

Takaki, Ronald. *A Different Mirror: A History of Multicultural America.* Boston: Little, Brown, 1994 [reissue].

Tate, Allen. *Essays of Four Decades.* Chicago: Swallow, 1968. 310–323.

Toklas, Alice B. *The Alice B. Toklas Cookbook.* New York: The Lyons Press, 1998.

Tonouchi, Lee. *Living Pidgin: Contemplations on Pidgin Culture.* Kane'ohe, HI: Tinfish Press, 2002.

Trask, Haunani-Kay. *Night Is a Sharkskin Drum.* Honolulu: U of Hawai'i P, 2002.

Tucker, Arthur Holmes. "Hope Atherton and His Times," a paper read at the annual meeting of the Pocumtuck Valley Memorial Association at Deerfield, Massachusetts, February 23, 1926.

Vickery, Ann. *Leaving Lines of Gender: A Feminist Genealogy of Language Writing.* Middletown, CT: Wesleyan UP, 2000.

Vincent, John. *Queer Lyrics: Difficulty and Closure in American Poetry.* New York: Palgrave, 2002.

Wa Thiong'o, Ngugi. *Decolonising the Mind: The Politics of Language in African Literature.* Portsmouth, NH: Heinemann, 1986.

Wexler, Joyce Piell. *Laura Riding's Pursuit of Truth.* Columbus: Ohio State UP, 1979.

White, Hayden. *Tropics of Discourse: Essays in Cultural Criticism.* Baltimore: Johns Hopkins UP, 1978.

Whitman, Walt. *Complete Poetry and Collected Prose.* Ed. Justin Kaplan. New York: The Library of America, 1982.

Wilder, Thornton. "Four in America." In Harold Bloom, ed. *Modern Critical Views: Gertrude Stein*. New York: Chelsea House, 1986. 25–45.

Williams, William Carlos. *In the American Grain*. New York: New Directions, originally published 1925.

———. "Marianne Moore." In *Imaginations*. Ed. Webster Schott. New York: New Directions, 1970. 310–20.

Wilson, Rob. "Bloody Mary Meets Lois-Ann Yamanaka: Imagining Hawaiian Locality from *South Pacific* to Bamboo Ridge." *Public Culture* 8 (1995): 127–58.

———. *Pacific Postmodern: From the Sublime to the Devious, Writing the Experimental / Local Pacific in Hawai'i*. Kane'ohe, HI; Tinfish, 2000.

———. *Reimagining the American Pacific: From South Pacific to Bamboo Ridge and Beyond*. Durham: Duke UP, 2000.

Yamanaka, Lois-Ann. *Saturday Night at the Pahala Theatre*. Honolulu: Bamboo Ridge Press, 1993. Selections on tape.

———. *Wild Meat and the Bully Burgers*. New York: Farrar, Straus & Giroux, 1996.

Yingling, Thomas E. *Hart Crane and the Homosexual Text: New Thresholds, New Anatomies*. Chicago: U of Chicago P, 1990.

Yoshinaga, Ida. "Pacific (War) Time at Punchbowl: A *Nembutsu* for Unclaiming Nation." Chain 11: Public Forms (Summer 2004): 328–43.

———. "*Uyesugi Gumi*: Sonnets from the Non-*Samurai Sansei* Boys' Club. *Tinfish* 13 (September 2003): 11–12.

Zumthor, Paul. *Oral Poetry: An Introduction*. Trans. Kathryn Murphy-Judy. Minneapolis: U of Minnesota P, 1990.

Index